P9-BYJ-663

Adult Education

Adult Education: Foundations of Practice

Gordon G. Darkenwald
RUTGERS UNIVERSITY

Sharan B. Merriam
NORTHERN ILLINOIS UNIVERSITY

HARPER & ROW, PUBLISHERS, New York
Cambridge, Philadelphia, San Francisco,
London, Mexico City, São Paulo, Sydney

1817

Sponsoring Editor: George A. Middendorf
Project Editor: Rita Williams/Elizabeth Krache
Cover Design: Betty Sokol
Production Manager: Willie Lane
Compositor: Lexigraphics, Inc.

Art Studio: Vantage Art, Inc.

Adult Education: Foundations of Practice

Copyright © 1982 by Harper & Row, Publishers, Inc.

All rights reserved. Printed in the United States of America. No part of this book
may be used or reproduced in any manner whatsoever without written
permission, except in the case of brief quotations embodied in critical articles
and reviews. For information address Harper & Row, Publishers, Inc., 10 East
53d Street, New York, NY 10022.

Library of Congress Cataloging in Publication Data

Darkenwald, Gordon G.
  Adult education
  Includes index.
  1. Adult education. I. Merriam, Sharan B. II. Title.
LC5215.D375   374   81-6861
ISBN 0-690-01541-0   AACR2

*To Jessica and Andrew Darkenwald
and
Paul and Laura Merriam*

Contents

Preface

Most fields of professional study are blessed with an abundance of works designed to introduce the body of knowledge undergirding professional practice. Adult education has not been so fortunate. Despite a growing corpus of literature, no comprehensive statement of the conceptual basis of the field has been published in nearly 20 years. We hope to remedy this deficiency to some degree with the present volume.

The subtitle, *Foundations of Practice*, underscores our goal of synthesizing and interpreting the general knowledge base on which informed professional action in large part rests. The book does not directly address professional action itself. While implications for teaching, program planning, and administration are noted, our work is in no way a substitute for the existing professional literature on these topics. Instead, it is meant to help graduate students and professionals in adult education and related fields understand more fully the contexts of practice and the concepts and perspectives that are essential to informed professional work.

In the broad and rapidly developing field of adult education, what constitutes the foundations of practice is not at all self-evident; indeed, it is often hotly debated. Our view is that disciplined inquiry in adult education and the social sciences is the source of most of the knowledge that is important for understanding and advancing professional action. Consequently, this volume emphasizes research and theory as they relate to adults as learners and the adult education enterprise broadly conceived. This text is not, of course, all-inclusive. Because it is intended as an introduction, important work in specialized areas such as group dynamics, social change, and organizational behavior has been omitted. We have addressed what we consider the basic topics and basic literature, with the partial exception of the history of adult education. Given the magnitude of the topic, we felt we could not do it justice in a single chapter. However, where feasible, we have incorporated historical material or perspectives throughout the volume.

This book is in some ways a successor to *Adult Education: Outlines of an Emerging Field of University Study* (1964) and the 1970 *Handbook of Adult Education*, two works with a similar purpose. It differs from these earlier volumes, however, in that it is intended to serve as a textbook for an introductory course as well as a professional reference work. The chapters are thus organized around the topics typically dealt with in an introductory course. They include a general introduction to adult education as a field of study and professional practice, and in-depth treatments of the philosophy of adult education, the adult as a learner, participation in adult education, agencies and programs, the international dimension of the field, and current problems and issues.

A great many people contributed in different ways to bringing this work to fruition. For more than a decade, the first author has continued to learn from his initial mentors at Columbia University, Jack Mezirow and Alan Knox, and from his friend and colleague at Rutgers University, Hal Beder. While their influence has been great and is gratefully acknowledged, they are not of course responsible for any of the book's shortcomings. We are grateful also to our students for all they have taught us, and to our families for their patience and support over the last four years. Finally, we wish to thank our colleagues Hal Beder, Gordon Larson, Alan Knox, Franceska Smith, and Travis Shipp for their helpful criticisms of the initial manuscript, and Mary Ann Takash, who deftly and cheerfully typed the bulk of it.

GORDON G. DARKENWALD
SHARAN B. MERRIAM

Chapter 1
Adult Education

The purpose of this book is to describe and interpret the field of adult education and the knowledge base that constitutes the foundations of professional practice. This chapter attempts to provide a context for those that follow by looking closely at what adult education is and is not and how it differs in both theory and practice from the preparatory education of children and young people. Thus the chapter focuses on the professional field of adult education, its development, and its current status. Subsequent chapters deal with the philosophy of adult education, adult learning and development, participation in adult education, organizations and programs, the international dimension, and problems and issues of the 1980s and beyond.

This chapter begins with a brief consideration of the changing character of education in general and then discusses the concept of lifelong learning and the social forces that have led to increased concern for education as a lifelong process. Adult education is defined and described and considered in relation to other human service professions. The final part of the chapter describes what adult educators do; reviews career opportunities, graduate training, and research; and discusses professional organizations and the issue of professional identity.

EDUCATION AND SCHOOLING

The word *education* is so deeply associated with young people and with schools that for much of the public and even for many professional educators the phrase *adult education* has a slightly incongruous ring. Nonetheless the realization is rapidly growing that education and schooling are not synonymous; in fact, it has become increasingly clear that education and our understanding of it are undergoing a fundamental transformation. The basic reason for this transformation was succinctly described some years ago in the influential report of the International Commission on the Development of Education:

> For far too long education had the task of preparing for stereotyped functions, stable situations, for one moment in existence, for a particular trade or a given job. It inculcated conventional knowledge, in time-honored categories. This concept is still far too prevalent. And yet, the idea of acquiring, at an early age, a set of intellectual or technical equipment valid for a lifetime is out of date. This fundamental axiom of traditional education is crumbling.[1]

In many respects the traditional view of education never was realistic. If education is broadly conceived as the deliberate, systematic, and sustained effort to transmit, evoke, or acquire knowledge, attitudes, values, or skills, as well as any outcomes of that effort,* then it is clear that the education of adults and children alike occurs today and has always occurred in many settings and through many kinds of activities. Schools and colleges are not the only or even necessarily the most potent institutions that educate. The family, the church, the work place, the mass media, the library, and many other institutions also play important roles in the education of people, both young and old. Moreover, as Lawrence Cremin has observed, each of these institutions educates deliberately and systematically; each has, in a very real sense, its own curriculum.[2] Thus an accurate understanding of education must take into account all the institutions and interactions that help to shape the development of individuals across the life span.

LIFELONG LEARNING

In recent years this broader view of education has been given wide currency by scholars and planners who have promoted the concept of lifelong learning. Advocates of lifelong learning assert that education is a process that continues in one form or another throughout life, and that its

---

*This is basically a restatement of Lawrence Cremin's definition, but we have added the word *acquire* to underscore the fact that self-education is included. See Lawrence A. Cremin, *Public Education* (New York: Basic Books, 1976), p. 27.

purposes and forms must be adapted to the needs of individuals at different stages in their development. Education is seen as an integral part of living and all the institutions of society with an educative potential are considered resources for learning. These ideas, as the International Commission on the Development of Education noted, are not new, but the potential for their realization is greater today than ever before:

> Whether they do so consciously or not, human beings keep on learning and training themselves throughout their lives, above all through the influence of the surrounding environment and through the experiences which mold their behavior, their conceptions of life, and the content of their knowledge. However, until the present day, there were few structures in which this natural dynamic could find support, so as to transcend chance and become a deliberate project. Especially, preconceived ideas about instruction—it was for the young and took place in schools—prevented people generally from conceiving lifelong education in normal educational terms. Yet it is true that in the space of only a few years the same obvious fact has come home to people from one end of the world to the other: most men are not sufficiently equipped to face the conditions and vicissitudes of life as lived in the second half of the twentieth century.[3]

While ideas about lifelong learning may sound like little more than enlightened common sense, in fact they represent a design for the restructuring of educational systems that has revolutionary implications for preparatory as well as adult education. First, the concept of lifelong learning contradicts the tenacious conventional wisdom, and the ramifications thereof, that education is limited to what goes on in schools and colleges to prepare children and young people for adulthood. A second profound implication is that society must make adequate provision to meet the educational needs of adults who have left formal schooling. A third implication, and perhaps the most far-reaching, is that the formal educational system must be reorganized so that it is flexible enough to accommodate individual options and to prepare young people to continue their education as self-directed and competent adult learners. At the very least, this last goal would require much greater emphasis in schools and colleges on learning how to learn.[4]

Societal Context of Lifelong Learning

What are the "conditions and vicissitudes of life" today that have led us to the threshold of a learning society? There is no simple answer to this question, but some insight can be gained through an examination of certain fundamental social and economic trends that have gained momentum since the end of World War II.

The science-based, postindustrial technology of modern economies has, among other things, led to vast increases in productivity, disposable income, leisure time, and educational attainment. Growing complexity and change characterize not only technology and work, but also social relations in marriage, family, and community. Obviously, as the society changes so, too, do individuals, and education is an important vehicle for such individual change. It would be a mistake, however, to assume that lifelong education is or should be merely a mechanism for adapting the individual to inexorable social and technological forces. As the Brazilian adult educator Paulo Freire has demonstrated, education can also be a vehicle for transforming society, for enabling people to direct the course of change rather than merely to react to it.[5]

Rapid technological and social change has direct consequences for the future of adult education. Consider the implications of the "knowledge explosion," particularly in science, technology, and the professions. It has been estimated that for some fields, such as engineering and medicine, the "half-life" of knowledge acquired in professional school is roughly five years.[6] Thus in a few years half of what the doctor or engineer learned in the classroom has become obsolete. Not only does the absolute amount of knowledge continue to grow exponentially, but the structure of knowledge, technology, and work is becoming ever more complex and specialized. As a consequence, most people must continue to learn throughout their lives merely to keep up with the demands of their jobs. Moreover, professionals in particular must stay abreast of an ever-broader range of concerns as the complexity and interdependency of the professions increase. Physicians, for example, must cope with complicated legal regulations, with unfamiliar new drugs, with changing professional relationships with those both within and outside the health field, and with new ethical dilemmas involving decisions of life and death.

Economic and social forces in the postindustrial society also have affected the socio-demographic composition of most industrialized nations in ways that almost surely will encourage the continuing expansion of lifelong learning opportunities. In the United States, and most other industrialized nations, several trends are of particular importance. First, the number of mature adults is increasing in proportion to the total population as well as in absolute size. This aging of the American population is a consequence of declining birth rates, increased life expectancy, and the entry into adulthood of the postwar baby boom cohort, which now makes up about one-fifth of the total population. Of particular note is the birth rate, which dropped from 25 per thousand in 1955 to 15.3 per thousand in 1978 and which will probably increase only slightly, if at all, in the 1980s.[7] In the 1980s and 1990s the baby boom cohort will be entering middle age; by the year 2000, the number of those in the 35-to-44 age group will have increased by 40 percent from about 25 million in 1980 to 41 million.[8] Looked at another way, in 1970 the median age was 27.9, and if fertility rates do not increase it will be 32.8 in 1990 and 35.5 in 2000.[9]

Perhaps even more important for the future of adult education is the increase in educational attainment by the population of the United States, Canada, and other industrialized nations.* In the United States the median number of years of schooling completed by adults 25 and over increased from 8.6 in 1940 to 12.5 in 1979. Over the same time span, the percentage of adults 25 and over who completed four or more years of college rose from 4.6 to 16.4.[10] Numerous studies have shown that those with more preparatory schooling are much more likely to continue their education as adults than those with less schooling.[11] The reasons for this phenomenon are complex, but even disregarding the effects of the higher income and occupational status associated with higher levels of educational attainment, there is still a strong relationship between amount of formal schooling and participation in adult education.[12]

The changing status of women in advanced industrial societies also has important implications for the future of adult education. Of particular relevance is the continuing trend toward married women in the labor force. In 1950, only 24.8 percent of married women were employed or looking for employment; by 1979 that figure had jumped to 50 percent, and it continues to rise.[13] As women increasingly combine marriage and jobs, their need to acquire work-related skills and credentials becomes ever greater. While this is true for women of all ages, it is particularly so for "reentering women," who dropped out of the labor market to raise children and wish or need to return to work but often lack the necessary skills.

One of the most profound changes in the work place in recent years, affecting both men and women, has been greatly increased individual movement between jobs and even between occupations. A study by Wirtz and his colleagues at the National Manpower Institute concluded that "about 1.3 million people in this country move each year from one major occupational area to another under circumstances requiring significant retraining or education in order to make this change."[14] Wirtz was not referring to routine promotions or reassignment of duties, but to changes across occupational categories (for example, from farmer to teacher) and to significant changes within an occupational group (such as from carpenter to tool-and-die maker). Wirtz goes on to cite a Department of Labor study that estimates that a 20-year-old man will make six to seven job changes in the course of his working life. While no comparable figures are available for women, it seems likely that the rate of job mobility has increased for both sexes and with it the need for further education or training.

Underlying these changes in the work place has been the long-term

*The emphasis on industrialized nations is not meant to denigrate the importance of adult education in developing countries, but rather to highlight the effects of economic and social forces typical of the modernizing process.

structural transformation of the labor market. The decline in jobs in the agricultural sector, for unskilled labor, and for blue-collar workers in general has been enormous, with demand shifting to the clerical, service, and technical/professional sectors. Thus the jobs that require the least education and training are disappearing, and much of the work that people perform today and will perform in the future requires an expanding base of knowledge and skills.

Finally, the last quarter century (or at least the period up to the late 1970s) has seen a general increase in disposable income and in the amount of leisure time available to most workers in the United States and other developed countries. Median family income, as measured in constant 1978 dollars, nearly doubled from $8,991 in 1950 to $17,640 in 1978.[15] While real income is not expected to grow much in the 1980s, today's standard of living compared with that of 1960 or 1950 is, for most Americans, enormously improved.

Americans not only have more money, but have more time to spend it. Total leisure time for the average urban adult increased from 34.8 hours per week in 1965 to 38.5 hours in 1975.[16] Changes in the work/leisure ratio are underscored by the continuing trend toward longer paid vacations, more paid holidays, flexible work hours, and the four-day work week. More money and more free time have reduced two of the major barriers to participation by adults in educational activities.

In summary, specific socioeconomic, cultural, and demographic forces, and not simply the wishful thinking of enlightened educators, are helping to make lifelong learning a reality. A survey conducted in 1972 found that nearly one adult in three participated in some form of organized learning activity, including self-study.[17] Government statistics, which do not include self-study, show substantial increases in participation in organized adult education between 1969 and 1978.[18] While adult education never was a marginal part of the education of the American public, today its significance is greater and more widely acknowledged than ever before.

NATURE OF ADULT EDUCATION

In order to arrive at a definition of adult education, it is first necessary to examine the terms *education* and *adult*. Few would disagree that it is important to distinguish between education and learning. All education surely involves learning, but not all learning involves education. In the concept of education there is an element of design, of human contrivance, that is not integral to the meaning of learning. This element of design is clear in the definition of education offered earlier: the deliberate, systematic, and sustained effort to transmit, evoke, or acquire knowledge, attitudes, values, or skills. Education, in this view, is purposeful (deliberate), organized (systematic), and of consequential duration (sustained). On the other hand, learning can be nondeliberate or incidental, unorganized, and of very short duration. The word *acquire* in the definition above is crucial because it emphasizes the fact that education includes self-directed learning that is deliberate, systematic, and sustained. Other definitions of education and adult education emphasize the role of an "educational agent," but it seems to us that the defining characteristic of education is the element of deliberateness or design, not the presence of a teacher or leader.[19] From this point of view, then, the construct of adult learning subsumes both natural, unplanned learning and adult education. Adult education itself takes in both self-education, whereby the learner is primarily responsible for the design and conduct of his or her learning activities, and other-directed education, whereby a teacher, leader, media production team, or some other educational agent is primarily responsible for the management of learning.

The preceding discussion obviously does not address all the distinctions and issues involved in defining education, but unless one employs an excessively rigid definition, there will always be some ambiguity and debate over what can properly be called education. Is viewing a two-hour TV documentary on the origins of the Vietnam War an example of adult education? Immediately questions leap to mind about the producer's intent, the content of the broadcast, the viewer's intent. Clearly, there is no one answer to whether or not this activity constitutes adult education. Furthermore, this discussion has stressed the activity or process of education from a perspective that is useful to educators, but which also is limiting. If one looks at individual human beings and their "education" in terms of the sum total of knowledge, skills, values, and attitudes they acquire in the course of their lives, it is clear that the multiplicity of institutions and experiences that educate overwhelms the few that our definition strictly allows. As Grattan put it, one must be mindful of the distinction between the education of adults and adult education, as the former is much more encompassing.[20] John Stuart Mill spoke to this point more than a century ago:

> Education, in its larger sense, is one of the most inexhaustible of all topics. . . . Not only does it include whatever we do for ourselves, and whatever is done for us by others, for the express purpose of bringing us somewhat nearer to the perfection of our nature; it does more: in its larger acceptation it comprehends even the indirect effects produced on character and on the human faculties, by things of which the direct purposes are quite different; by laws, by forms of government, by the industrial arts, by modes of social life; nay, even by physical facts not dependent on human will, by climate, soil, and local position. Whatever helps to shape the human being . . . is part of his education.[21]

If defining *education* is at best problematic, defining *adult* is no less so. Biological maturity is a necessary but hardly sufficient condition for adult status in most modern societies, for the word *adult* connotes not only biological but also social and psychological maturity in regard to judgment, autonomy, responsibility, and the assumption of adult life roles. The arbitrariness of using chronological age in defining who is an adult is obvious. Recognizing that an age- or trait-specific definition of adulthood is of little use, most adult educators long ago adopted a functional definition based on social role. In this view, an adult is someone who has left the role of full-time student (the principal social role of childhood and adolescence) and assumed the role of worker, spouse, and/or parent. This definition, while not totally satisfactory, does at least acknowledge that an adult is a person who performs socially productive roles and who has assumed primary responsibility for his or her own life.

As with that of education, our discussion of adult status leaves many important issues unresolved. Strictly applied, the social role definition would award adult status to a 16-year-old high school dropout and deny it to a 25-year-old medical student. For purposes of defining adult education, however, it makes little sense to view as adults persons who are full-time students in colleges and universities and who are not, in Bryson's words, fully engaged in the "ordinary business of life."[22] Nonetheless, persons who have been engaged in the "ordinary business" of life as workers, parents, and citizens, and who return to schools or colleges as full-time students can be considered as engaging in adult education. It is not the technical definition of full-time student (e.g., one who is enrolled for at least 12 credits) that is important but the salience of the student role vis-à-vis other social roles. The 40-year-old woman who returns full-time to college to complete a bachelor's degree is not a student in the same sense as is a 19-year-old adolescent. For such adults, with rare exceptions, the ordinary business of life continues and the role of student is subordinate to it.

Toward a Definition

How then might adult education be defined? It is important to recognize that no universally acceptable definition is possible, for any definition must ultimately be based on certain assumptions and value judgments that will not be acceptable to everyone. Rather than simply assert that this or that is adult education, it may be useful first to ask how the functions of the adult education enterprise differ from those of the preparatory schooling enterprise.

To consider every function of preparatory schooling is beyond our scope here. Schools and colleges keep young people off the streets and out of the labor market, select and sort them for various social statuses, inculcate the values of the dominant culture, and educate in the sense that we have described earlier. Above all, however, schools and colleges are agencies of socialization whose principal purpose is to *prepare* children and young people for adult life. Quite obviously, this cannot be the overarching purpose of the adult education enterprise.* Adult education is concerned not with preparing people for life, but rather with helping people to live more successfully. Thus if there is an overarching function of the adult education enterprise, it is to assist adults to increase their competence, or negotiate transitions, in their social roles (worker, parent, retiree, etc.), to help them gain greater fulfillment in their personal lives, and to assist them in solving personal and community problems.

Given the preceding assumptions and definitions, we would define adult education as follows:

> Adult education is a process whereby persons whose major social roles are characteristic of adult status undertake systematic and sustained learning activities for the purpose of bringing about changes in knowledge, attitudes, values, or skills.

Purposes and Issues

The definition given above emphasizes the learner's characteristics and intentions and the processes and outcomes of educative activity. It does not address other important concerns such as the content, sponsorship, methodology, or purposes of adult education. Yet if we are to gain a fuller appreciation of how the enterprise of adult education is distinct from that of preparatory education, and of the ongoing debate centering on this question, then it is necessary to take the matter of definition one step further. With this purpose in mind, it may be fruitful to consider the more encompassing definition adopted in 1976 by the General Conference of UNESCO. It is the official world definition:

> The term *adult education* denotes the entire body of organized educational processes, whatever the content, level, and method, whether formal or otherwise, whether they prolong or replace initial education in schools, colleges, and universities as well as in apprenticeship, whereby persons regarded as adult by the society to which they belong develop their abilities, enrich their knowledge, improve their technical or professional qualifications, or turn them in a new direction and bring about changes in their attitudes or behavior in the two-fold perspective of full personal development and participation in balanced and independent social, economic, and cultural development. . . .[23]

The definition goes on to state that adult education should be seen as an

---

*Socialization in the sense of helping people learn new roles or improve their role performance is an important feature of adult education.

integral component of a "global scheme for lifelong education and learning."

Not surprisingly, the UNESCO statement minimizes long-standing controversies regarding goals, content, and objectives as well as the matter of who is an adult. (A number of these controversies will be discussed in more detail in Chapter 2.) While UNESCO sees both individual and social (that is, community and national) development as equally legitimate goals for adult education, others disagree and sometimes even deny the validity of social development as an educational goal.[24] Moreover, while it appears to be implicit in the UNESCO definition, some have voiced concern that education be distinguished from indoctrination, a distinction that is perhaps easier to make in adult than in preparatory education.[25] Content is less controversial, but in certain countries, particularly in the past, nonliberal or vocational studies and studies below university level have been deemed unworthy of consideration as adult education.[26]

In the United States and Canada, the leaders of the adult education movement in its formative years tended to deemphasize formal instruction and to stress the importance of informal learning for personal development and civic improvement. Thus, for much of the present century, adult education was not always seen as including vocational subjects or learning geared toward the acquisition of degrees and credentials.[27] This perspective also was reflected in a preference for less formal, "adult-oriented" learning processes, especially the group discussion method. The preoccupation with group work and discussion methods among leaders in the field, even as recently as the 1950s, is revealed by the search for a title for the Adult Education Association's practitioner-oriented journal, which was established in 1951. The journal's editorial board, which included such prominent leaders in the field as Malcolm Knowles, Howard McClusky, and Leland Bradford, decided to survey its potential readers in order to determine a name democratically. Those surveyed chose *Adult Leadership* from a list of titles including *Groups and Leaders, Group Leadership, Together*, and *Democratic Leadership*. Interestingly, the editors were disappointed with this choice; their initial preference had been *Together*.[28] In 1977, in an action symbolic of the current conception of the field, the name of the periodical was changed to *Lifelong Learning: The Adult Years*.

Some adult educators still feel that the essence of "true" adult education is not to be found in the remedial or second-chance programs associated with formal schooling. Grattan expressed this point of view succinctly: "Far more important than adult education simply calculated to bring adults up to some chosen mark of formal schooling, is that kind of adult education addressed to *adults as adults* and designed to assist them

to live more successfully. This is the real field of *adult* education."
(Grattan's italics.)[29]

At the root of debates over goals, content, and methods—and
ultimately the definition of the field—is the contrasting nature of the
activities subsumed under the broad rubric of adult education. The
perspectives of two influential philosophers of adult education illustrate
the point. For the contemporary philosopher and adult educator Paulo
Freire, who has worked with illiterate adults in Brazil, Chile, and
Guinea-Bissau, adult education has a special meaning formed by the hard
realities of social and economic oppression in Third World countries.[30]
For Eduard Lindeman, a naturalized American whose major work was
first published in 1926, adult education had a very different meaning that
was tempered by the American experience of the first decades of this
century.[31] While Freire looks to Christian humanism and Marxism for
intellectual guidance, Lindeman looked in a different direction toward
secular pragmatism and the philosophy of John Dewey. Yet, divergent as
their backgrounds are, both men have made important contributions to
our understanding of adult education. The same can be said of the other
scholars and practitioners who have brought to the field a complex
pluralism of experience and perspective.

Scope of the Field

There seems to be increasing agreement that the maturity of the adult
learner and the needs and problems of adulthood are what give adult
education its special quality. Some of these needs and interests are met by
academic and vocational programs for adults sponsored by schools and
colleges, but many more of them are addressed by the less visible but
nonetheless widespread efforts of nonschool agencies. Consider, for
example, the multitude of organizations that earmark a substantial part of
their resources for the education and training of their employees,
members, clients, or customers. In the public sector these include the
federal, state, and local government agencies that employ millions of
persons in every conceivable occupation—as clerks, scientists, judges,
teachers, nurses, prison guards—in addition to the military, which
employs more than two million men and women. In the private sector,
business and industry likewise employ millions of adults and provide
training and education ranging from job orientation to retirement planning for employees at all levels, and from classes in basic skills for
entry-level workers to advanced seminars for managers and scientists.
Often overlooked, moreover, are the extensive educational programs of
the corporate sector designed to help customers use the products or
services they purchase, an activity similar to the programs of hospitals and

health maintenance organizations for patient education. Labor unions, too, provide a wide range of educational programs for their members and employees. Voluntary organizations such as the League of Women Voters and the American Cancer Society are heavily engaged in the mass education of the adult public as well as in the training of employees and volunteers. Churches, synagogues, and other religious organizations offer opportunities for study not only in religion but often in other areas, such as parent training. Museums and libraries are major resources for self-education as well as providers of more formal educational programs for both young people and adults. The broadcast media, particularly television, offer not only formal lecture-style courses but also a variety of less formal programs with educational value, including series based on great literary works, or dealing with cooking and gardening, and a variety of special programs on such topics as health, science, public affairs, and religion. In whatever setting adults come together there are likely to be opportunities for purposeful learning. Often these opportunities are planned for or with the learner by an organization or group, but often it is the individual who initiates, plans, and carries out his or her own learning project without the direction of a teacher or other expert.[32]

Synonyms and Related Terms

The term *adult education* has not won universal acceptance by those involved with the education of adults. Perhaps this is because it has overtones of night school or invokes in the public mind the specter of basketweaving or similar "recreational" activities. The most widely used synonym is *continuing education,* which implies that the adult learner is pursuing education beyond the point where he or she left formal schooling, thus underscoring the ideal of continuous learning throughout the lifespan. Colleges and universities, as well as many professional organizations, generally refer to their adult education activities as *continuing education,* while public school systems more frequently use the term *adult education.*

Other related terms include *lifelong learning* (or *lifelong education*), *recurrent education, nontraditional education, community education,* and *andragogy.* While it is often used synonymously with *adult education, lifelong learning,* as noted earlier, more correctly refers to a reconceptualization of the entire educational process, of which adult education is an integral part. In the words of UNESCO, the term *lifelong learning*

> denotes an overall scheme aimed both at restructuring the existing education system and at developing the entire educational potential outside the education system; in such a scheme men and women are the agents of their own education through continual interaction between their thoughts and

action; education and learning . . . should extend throughout life, include all skills and branches of knowledge, use all possible means, and give the opportunity to all people for full development of the personality.[33]

As a comprehensive theory of education and an agenda for reform, lifelong learning provides both intellectual justification and a plan of action for the fuller realization of the potential of adult education. It is noteworthy that much of the recent impetus for reconceptualizing education as lifelong learning came not from the United States and Canada, but rather from Western Europe. Moreover, the concept is not new. Its origins can be traced back at least as far as 1919, when the Adult Education Committee of the British Ministry of Reconstruction issued its influential report asserting that adult education is a "permanent national necessity" and therefore "should be both universal and lifelong."[34]

Recurrent education refers to another concept of European origin that underscores the principle of lifelong learning that work and study should alternate or that learning should recur periodically throughout one's life as needs and circumstances change. In practice, *recurrent education* is used principally as a synonym for *adult education,* particularly in the international literature produced by such agencies as the Organization for Economic Cooperation and Development.

The term *nontraditional education* is an American invention popularized by the Commission on Non-Traditional Study, a foundation-supported panel of educational leaders that sponsored several studies in the early 1970s.[35] The basic concerns of the commission were the new developments epitomized by the external degree and by corollary approaches to awarding degree credit through such vehicles as examinations and assessment of experiential learning. The commission's work, like its understanding of nontraditional education, was largely limited to developments in higher education.

Community education is used sometimes in a generic sense, and at other times to denote a particular educational philosophy and movement. In its generic sense, *community education* refers to any kind of educational program or activity designed to serve people "out in the community," whether preschoolers or the elderly. It should be noted that community education is not the same as *community development.* The latter is characterized by action-oriented community problem solving, in which learning and doing are intimately bound together.[36] Community development has long been associated with adult education. Community education, however, is often associated with the community school movement, supported for many years by the Mott Foundation and dedicated to making neighborhood public schools centers for educational, cultural, and recreational activity for people of all ages.

Andragogy is derived from the Greek word *aner,* meaning *man,* and thus, in contrast to *pedagogy* (*paid* meaning *child*), it is the "art and science of helping adults learn."[37] The term *andragogy* is widely used in certain European countries, most notably Yugoslavia, where university departments of andragogy have been established apart from the traditional departments of pedagogy. In North America, except in the French-speaking provinces of Canada, the term has not gained much currency, nor is it widely used in Britain or the Commonwealth nations. Resistance to the use of *andragogy* stems in large part from the prevailing view that education is not fundamentally different for adults and children.[38] Thus those who stress the continuities in the educational process reject the notion of a special field of andragogy, while those who emphasize the unique qualities of the adult as learner often favor the term. Nonetheless, *andragogy* seems to be increasingly employed in its narrower denotation as a set of assumptions and methods pertaining to the process of helping adults learn.

Persons unfamiliar with adult education are often puzzled by the terms used to describe the adult education units or activities of particular kinds of organizations. While colleges and universities often refer to their adult education units as divisions or schools of continuing education, there are other terms in use as well. Some higher education institutions, especially land grant state universities, employ the term *general* or *university extension* to denote units responsible for general adult education programming. The *Cooperative Extension Service*, in contrast, refers to a separately funded (and usually separately administered) unit that sponsors educational and informational services for the public, related mainly to agriculture, nutrition, homemaking, consumer economics, and 4-H youth development. On many campuses, one finds a university college or school of general studies or similar unit that provides evening and weekend degree-credit offerings for a mainly part-time adult clientele. Community colleges, like private four-year colleges, rarely use the word *extension*. Instead, the majority of these institutions employ the terms *continuing education* and *community services* to refer to adult education, with *community services* often restricted to noncredit courses and cultural activities such as concerts and art exhibits.

When an organization provides education for its employees, the terms *adult* or *continuing education* are seldom used. In business and industry, adult education is generally referred to as *training* or *human resource development* (or simply *development*) and the units called departments or divisions of training, human resource development, or employee development. Other employers, too, including the armed forces and many government agencies, often prefer the word *training* and its variants, although human service organizations such as hospitals often use the terms *in-service* and *continuing education* rather than *training*. There are of course other labels particular to other settings, but the above terms are those most frequently encountered.

Related Activities

While the conception of adult education espoused here is a broad one, it nonetheless implies definite boundaries. As discussed earlier, college students in their late teens and early twenties are in many ways adults, but because they have not assumed the full responsibilities implicit in adult status they cannot be considered as engaged in adult education. Adult education blends with higher education only when the learners' principal social roles signify full adult status—in which case they are usually part-time students. Admittedly this distinction is increasingly difficult to make as more and more older people become full-time students for extended periods of time.

Many of the human service professions, such as social work and psychiatry, are concerned in one way or another with adult learning and education, but education in these contexts is generally considered subordinate to other purposes and processes. While purposeful learning is involved in any kind of therapy, including physical therapy, it does not follow that therapy and education are the same. This is not to deny that in certain respects all professionals are educators and their clients learners.

Professionals who work with adults in a purely educational capacity are adult educators and what they do is adult education, whether it is recognized as such or not. Thus, persons in business, organized labor, government, and the armed forces who design and conduct learning activities for adults are engaged in adult education, although they may refer to what they do as development or something else that obscures its educational nature. Likewise, there are people who work in certain fields, such as public health or recreation, and in certain settings, such as libraries, museums, churches, and broadcast studios, where their work is sometimes educational and sometimes not and where the education may or may not be directed at adults. Librarians, public health officers, social workers, recreation directors, TV producers, the clergy, and many other community service professionals are often partly or almost fully engaged in adult education, although their professional identities lie elsewhere. Clearly, adult education does not encompass all such roles and settings, but it does play an increasingly important part in the larger configuration of social institutions and processes that shapes the life of every member of society.

PROFESSIONAL FUNCTIONS AND ROLES

While organized adult education can be traced at least as far back as the early eighteenth century, it was not established in the United States as a field of professional practice until the founding of the American Association for Adult Education in 1926. As Knowles has pointed out, adult education is one of the newest fields of social practice in the United States, inasmuch as the library field can be similarly defined as originating in 1876, the social work field in 1873, and the broader field of education (that is, public schooling) in 1857.[39]

While adult education has developed rapidly in the years since 1926 and undergone many changes, the functions and roles of adult educators have not been greatly altered by time. A distinction is made between function and role because, unlike the field of preparatory education, in adult education there is often a great disparity between the formal roles educators occupy and the functions they perform. In general, adult educators, whatever their designated role, perform a greater variety of educative functions than do their counterparts in preparatory education.

Basic Functions

The basic functions of adult education are instruction, counseling, program development, and administration. Three of these four functions have clear analogues in preparatory education, but program development does not. In broad terms, program development refers to the design, implementation, and evaluation of educational activities. Among other things, the program development process involves assessing learner needs, setting objectives, selecting learning activities and resources for learning, making and executing decisions necessary for learning activities to take place, and evaluating outcomes. These and other activities involved in program development are described in detail in the professional literature.[40]

What is distinctive about program development in adult education is the blending of roles and tasks that are typically separate and distinct in preparatory education. Program development obviously incorporates major elements of the functions of instruction and administration (and often counseling too) and therefore involves tasks traditionally associated with the roles of both teacher and administrator.

The uniqueness and centrality of the program development function in adult education derive ultimately from the diversity of purposes and needs adult educators and adult education agencies must address. The curricula of schools and colleges tend to be relatively uniform and to remain fairly stable over time. In contrast, adult education agencies generally do not process large numbers of learners through a relatively standardized curriculum. Instead, usually an effort is made to meet a variety of changing individual and group needs through short-term programs. It follows that where adult education is more standardized, as in remedial or second-chance programs that parallel the curricula of preparatory education, the program development function is less important. This tends to be true of degree-oriented higher education for part-time adult students, occupational education designed to prepare persons for the labor market rather than to upgrade skills and knowledge, and adult basic education and high school completion programs.

As the preceding discussion of the program development function suggests, it is not always easy in adult education to make clear distinctions among professional roles, especially for administrators. While the key role in the majority of adult education settings might well be identified as program developer, in practice this role is usually not formally differentiated from that of administrator. Consequently, a brief overview of the roles of teacher and of counselor will be followed by a more extended discussion of the multifaceted and often interconnected roles of program developer and administrator.

Teachers

The teacher of adults, like the teacher of children and young people, is concerned with transmitting or evoking knowledge, attitudes, values, or skills in a systematic way. There are, of course, differences between teaching adults and teaching young people; in practice the extent of these differences varies. As a rule, the role of adult teacher is most similar to the traditional teaching role in the more formal programs that parallel the preparatory curricula of schools and colleges, and most unlike it in the less formal, nonschool settings. The phrase "transmitting or evoking" used above captures the essence of these crucial differences. Partly because of tradition and training, and partly because of the highly structured nature of academic and vocational subjects, the emphasis in more formal, school-like settings tends to be on the transmission of knowledge by the teacher. In less formal settings, especially where the expectation is that the adults involved will learn from each other, where problem solving is a principal concern, or where self-direction is otherwise necessary or appropriate, the tendency is for teachers to arrange conditions to facilitate the evocation, rather than the transmission, of knowledge and skills. This latter conception of teaching has long been emphasized in the professional literature because it takes into account certain special characteristics of adults as learners. In fact the literature of adult education often does not mention the word *teacher*, but employs instead such terms as *leader*, *mentor*, and *facilitator*. The word *teacher* is used here because it is familiar, but it is defined in its broader sense to denote anyone who directly facilitates learning.

The majority of the teachers of adults teach on a part-time basis, and often in the evening. The percentage of adult education teachers who work full-time is not known (nor is much else about the nature of the adult education teaching force) because of a lack of reliable statistics. Some data, however, have been collected on certain aspects of adult education.

A 1972 study of adult education in community organizations such as churches, Y's, and civic and social service agencies reported a total of 654,100 staff members involved. Significantly, the great majority (510,900) were volunteers; only 143,200 were employed full-time.[41] Statistics on instructional personnel employed in adult education programs by local school systems show a total of 141,015 employed as "classroom teachers," with approximately 8 percent classified as full-time employees.[42]

The total number of teachers probably will never be known, although some rough estimates can be made. Using the most conservative recent statistics showing 18 million participants in organized adult education in the United States, and assuming a ratio of learners to teachers of eight or nine to one, the total number of teachers would be about two million.[43] This estimate is crude, but does suggest the enormous numbers involved.

The settings, purposes, and activities of teachers of adults are so diverse as to preclude all but the most general descriptions. As Houle has pointed out, a great many teachers of adults are volunteers who teach in a multitude of community settings, for example, in the educational programs of voluntary associations like the League of Women Voters and the American Heart Association, in museums and libraries, and in churches and synagogues.[44] Persons employed in basically noneducational roles may also teach adults as part of their work. One thinks immediately of social workers, recreation specialists, the clergy, and many other human service workers. Less visible are the specialists of all kinds in government and industry who share their knowledge and expertise with fellow employees and the technical sales personnel who spend much of their time in customer education. Then there is the large corps of full-time teachers of adults, some of whom have program development responsibilities as well. They probably number more than 100,000. Very few are employed by schools and colleges (some 45,000 are employed in business and industry).[45] In this category fall the full-time trainers who teach subjects and skills of all kinds in business and industry, in government agencies, and in the military, as well as the full-time staff members of voluntary associations who train volunteers.

As is evident at this point, the overwhelming majority of teachers of adults are not professional educators. Few have received training in education, few hold teaching licenses, and most are employed by noneducational organizations. Even teachers of adults employed by educational institutions are usually selected for their specialized knowledge or expertise, not for their training in teaching.

While full-time career opportunities for teachers of adults are limited, there is reason to believe that this situation is changing, particularly for teachers of basic skills and vocational subjects. In the 1960s and 1970s there was a steady increase in government funding of vocational training and adult basic education programs. As a result, school systems and some postsecondary institutions began to provide separate facilities for adult education and to operate programs throughout the day and evening. More and more full-time teachers were hired, and this trend will probably continue despite recent cutbacks in government spending. Employers, too, seem to be hiring increasing numbers of teachers of basic skills to upgrade the communication and computation skills of entry-level clerical employees and to provide greater opportunities for occupational advancement by women and minorities.

Counselors

There is even less concrete data available on the counselors of adults than on teachers. Our concern here is with counseling functions that directly enhance the educational activities and purposes of adults. Those functions include the provision of information about educational and career opportunities, assistance in making educational and occupational choices, and help in dealing with problems that interfere with the learning process. There is reason to believe that these functions are widely neglected, especially in less formal adult education settings, but also in schools and colleges.[46] The number of formally designated adult counselors is very small, and thus for the most part the counseling that does occur is done by teachers, program developers, or administrators. A study of big-city adult basic education programs reported that the need for counseling was so great, and the supply of counselors so small, that teachers had this role thrust upon them whether or not they were prepared to accept it.[47] The ratio of counselors to learners in comprehensive public school adult education agencies in New Jersey was estimated at 1 to 5000.[48] In higher education settings, particularly community colleges, this ratio is generally smaller, but counseling resources are seldom commensurate with the need. As a rule, counselors are most widely available to adult learners in basic education, high school completion, and college degree programs and least available in less formal educational settings. Testing and referral to health and social service agencies tend to be prominent counseling functions in ABE and high school completion programs, while vocational counseling (often using groups), academic advising, and study skills development are more characteristic of higher education settings.

The recent development of a new counseling role—that of educational broker—and of community-based educational information and guidance centers holds promise for extending counseling services to a much wider segment of the adult population. The role of educational broker was first created by external degree institutions, but brokers are now employed in other settings as well, most notably in libraries and community-based educational information and guidance centers. Unlike the traditional counselor, the educational broker acts as a liaison between the learner and the educational resources of the community. In trying to match educational resources with learner needs, the broker acts in the interest of the learner, not on behalf of an educational institution. In fact, an essential dimension of the broker role is client advocacy—which might involve, for example, persuading an educational institution to waive an application deadline or provide financial assistance for an adult learner.

Legislation enacted by Congress in 1976 authorizing funds for states to plan and operate Educational Information Centers (EICs) provided an impetus for the development of community-based information and guidance services. Some states are experimenting with the use of public libraries as the delivery system for such services, while others are looking to external degree institutions or various combinations of new and existing agencies to serve as the structure for an EIC network. While much depends on the amount of money appropriated for EICs in the years ahead, it is clear that the need for such services is very great.

Counseling adult learners, like teaching them, is still performed largely by persons who devote only part of their working time to it. It seems likely, however, that the number of full-time positions for counselors of adults will continue to grow. At present, only a small minority of adult counselors and educational brokers have had professional training in counseling or adult education. Those with professional credentials have generally been trained in school guidance or vocational counseling. However, specialized graduate training in adult counseling is available today at a number of American universities.

Program Developers/Administrators

The great majority of full-time adult educators are employed in administrative or semi-administrative roles that involve both program development and management functions. Part-time adult educators, of course, also serve in such roles. This is true in almost all the institutional settings where adult education takes place—hospitals, industries, unions, colleges, voluntary associations, and so forth. As noted earlier, the centrality of the program development process reflects the diverse and changing learner needs that most adult education agencies attempt to serve. Of course, when the needs an agency attempts to meet are relatively uniform and stable, the program development function becomes less central and the traditional distinction between instruction and administration tends to become sharper.

There are other factors that serve to reinforce the blending of administrative and program development roles in adult education. The lack of a full-time faculty in most adult education settings makes it necessary for administrators to assume certain functions that faculty members normally would perform. Thus, for example, decisions about what courses or programs will be offered and what instructional formats (e.g., lecture, workshop, discussion group) will be employed typically are made by administrators. It follows that where there is a full-time faculty, for example, in some adult learning centers and evening colleges, the administrator's role tends to center on management rather than instructional tasks. Another important factor is the small size of most adult education agencies in terms of the number of full-time professional personnel. When the full-time staff consists of only one or two people (as it often does), then responsibility for both program development and administrative functions is almost unavoidable. However, in relatively large agencies—such as the training unit of a large corporation or the extension division of a land grant university—the highest-ranking administrators tend to devote most of their time to management rather than program development tasks. As a general rule, the higher one's rank in an adult education agency, the less involvement one has in routine program development activities. Nonetheless, many deans, directors, and other managers, especially in smaller agencies, are heavily involved in the day-to-day work of organizing educational activities.

The full-time professional adult educator then typically plays a variety of roles. He or she is simultaneously an administrator, supervisor, program developer, counselor, and, sometimes, even a teacher. Moreover, certain organizational characteristics typical of many adult education agencies impose special demands on the administrator. In most cases the adult education agency is a subunit of a larger organization where the primary goals are not adult education or even education. Very often, as Clark has pointed out, the low priority of adult education within the larger parent organization leads to institutional marginality and insecurity.[49] When budget cuts are made, adult education is often particularly vulnerable. Consequently, the adult education administrator must strive continually to convince administrators in the parent organization of the value and importance of his or her programs. Dependence on the parent organization for facilities and support services also means that a good deal of time and effort must be spent in negotiating and maintaining relationships with other institutional units.

Thus, in many cases the adult education administrator must be something of an entrepreneur, selling the importance of his or her programs within the parent organization and continually making arrangements with other organizational units to secure necessary support services related to personnel, finances, student records, and so forth. Similarly, because most programs rely on voluntary participation by learners and must be largely self-supporting, the administrator also must be an entrepreneur in relation to the larger community. The visibility of the program and the continuing flow of new learners and even teachers often depend on contacts and linkages with various groups and organizations in the larger community. As Beder has argued, such contacts and linkages can be crucial in securing needed resources such as learners, teachers, political support, and sometimes even facilities, as well as services such as child care and job placement.[50] Even relatively secure and self-contained education and training units in the military and industry often find it advantageous to form outside linkages, particularly with colleges and universities.

In terms of background and training, administrators or program developers are as diverse as teachers of adults. Typically, however, there is a relationship between work setting and background. Education directors in labor unions generally have a background in union leadership; training directors in business and industry usually have business experience or training; and public school adult education directors usually have a background in teaching. While most persons with graduate training in adult education enter administrative and program development positions, professionals with such preparation constitute only a small portion of the total leadership force. Initial occupational identity tends in many cases to block the awareness or acknowledgement of many in the field that they are in fact adult educators. Those nurses who work full-time directing in-service education programs may continue to identify themselves professionally as nurses despite the fact that they have long since given up any nursing duties. Similarly, training directors in industry often see themselves as engaged in "human resource development," not in education, perhaps because education connotes impractical academicism to many businesspeople.

GRADUATE STUDY

As noted previously, only a small proportion of the educators of adults have had university preparation in the field of adult education. Since the 1960s, however, the number of university programs in adult education and the number of degrees awarded have grown enormously. Today, especially in the United States and Canada, and increasingly in Europe, Africa, and other parts of the world, universities play an important role in preparing adult educators and in generating new knowledge for the improvement of professional practice.

The first university courses in adult education were offered at Teachers College, Columbia University, in the 1920s, but it was not until 1935 that Columbia awarded the first doctorates in the field.[51] In that same year the University of Chicago and Ohio State University organized doctoral programs in adult education, and several other universities became involved in the 1940s and 1950s. Graduate programs grew slowly, however; by 1949 only 36 persons held doctorates in adult education from

American universities (there are no statistics even today on master's and bachelor's level graduates).[52] By 1965, approximately 500 people held Ed.D's or Ph.D's in adult education from American universities, and doctoral programs were offered by 15 institutions in the United States as well as by universities in Canada and Yugoslavia.[53] By the 1970s the number of graduate programs as well as their average size had increased greatly. Unfortunately, there are no recent reliable statistics on graduate study in adult education. We can, however, obtain some idea of the extent of such preparation today by examining the membership of the Commission of Professors of Adult Education. In 1980 there were 407 full members of the commission, representing more than 100 colleges and universities in the United States and 8 in Canada. In contrast, in 1960 there were only 20 members of the commission, representing some 15 universities.[54] It should be noted that not all of the institutions represented by commission members offer formal master's and doctoral programs in adult education, while at least a few institutions that do offer programs are not represented on the commission. Nonetheless, these statistics do provide a rough measure of the phenomenal growth in university preparation programs over the past two decades. Today, one can earn a master's degree in adult education at more than 50 universities in North America and a doctoral degree at 25 or so.

Despite the rapid growth in the number of graduate programs and the number of graduates with formal preparation in adult education, the majority of university-based programs are of modest size, at least when measured in terms of full-time faculty members. While perhaps half a dozen programs have six or more full-time professors, more typical is a staff of one or two full-time professors whose efforts are supplemented by faculty in other departments or by part-time adjunct instructors. In most cases, the adult education program is part of a larger department. Administrative arrangements vary greatly, but often adult education is combined with programs that are ostensibly complementary, such as vocational education, higher education, or educational administration.

Educational goals, curricula, and orientations to the field of adult education vary among graduate programs. Some newer programs, particularly those established with federal assistance in the South during the late 1960s, are heavily oriented toward training adult basic education personnel.[55] Others, at major land grant universities such as Cornell and Wisconsin, historically have placed emphasis on extension education, that is, the training of personnel for the Cooperative Extension Service. Such specialized goals, however, are not the norm. Because of the scarcity of full-time positions for teachers of adults, graduate study in most universities is geared to preparation for program development and administrative roles in a broad spectrum of settings.

What might be called a core curriculum in adult education graduate programs usually is found in one form or another at most universities. As described by Knox, the core curriculum consists of an introductory or survey course, a course dealing with adult learning and development (sometimes offered by the psychology department), and courses in program development and administration.[56] Many universities also offer more specialized courses in the core areas, for example, in history or philosophy of adult education, group dynamics, and methods of teaching adults. In many institutions flexibility is provided by topics courses and advanced seminars that change their focus from time to time. Flexibility is also typically available through individualized, self-directed learning using such vehicles as independent study, fieldwork, and internship courses. Where the doctorate is offered, there is usually at least one course geared toward preparation for a dissertation. Finally, as Knox notes, most programs offer specialized courses that reflect particular faculty interests or institutional resources, for example, courses dealing with adult basic education, comparative adult education, or educational gerontology.[57]

Adult education might be termed an adventitious profession in that most people enter it perhaps not really by accident but also seldom by design. A teenager may aspire to be a schoolteacher but seldom to be an adult educator. Consequently, graduate students come from varied backgrounds and usually have had some professional experience in adult education or a related field before beginning graduate study. However, while graduate students generally range in age from their mid-twenties to their mid-forties, there has been a tendency, first noted by Houle nearly a decade ago, for an increasing number to come directly from undergraduate school.[58] While this is probably due mostly to the increased status and visibility of the field in recent years, it may also be related to the recent institution of undergraduate courses in adult education at a number of universities. Interestingly, a very different trend also seems to be developing. More people in their forties and fifties are entering graduate programs, sometimes motivated in part by their experience as adult students in undergraduate degree programs. If there is such a trend, it should hardly be surprising in light of the increasing number of adults, particularly women, who are returning to education or the work place or changing careers.

Graduates of university degree programs in adult education—at least doctoral graduates—seem to find employment most often in colleges and universities. In their 1965 survey of doctorate holders, Houle and Buskey reported that 69 percent were employed by colleges and universities, the majority in administrative and program development positions. Employment in public school settings ranked a distant second, only 8 percent of the total.[59] A more up-to-date survey might well show somewhat different results, but there is little doubt that most doctoral graduates still are employed by colleges and universities.

Universities, of course, are not the only institutions that prepare adult educators. As Houle observed a decade ago, "the largest volume of organized . . . training of adult educational leaders occurs within the institutions which sponsor programs, such as industrial and commercial establishments, public schools, substantive government departments, and voluntary associations."[60] This is still the case today and undoubtedly will remain so. The university, however, has increasingly become the trainer of trainers for these other settings. The university plays a unique and essential role too in the professionalization of the field and in the improvement of practice through the creation as well as the dissemination of knowledge.

RESEARCH

The creation of a body of knowledge in adult education through systematic and disciplined inquiry has lagged behind the development of graduate training programs. Adult educators have of necessity relied extensively on the general body of theory and research findings in education and the social sciences, which is of great importance to all educators. However, this general store of tested knowledge has not been sufficient. There is an urgent need for the development of a body of research and theory unique to adult education so that adult educators may gain a better understanding of the nature of their particular enterprise and the conditions that facilitate successful educational practice with adults.

To date, most of the significant research bearing directly on adult education has been produced by social scientists in such disciplines as psychology and sociology. Some of this work was done more than 50 years ago. A milestone was the publication in 1928 of *Adult Learning* by the distinguished psychologist Edward L. Thorndike.[61] Using the methods of scientific psychology, Thorndike demonstrated that one's learning ability increases to age 25 and declines thereafter only very gradually (recent research suggests there is no decline until old age). In effect, Thorndike pronounced that adults could learn as well or better than children—a startling discovery at that time. Thorndike continued his work on adult learning into the 1930s, focusing on more pragmatic concerns in his volume *Adult Interests*.[62]

While a thorough review of the contributions of social scientists to our understanding of adult learning and education is not possible here, we shall note briefly a few of the most influential developments. The studies of Kurt Lewin and his associates, beginning in the late 1940s and focusing on group dynamics and change theory, stand out. Many of Lewin's associates were prominently identified with adult education and had enormous influence on the field's development, especially in the 1950s when group discussion was widely advocated as the preferred method of adult education. Also in the 1950s pioneering work in adult psychosocial development was undertaken by several scholars whose influence is still felt. Two of the most prominent are Bernice Neugarten and Robert Havighurst. *Adult Education in Transition,* a sophisticated study of the organizational dynamics of public school adult education agencies by the sociologist Burton Clark, also appeared in the 1950s.[63] Clark's analysis of the causes and effects of institutional marginality is still of value in understanding administrative roles and organizational processes in adult education, especially in school and college settings. During the 1960s and 1970s the number of studies by social scientists directly related to adult education increased enormously, especially in the area of adult development and learning. A landmark volume of the mid-1960s was the first comprehensive analysis of participation in adult education, *Volunteers for Learning.*[64]

There is no doubt that social scientists will continue to make important contributions to our understanding of adult education and that adult education researchers will continue to use concepts and research findings from sociology, psychology, economics, and other disciplines. However, many research problems that are of little interest to social scientists are of central importance for advancing understanding of adult education and for improving professional practice.

Several attempts have been made to identify research priorities in adult education, but any such judgments are essentially a matter of preference and opinion.[65] Certainly few researchers in the field would contest the assertion that no problem or topic has been overstudied and that many important questions have scarcely been examined. Even the most fundamental and widely held assumptions about adult learners and the conditions that facilitate adult learning have been subject to very little scientific scrutiny. It has not been clearly demonstrated, for example, that active participation by adults in planning or implementing their learning activities has any particular beneficial effect on educational outcomes. There are good theoretical grounds for believing that learner involvement has certain desirable consequences, but convincing evidence is lacking. Even in the area of participation, where a good deal is known about the differences between participants and nonparticipants in terms of age, educational background, sex, race, and so on, the information has limited explanatory or predictive value. Little is known about the fundamental factors—for example, attitudes toward education or major changes in family or work life—that affect an individual's decision to participate in adult education. Historical scholarship, too, has touched on only a few of the many important questions that must be explored if we are to understand better the development of American adult education, particularly in its less formal manifestations outside institutions such as Chautauqua and university extension.[66]

Most research on adult education takes place in universities, and by far the largest share is produced by doctoral students in the form of dissertations. While the volume and quality of research in adult education has increased considerably over the past decade, the number of active researchers is still small and the financial support available for research on fundamental problems is limited. Another serious weakness of the research in the field is its fragmented nature; few lines of inquiry have been pursued in a systematic and cumulative fashion, although there are exceptions such as the work on motivational orientations[67] and on processes of self-education.[68]

Forums held for adult education researchers play important roles in encouraging the production and dissemination of new knowledge. The Commission of Professors of Adult Education, a group founded in the 1950s and affiliated with the Adult Education Association, continues to play a vigorous role in encouraging research through the work of various ad hoc committees, through sponsorship of publications, and through an annual meeting devoted in part to the discussion of scholarly issues. The Adult Education Research Conference, established in 1960, meets each year in a different American or Canadian city and provides a forum where not only professors but also graduate students and other interested professionals can share research findings and discuss research methods and related issues. In recent years adult education researchers have been increasingly active in the American Educational Research Association and in other professional societies in such fields as reading and gerontology.

Dissemination of research occurs through other vehicles as well. The most important are the scholarly journals and the federally supported ERIC system, which provides microfiche copies of unpublished reports, papers, and studies that otherwise would not be readily available. The oldest and most prominent research periodical is *Adult Education*, published quarterly by the Adult Education Association. *Convergence*, published by the International Council for Adult Education in Toronto, is another periodical of worldwide circulation and is a major outlet for scholarship with an international and comparative focus. Of the scholarly journals published outside the United States, one of the most highly regarded is the British *Studies in Adult Education*. An indicator of the increasing maturity of the research in adult education is the recent development of several specialized scholarly periodicals, including *Educational Gerontology* and *Adult Literacy and Basic Education*. Finally, a considerable number of periodicals oriented mainly to the interests of professional practitioners sometimes publish work of interest to researchers, as well as less technical articles by researchers themselves: *Lifelong Learning: The Adult Years*, published by the Adult Education Association; the *Canadian Journal of University Continuing Education; The Journal of Extension; Continuum;* and the British *Adult Education*. A 1976 directory lists some 80 periodicals published in all parts of the world concerned with disseminating information about adult education or related fields.[69]

PROFESSIONAL ORGANIZATIONS

The numerous organizations to which adult educators and adult education institutions belong mirror the multitude of purposes and settings that characterize adult education today. These organizations serve several functions that are vital to the continuing development of the field and its practitioners. Perhaps the most important function served by organizations of adult educators is professional development. Virtually all such organizations or associations provide vehicles for the formulation and exchange of professional information, attitudes, and values. Professional development is fostered in many ways—for example, through publications, committee work, and participation in organized learning activities such as lectures, symposia, and workshops. Another important function served by organizations with both individual and institutional membership is advocacy, sometimes on behalf of adult learners in general or the field as a whole, but more often for special interests. Activities involved in advocacy can range from routine public relations duties to aggressive political lobbying in the state legislatures and in Congress. Another function is coordination. Local adult education councils often serve as informal mechanisms for communication and coordination among agencies in a specific geographical area. At the national level, the Coalition of Adult Education Organizations functions both as a coordinating body for some 20 national organizations and as an advocate for the interests of organized adult education as a whole. At the global level, the International Council for Adult Education performs similar functions and in addition places emphasis on professional development activities. A final function, although one performed by only a few organizations, might be termed regulation. A regulatory organization is one that imposes rules or standards on other organizations. The most explicit example of regulation is accreditation, which is the major purpose of at least one organization— the Council on Non-Collegiate Continuing Education—and an important function of a few others, such as the National Home Study Council.

The full range and diversity of the functions that professional organizations serve are broader than we can show here. After discussing Houle's work on the classification of adult education organizations, Griffith set forth a useful descriptive typology of associations of adult educators "oriented toward one or more of . . . five bases."[70] These bases are content, sponsoring agency, method, place, and clientele. As Griffith noted, these categories are not mutually exclusive and educators often belong to more than one type of association. It might also be noted that the functions discussed above tend to cut across these categories, except for the regulatory function, which perhaps constitutes an additional "base." Yet another base might be "role" as exemplified by teacher and counselor groups in state-level adult education associations and by such role-based national organizations as the National Council of State Directors of Adult Education.

Associations based on content tend to be the least institutionalized and perhaps the least widespread. Typically they consist of committees or special interest groups within the Adult Education Association or of groups concerned with adult education within "content-based" professional organizations such as the American Vocational Association, the Religious Education Association, and various associations in the fields of reading and teaching English as a second language. In contrast, associations based on institutional sponsorship of adult education tend to be more institutionalized and also influential in terms of both advocacy and professional development. Examples include the National University Continuing Education Association, the Association for Continuing Higher Education, the National Association for Public Continuing and Adult Education, and the American Society for Training and Development. Associations based on methods of instruction or delivery of education include the National Home Study Council, media associations such as the National Association of Educational Broadcasters, and special interest groups such as the Adult Education Association's section on residential adult education. Like institutional sponsorship, place or geography is an important base for the development of professional associations. General-purpose adult education associations can be found at the local level, the state level, and the regional level (e.g., associations in the Missouri Valley, Rocky Mountain States, and Pacific Northwest). Finally, there are the national general-purpose organizations such as the Adult Education Association of the U.S.A. and the Canadian Association for Adult Education.

This profusion of associations of adult educators might be interpreted as an example of healthy pluralism or as a symptom of parochialism and fragmentation. Depending on how one views it, it can be either or both. If we consider the larger picture at the national and state levels, it is clear that fragmentation has negative consequences for such vital professional functions as advocacy, professional development, and coordination. In regard to political action at the national level, organized adult education seldom speaks with one voice and has been singularly ineffective in influencing public policy through lobbying efforts in Congress or with administrative agencies of the government.[71] Despite some joint national conferences and other occasional efforts at cooperation, the major national organizations concerned directly with adult education have consistently gone their separate ways. Institutional loyalties and parochial interests have so far vitiated any efforts to bring greater unity and coherence to the field.

PROFESSIONAL IDENTITY

Most professional occupations are bound together by a common body of knowledge and technique and by common institutional settings, roles, and purposes. As we have seen, however, this is not true of adult education. Adult education by its very nature is an enterprise that cannot be dominated by any one institution and that can never be reduced to any single purpose or function other than the broadest commitment to human and societal development. In some respects adult education is similar to other subfields within the broad profession of education, such as special education or guidance, but in other respects it is very different, for it is not bound to schools or school-like settings and purposes.

That the majority of the educators of adults do not identify professionally with the field of adult education is to be expected. Most, as we have seen, are volunteers or persons who devote only part of their time to educational work with adults. Social workers, museum curators, public health officials, and the various human service professionals who engage in adult education work identify with their primary occupations. This does not preclude, however, the possibility of greater awareness among professionals in related fields that some or much of their work is essentially adult education, and such awareness seems to be growing.

The real issue of professional identity concerns the increasing number of persons whose energies are principally devoted to educational work with adults. Included are the full-time "trainers" in industry and government agencies; the education staff of unions, Y's, voluntary associations, and various community organizations; the directors of continuing education in medical centers and professional associations; and the many other professionals who work with adults in different settings, including colleges and schools. Despite strong institutional loyalties, a growing number of adult educators who have not identified themselves as such in the past are beginning to do so, as greater enrollments in graduate degree programs in adult education show. Given the fact that before the 1950s adult education barely existed as a field of study and as an organized profession, the lack of widespread professional identification with the field is not surprising.

The lack of professional identity may be less acute now than in the past, but it is still a serious concern because of its implications for standards of professional practice and for the political effectiveness of organized adult education. It is doubtful that there is any short-term solution to the problem. Ultimately, the credibility and vitality of any profession rests on the development and dissemination of a specialized body of theory and technique. A few decades ago it would have been presumptuous for adult education to have made any claims in this regard. Today there is a sufficient body of specialized knowledge and technique to justify the assertion that adult education is a credible field of professional specialization. However, this knowledge base is still fragmentary and the techniques of professional practice still relatively rudimentary. The greatest challenge adult education confronts therefore is to expand its knowledge base and to refine its unique body of specialized technique. For most practitioners, identification with the profession of adult education will depend on the efficacy of its concepts and practical tools in helping adults to learn.

NOTES

1. United Nations Educational, Scientific, and Cultural Organizations (UNESCO), *Learning to Be*, prepared by Edgar Faure et al., 1972, p. 69.
2. Lawrence A. Cremin, *Public Education* (New York: Basic Books, 1976).
3. UNESCO, *Learning to Be*, p. 142.
4. Robert M. Smith and Kay K. Haverkamp, "Toward a Theory of Learning How to Learn," *Adult Education* 28, no. 1 (1977): 3—21.
5. Paulo Freire, *Pedagogy of the Oppressed* (New York: Herder and Herder, 1970).
6. Carl Lindsay, James Morrison, and E. James Kelley, "Professional Obsolescence: Implications for Continuing Professional Education," *Adult Education* 25, no. 1 (1974): 3—22.
7. U.S., Bureau of the Census, *Statistical Abstract of the United States: 1980* (Washington, D.C.: Government Printing Office, 1980), p. 62.
8. Ibid., p. 30.
9. Ibid.
10. Ibid., p. 148.
11. John W. C. Johnstone and Ramon J. Rivera, *Volunteers for Learning: A Study of the Educational Pursuits of American Adults* (Chicago: Aldine, 1965).
12. Richard E. Anderson and Gordon G. Darkenwald, *Participation and Persistence in American Adult Education* (New York: College Board, 1979).
13. U.S., Bureau of the Census, *Statistical Abstract: 1980*, p. 402.
14. Willard Wirtz, *The Boundless Resource* (Washington, D.C.: New Republic Books, 1975), p. 108.
15. U.S., Bureau of the Census, *Money Income of Families and Persons in the United States: 1978* (Current Population Reports, Series P—60, no. 123, June, 1980), p. 54.
16. U.S., Department of Commerce, *Social Indicators 1976* (Washington, D.C.: Government Printing Office, 1977), p. 509.
17. Abraham Carp, Richard Peterson, and Pamela Roelfs, "Adult Learning Interests and Experiences," in *Planning Non-Traditional Programs*, ed. K. Patricia Cross and John Valley (San Francisco: Jossey-Bass, 1974), pp. 11—52.

18. National Center for Education Statistics, *Participation of Adults in Education: 1978 Preliminary Report* (Washington, D.C.: U.S. Department of Education, 1980).

19. Coolie Verner, "Definition of Terms," in *Adult Education: Outlines of an Emerging Field of University Study*, ed. Gale Jensen, A.A. Liveright, and Wilbur Hallenbeck (Chicago: Adult Education Association of the U.S.A., 1964), pp. 30–32.

20. C. Hartley Grattan, *In Quest of Knowledge* (New York: Association Press, 1955), p. 9.

21. F. A. Cavenaugh, ed., *James and John Stuart Mill on Education* (Cambridge, England: 1931), pp. 132–133. Quoted in Grattan, *In Quest of Knowledge*, p. 8.

22. Lyman Bryson, *Adult Education* (New York: American Book, 1936), p. 3.

23. UNESCO, *The General Conference Adopts a Recommendation on Adult Education* (Adult Education Information Notes, no. 1), 1977, p. 2.

24. See the discussion in K. H. Lawson, *Philosophical Concepts and Values in Adult Education* (Nottingham, England: Department of Adult Education, University of Nottingham, and the National Institute of Adult Education, 1975).

25. See, for example, Jack Mezirow, "Perspective Transformation," *Adult Education* 28, no. 2 (1978): 100–110.

26. For a discussion of how this situation has changed in Germany, see Robert A. Carlson, "Liberal Adult Education Adapts to the Technological Society: A Study of West Germany's Adult Education Centers," *Adult Education* 27, no. 1 (1976): 3–12.

27. See, for example, Eduard Lindeman's influential book, first published in 1927: *The Meaning of Adult Education* (Montreal: Harvest House, 1961).

28. *Adult Leadership* 1 (May 1952): 32.

29. Grattan, *In Quest of Knowledge*, p. 4.

30. Freire, *Pedagogy of the Oppressed*.

31. Lindeman, *Meaning of Adult Education*.

32. For a review of research on this topic, see Allen Tough, "Major Learning Efforts: Recent Research and Future Directions," *Adult Education* 28, no. 1. (1978): 250–263.

33. UNESCO, *General Conference Adopts a Recommendation*, p. 2.

34. Grattan, *In Quest of Knowledge*, p. 119. Portions of the original report were published in R. D. Waller, ed., *Design for Democracy* (New York: Association Press, 1956).

35. Commission on Non-Traditional Study, *Diversity by Design* (San Francisco: Jossey-Bass, 1973).

36. Lee J. Cary, ed., *Community Development as a Process* (Columbia, Mo.: University of Missouri Press, 1970).

37. Malcolm Knowles, *The Modern Practice of Adult Education*, rev. ed. (Chicago: Association Press/Follett Publishing Co., 1980), p. 43.

38. See, for example, Cyril O. Houle, *The Design of Education* (San Francisco: Jossey-Bass, 1972), p. 5.

39. Malcolm Knowles, "What We Know About the Field of Adult Education," *Adult Education*, 14, no. 2 (1964): 67.

40. See, for example, Knowles, *Modern Practice of Adult Education*.
41. J. M. Daly et al., *Survey of Adult Education in Community Organizations* (Rockville, Md.: Westat, 1973).
42. *Yearbook of Adult and Continuing Education, 1975–76* (Chicago: Marquis Academic Media, 1975).
43. National Center for Education Statistics, *Participation of Adults in Education: 1978*.
44. Cyril O. Houle, "The Educators of Adults," in *Handbook of Adult Education*, ed. Robert M. Smith, George F. Aker, and J. R. Kidd (New York: Macmillan, 1970), pp. 109–119.
45. Seymour Lusterman, *Education in Industry* (New York: Conference Board, 1977).
46. Carnegie Commission on Higher Education, *Toward a Learning Society* (New York: McGraw-Hill, 1973).
47. Jack Mezirow, Gordon G. Darkenwald, and Alan B. Knox, *Last Gamble on Education: Dynamics of Adult Basic Education* (Washington, D.C.: Adult Education Association of the U.S.A., 1975).
48. Gordon G. Darkenwald, "Educational and Career Guidance for Adults: Delivery System Alternatives," *Vocational Guidance Quarterly* 28 (March 1980): 200–207.
49. Burton R. Clark, *Adult Education in Transition* (Berkeley, Calif.: University of California Press, 1968).
50. Harold W. Beder, "An Environmental Interaction Model for Agency Development in Adult Education," *Adult Education* 28, no. 3 (1978).
51. Cyril O. Houle and John H. Buskey, "The Doctorate in Adult Education," *Adult Education* 16, no. 3 (1966): 133.
52. Ibid., pp. 131–141.
53. Ibid., pp. 133–134.
54. Commission of Professors of Adult Education, *1960 Conference Proceedings* (Chicago: Adult Education Association of the U.S.A., 1960).
55. Charles E. Kozoll, *Response to a Need: A Case Study of Adult Education Graduate Program Development in the Southeast* (Syracuse, N.Y.: Syracuse University Publications in Continuing Education, 1972).
56. Alan B. Knox, *Development of Adult Education Graduate Programs* (Washington, D.C.: Adult Education Association of the U.S.A., 1973), pp. 27–28.
57. Ibid., p. 28.
58. Houle, "Educators of Adults," p. 117.
59. Houle and Buskey, "Doctorate in Adult Education," pp. 138–139.
60. Houle, "Educators of Adults," p. 115.
61. Edward L. Thorndike, *Adult Learning* (New York: Macmillan, 1928).
62. Edward L. Thorndike, *Adult Interests* (New York: Macmillan, 1935).
63. Clark, *Adult Education in Transition*.
64. Johnstone and Rivera, *Volunteers for Learning*.
65. See, for example, Burton W. Kreitlow, *Educating the Adult Educator: Part 2, Taxonomy of Needed Research* (Wisconsin Research and Development Center, University of Wisconsin, 1968), and The Advisory Panel on Research Needs in Lifelong Learning During Adulthood, *Lifelong Learning During*

Adulthood: An Agenda for Research (New York: College Board, 1978).

66. For examples of recent historical work of this kind, see *Adult Education* 26, no. 4 (1976).

67. For a review, see Roger Boshier, "Factor Analysts at Large: A Critical Review of the Motivational Orientation Literature," *Adult Education* 27, no. 1 (1976).

68. For a review, see Tough, "Major Learning Efforts."

69. John A. Niemi and Daniel C. Jessen, *Directory of Resources in Adult Education* (Washington, D.C.: Adult Education Association of the U.S.A.; and DeKalb, Ill.: ERIC Clearinghouse in Career Education, 1976).

70. William S. Griffith, "Adult Education Institutions," in *Handbook of Adult Education*, ed. Smith, Aker, and Kidd, p. 174.

71. William S. Griffith, "Adult Educators and Politics," *Adult Education* 26, no. 1 (1976): 270–297.

Chapter 2
Philosophy and Adult Education

The philosophy of education involves the systematic examination of the assumptions that underlie practice. How one analyzes and interprets practice in adult education depends upon the philosophical orientation one brings to the task. Just as adult education in the United States is characterized by a diversity of programs, sponsors, and clienteles, so, too, a wide range of thought characterizes the philosophy of adult education. There exists no single conceptual framework, no single set of basic assumptions and principles from which all educators view the field.

This diversity in both the theory and practice of adult education is not particularly surprising. Institutions and movements and philosophies evolve from sociocultural contexts. While some argue that the adult education movement should have a single comprehensive philosophy "so that no matter what problems adult educators are facing they share a common course,"[1] it is much more likely that adult education philosophy will continue to reflect our pluralistic society. As one writer has pointed out:

> As long as we are a pluralistic society, as long as our public is made up of many publics, we shall continue to have philosophies of education in conflict

with one another. Meanwhile, educators will continue to muddle along as best they can (which is very well indeed) on the basis of different philosophies (or different assumptions), often not formulated at all; and they will continue to feel pressure from different individuals and publics with varied philosophies and assumptions. It has been said that the United States does not have an ideology; it is one. The same may be said of American education. Like the American ideology, the philosophy of education is tentative, changing, and eclectic.[2]

This chapter's purpose is to review and analyze the ways in which philosophy has been applied to adult education. Acquainting readers with this topic could be done through a discussion of the views of individual theorists such as Lindeman, Bergevin, and Freire. A second approach might be to analyze the impact various schools of educational philosophy such as progressivism or existentialism have had upon the field. One might also look at the philosophy of adult education from a historical or developmental perspective, beginning with the earliest analyses of the field and ending with the major contemporary works. Our approach will be to probe the issues salient to the field of adult education—issues addressed by writers influenced by differing schools of educational thought.

The issue given the most attention by educational philosophers is that of the aims and objectives of adult education. Implicit in a discussion of the aims of education is a consideration of the relationship between education and the society in which education takes place. As will be seen, opinions range from those of the British philosophical linguists, who see adult education as "value-neutral," and its aim the seeking of truth, to those of the revolutionaries, who would use education to bring about radical social change. A second issue is the question of curriculum or subject matter. What one considers to be appropriate content depends to a certain extent upon one's view of the overall purpose of education. How the content is dealt with leads in turn to questions about the role of the teacher, the role of the learner, and instructional methodology.

THEORY AND PRACTICE

Before beginning a discussion of the purposes of adult education, it seems appropriate to address the question of the necessity of surveying the philosophic work in adult education. One might well ask why philosophy should be applied to education and whether or not it is important for educators to consider their own philosophic orientations.

Several writers have noted the desirability of formulating a philosophy of adult education. Roberts suggests that it is needed because those in adult education are too often concerned with "what to do without examining sufficiently why [they] should do it."[3] White notes that philosophy has an "immediate and intense attraction" to adult educators because, like adult education, it is concerned with "such basic problems as freedom and social justice, equal opportunity—in civil rights and power—and the participation of citizens in great decisions."[4] Bergevin, while recognizing that adult education philosophies vary, feels that there is value in having some basic philosophy to "establish a common point of reference, an integrated viewpoint, toward certain beliefs, ideas, attitudes, and practices."[5]

Many adult education practitioners engaged in the daily tasks of program planning, administration, or teaching have little time to reflect upon the meaning and direction of their activity. The educator is generally more concerned with skills than with principles, with means than with ends, with details than with the whole picture. Yet all practitioners make decisions and act in ways that presuppose certain values and beliefs. Whether or not it is articulated, a philosophical orientation underlies most individual and institutional practices in adult education. An evaluation and understanding of one's own philosophical orientation is one factor that distinguishes a professional adult educator from a nonprofessional or a novice. Thoughtful practitioners know not only what they are to do, but why they are to do it. Experience combined with reflection leads to purposeful and informed action. Philosophy does not equip a person with knowledge about what to do or how to do it; it is concerned with the why of education and with the logical analysis of the various elements of the educational process. Apps's monograph *Towards a Working Philosophy of Adult Education* presents a rationale for why philosophy can be of use to adult educators:

> The adult educator needs a foundation for looking at the relationship of educational problems.
> The adult educator needs to see the relationship of adult education activities to society.
> A well-developed working philosophy can provide the adult educator with an approach for dealing with such long-standing and basic questions as what is reality, what is the nature of man, what is education, etc.
> In a broader, personal sense, development of a working philosophy can provide a deeper meaning to the adult educator's life.[6]

The relationship between philosophy and action or between theory and practice has itself been the subject of debate. Some see philosophy and action as mutually exclusive concepts belonging to different realms. Another approach is to attempt to synthesize the two into one view. There appears to be an emerging consensus among philosophers that both are necessary: theory without practice leads to empty idealism, and action without philosophical reflection is mindless activism. In the early 1970s,

Silberman lamented the lack of philosophical interest in educational practice:

> If teachers make a botch of it, and an uncomfortably large number do, it is because it never simply occurs to more than a handful to ask *why* they are doing what they are doing, to think seriously or deeply about the purposes or consequences of education.
>
> This mindlessness—the failure to think seriously about educational purpose, the reluctance to question established practice—is not the monopoly of the public school; it is diffused remarkably throughout the entire educational system, and indeed the entire society.
>
> If mindlessness is the central problem, the solution must lie in infusing the various educating institutions with purpose, more important, with thought about purpose, and about the ways in which technique, content, and organization fulfill or alter purpose.[7]

Many current debates on educational policy and practice could be conducted more rationally if basic philosophic differences were clarified. A major purpose of philosophical inquiry, therefore, is to clarify issues so that decisions can be made on rational grounds. Arguments over means in education are fundamentally reduced to differences over ends or purposes to be achieved. For example, the debate over "back to basics" revolves around what types of persons we expect our educational system to produce. And the arguments between the proponents of liberal arts and of vocational education stem from basic philosophic issues related to the nature of the "good society."

In one sense, most actions are guided by some theory or some philosophy. We act for reasons, good or bad, and generally have some understanding of what we are doing, why we are doing it in the way we do it, and the consequences of our actions. What we have here in the ordinary course of human activity is common sense, which, though related to philosophy, can be distinguished from it. Long ago Socrates raised questions about common opinions and practices and demonstrated that the common-sense view of things could not always be trusted.

Philosophy is more reflective and systematic than common sense. Philosophy raises questions about what we do and why we do it, and it goes beyond individual cases and phenomena to treat questions of a general nature. When considering the interrelationship of philosophy and action, it is clear that philosophy inspires one's activities and gives direction to practice. The power of philosophy lies in its ability to enable individuals to better understand and appreciate the activities of everyday life.

By way of summary, Greene points to an even broader justification for engaging in philosophical inquiry: "We do not philosophize," she says, "to answer factual questions, establish guidelines for our behavior, or enhance our aesthetic awareness." Rather, we philosophize when, for some reason, we are aroused to wonder about how events and experiences are interpreted and should be interpreted. We philosophize when we can no longer tolerate the splits and fragmentations in our pictures of the world, when we desire some kind of wholeness and integration, some coherence which is our own.[8]

ADULT EDUCATION AND ADULTHOOD

The interrelationship between theory and practice in adult education provides a rationale for engaging in philosophical inquiry. Prior to looking at what various writers and schools of thought have said about the overall purpose of adult education, we should examine the concept of adult education, which presents, in itself, an important philosophical issue. Philosophy is interested in the general principles of any phenomenon, object, or process. Philosophy strives, as Scheffler notes, "for a maximum of vision and a minimum of mystery."[9] Lawson articulates the problem inherent in "minimizing" the mystery associated with the concept of adult education:

> Such a wide range of agencies engaging in such diverse fields of activity raises questions about the criteria which entitle us to bring them together in one portmanteau category. What is it about them which makes them examples of "the education of adults"?[10]

When one denotes diverse activities and delivery systems as adult education, philosophical issues emerge: Does "adult" indicate who the activities are for, or is there a special connotation about "education" when linked with "adult"?[11] As with other aspects of the educational process, one's definition of adult education reflects a particular philosophical orientation. Behaviorists, for example, would define adult education in terms of changes in behavior brought about by the educational process. Radical adult educators would find inadequate a definition of adult education that did not include raising people's consciousness of the social and political contradictions in their culture. And those who accept a humanist or existential orientation would define adult education in terms of inner growth and development. The questions inherent in defining adult education also relate to two other issues in the field: If adult education means learning activities especially for adults, what is the meaning of adulthood? and, If there is a special connotation for education when associated with adults, how is it distinguished from education in general? While these two issues are also dealt with in Chapter 3, they are philosophical questions.

The criteria one selects for defining adulthood are invariably dependent upon a particular sociocultural context. Age, psychological maturity, and social roles appear to be the essential ingredients in such a definition with the priority of these variables dependent upon the context of discussion. It is interesting to note that in American culture the concept of adulthood is a relatively recent one.[12] In writing about the emergence of this concept, Jordan notes that it evolved "by a process of exclusion, as a final product resulting from prior definitions of other stages in the human life cycle."[13] This notion of exclusion in part underlies Paterson's exploration of the concept of adulthood. "Adults are adults, in the last analysis," he says, "because they are older than children."[14] A person's age states a relationship to time that leads others to expect mature behavior:

> To say that someone is an adult is to say that he is entitled, for example, to a wide-ranging freedom of life-style and to a full participation in the making of social decisions; and it is also to say that he is obliged, among other things, to be mindful of his own deepest interests and to carry a full share of the burdens involved in conducting society and transmitting its benefits. His adulthood consists in his full enjoyment of such rights and his full subjection to such responsibilities. Those people (in most societies, the large majority) to whom we ascribe the status of adults may and do evince the widest possible variety of intellectual gifts, physical powers, character traits, beliefs, tastes, and habits. But we correctly deem them to be adults because, in virtue of their age, we are justified in requiring them to evince the basic qualities of maturity. Adults are not necessarily mature. But they are supposed to be mature, and it is on this necessary supposition that their adulthood justifiably rests.[15]

In analyzing the term *adulthood*, Paterson attempts to arrive at the essence of its meaning that is, to the extent possible, culture-free. An existentialist approach to adulthood would involve attention to the qualities and predicaments unique to humans. As Greene notes in *Teacher as Stranger*, "Acquainted with all the empirical data (if that were conceivable), capable of adjusting one construct to another, the teacher would still have to ask, 'Who am I?' and 'How am I to conceive the other—that child, that colleague, that man?'"[16] Humanistic psychologists such as Maslow and Rogers stress the idea that adulthood is a process rather than a condition, a process in which men and women continually strive toward self-actualization and self-fulfillment.

The concept of adulthood is intrinsically related to the question of whether adult education is fundamentally different from education in general. The disagreement between Knowles and Houle[17] over whether there is a distinct art and science of teaching adults to be termed andragogy implies an important definitional problem. One can emphasize the commonality of the educative process regardless of the clientele, as do Houle and others from various philosophical persuasions. Behaviorists, for example, are more concerned with arranging for reinforcement in the environment to bring about desired results than with whether the learners are children or adults. On the other hand, Knowles makes a case for approaching the educational process differently *because* one is dealing with adults rather than children. Others differentiate adult from child education on the basis of the centrality of socialization in the educational process.[18] Paterson, for example, finds adult education a neutral process because it does not require the transmission of attitudes and development of character as is the case in the education of children.[19]

In summary, the concepts of adult education and adulthood can be approached philosophically. One's assumptions about these concepts affect both practice and theory. Viewing adulthood as a process rather than a state, for example, leads to seeing education as a vehicle for individual development. Likewise, conceiving of adult education as a process of consciousness raising entails a special view of the student-teacher relationship.[20] These practical issues of content and curriculum, teacher-learner roles, and instructional methodology will be explored more fully in this chapter, as they evolve logically from the different views of the purpose of adult education.

AIMS AND OBJECTIVES

"The most important issue confronting educators and educational theorists," state Kohlberg and Meyer, "is the choice of ends for the instructional process."[21] One's attitude, one's choice of content and methodology, one's view of the learner and of the teacher logically evolve from what one considers to be the overall purpose of the educational process. Just as there exists no single philosophy of adult education, there is no single purpose around which all adult educators rally. A wide range of purposes, goals, and objectives has been characteristic of the field from the beginning of the movement. In *Adult Education in Action*, published in 1936, for example, 18 prominent educators, social scientists, and philosophers wrote about the need for adult education. The amazing variety of responses warrants reproducing the list of topics and authors.[22] "We need adult education," they wrote,

To Educate the Whole Man	L. P. Jacks
To Keep Our Minds Open	Nicholas Murray Butler
To Base Our Judgments on Facts	Newton D. Baker
To Meet the Challenge of Free Choice	Dorothy Canfield Fisher
To Keep Abreast of New Knowledge	William F. Ogburn
To Be Wisely Destructive	A. E. Heath
To Return to Creative Endeavor	John Erskine
To Prepare for New Occupations	Charles A. Beard

To Restore Unity to Life	Ernst Jonson
To Insure Social Stability	James E. Russell
To Direct Social Change	Harry Elmer Barnes
To Better Our Social Order	Glenn Frank
To Open a New Frontier	William F. Russell
To Liberalize the College Curriculum	Robert D. Leigh
To Improve Teachers and Teaching	H. A. Overstreet
To Attain True Security	Alvin Johnson
To Enlarge Our Horizons	Lucy Wilcox Adams
To See the View	William Bolitho

This list is representative of the several philosophical orientations from which it is possible to view the field of adult education. Purposes such as those listed are easily subsumed into several streams of educational ideology. Kohlberg and Meyer have identified three broad categories of educational thought: (1) romanticism, which stresses health, growth, and nurture of the inner self; (2) cultural transmission, which emphasizes the transmission of a culture's knowledge, values, and skills; and (3) progressivism, which focuses on practical problem solving for improving a person's life in society.[23] Erskine's response above, "To Return to Creative Endeavor" exemplifies the personal growth in romanticism, while "To Educate the Whole Man" and "To Better Our Social Order" are representative of cultural transmission and progressivism respectively. Other schemata such as Apps's five categories of essentialism, perennialism, progressivism, reconstructionism, and existentialism[24] or Elias and Merriam's framework of liberal education, progressivism, humanistic education, behaviorism, radicalism, and philosophical analysis[25] might also provide bases for viewing the purposes of adult education.

Both the diversity and interrelatedness of philosophical orientations can be seen through an analysis of the overall aims and objectives of adult education. Using the purposes of adult education as the basis for organizing the philosophical literature, it becomes apparent that there are at least five different emphases. The cultivation of the intellect, which draws on both liberal education and philosophical analysis, is one aim of adult educators. Societal advancement, a second aim, is often seen as a product of individual growth. A third clustering consists of educators influenced by the progressive education movement. For these, the aim of adult education is both personal growth and the maintenance and promotion of a better society. Fourth are the radicals who assign education a crucial role in bringing about a change in the social order. Finally, organizational effectiveness is the aim of adult education activities sponsored by employers in both the public and private sectors. Following is a discussion of the purposes of adult education based upon these differing emphases.

The Cultivation of the Intellect

The British philosophers K. H. Lawson and R. W. K. Paterson have introduced American adult educators to the notion that education should be valued for its own sake and considered apart from social goals and social action. The problem inherent in linking educational aims to social values becomes particularly acute in a pluralistic society where there is a difference of opinion as to what ends are most desirable. Broudy made this point in *Aims of Adult Education: A Realist's View*. There is a problem, he says, in preparing people to live the good life because there is no agreement as to what constitutes the good life. Likewise, the "social roles" approach, or attempting to teach people to play certain roles more effectively in society, produces a dangerous conformity to the view of the institutions that have defined those roles.[26]

Paterson, in an article devoted to the issue of social change as the aim of adult education, underscores what he sees as the inadequacy of this approach. The danger is twofold: the field of adult education will be turned into either "a political arena [as in an open democratic society] in which social, economic, and political questions loom larger than . . . educational questions," or into "a political closed shop."[27] It is not a prerogative, argues Paterson, of any one professional group such as educators or doctors to promote social change. Adult education should neither promote social change, "whether gentle and piecemeal or radical and sweeping," nor defend the status quo. The field cannot, he says, "take sides on any social questions."[28]

Paterson does, however, draw a distinction between the use of adult education for social ends and the social value of education. If adult education is conceived of as a "tool or instrument to be used as employers think fit," then "the education of adults has and can have no 'social purpose' or 'social relevance.' " If, however, adult education is conceived of as "an intrinsic *element* or essential *ingredient* in any society that is genuinely worth building and preserving," then "the education of adults fulfills a most vital social purpose and is always of the keenest relevance."[29]

Lawson also rejects social change as a function of adult education. Besides the argument that education is or should be inherently neutral, Lawson also points out the practical consideration that if adult education were to become involved in social causes, it would run the risk of not receiving adequate public funds for its management.[30]

What then is the proper aim of education? For Paterson the proper aim of adult education is to transmit knowledge that is "educationally worthwhile." Education, he says, is the "fearless transmission of truth," which is "morally, socially, and politically neutral."[31] Adult education should be designed to bring about a deepened awareness, "a meaningful touch with reality," which is accomplished by building up in a person "rich and coherent bodies of worthwhile knowledge." Paterson discusses what constitutes "worthwhile knowledge":

> It is the cognitive value of any piece of knowledge, that is, its intrinsic value *as* knowledge, which determines its educational value. It is not in its value as a means to economic advancement, either of the individual or of society as a whole, nor in its value as a means to the resolving of social problems, however grave or momentous, but in its intrinsic value as knowledge, as part of the fabric of the knowing mind, part of the very fabric of personhood, to develop which is the defining purpose of education, that the educational value of any piece of knowledge consists.[32]

Skills are included in the range of knowledge only if the skills are intrinsically worth learning and not merely instrumental. Overall, little attention is given to skills and affective learning in Paterson's discussion of objectives. An academic subject matter approach is central to his view of education. The subject matter of adult education involves nine different kinds of knowledge: mathematics, the physical sciences, history, the human sciences, languages, the arts, morals, religion, and philosophy. Paterson argues that the objective worth and richness of these disciplines has long been established and so they constitute "worthwhile" knowledge.[33]

Lawson proposes justifying adult education as education. It is not related to social service, recreation, or community work, he says, and need not be justified in those terms. Adult education, he feels, "has a claim to public support" purely because "it is a system of teaching and learning."[34] Like Paterson, Lawson contends that adult education does not need an external objective or purpose. It is enough to concentrate on the tasks intrinsic to adult education. Developing the rationality of human beings, educating them "because [they are] judged to be important" is justification enough. Developing the human being, Lawson writes, "serves the purpose of developing society, but it is a purpose internal to the concept of education and not one which is outside it."[35]

Lawson also agrees with Paterson about the content of adult education. Content consists of knowledge that is "publicly accredited, socially worthwhile, and any activity which contributes to the development of rational minds."[36] While seeming to prefer the traditional liberal studies conception of content, Lawson does make a case for the learning of skills as a legitimate form of knowledge within adult education. Yet his inclusion of craft subjects and skills is based on reducing these to a form of knowledge and intelligent behavior. Insofar as the learning of skills demands intelligence, these can be considered adult education activities. A craft qualifies as education insofar as it is a "system of skills, criteria, values, and cognitive knowledge."[37]

The view the two British philosophers hold of the educational objectives of adult education is consistent with their analysis of the concept of education. If the cognitive, rational, and intellectual dimensions of the educational process are the only dimensions worthy of being called education, then only those objectives that foster these forms of development can be appropriate for adult education. It is not that these analysts believe other objects and forms of human activity are not worthwhile, it is only that they feel they should not be classified under adult education. They believe that confusion arises when *adult education* is used as the umbrella term to embrace all types of learning activities. When it is so used it is difficult, in their opinion, to give an educational justification for the field of adult education.

In identifying adult education with the transmission of "neutral" knowledge, and thus primarily liberal studies, Paterson and Lawson support a traditional view of the roles of teachers and learners and the instructional process. For Lawson, the task of teachers in adult education is to make the choice about those things that are educationally worthwhile. The learners are of necessity subordinate to the teachers. Unless students are to be confined to what they already know, teachers are essential for introducing "learners to things beyond themselves."[38] It is the role of adult educators to identify what the learners do not know and to determine learning goals. The learners, because they lack knowledge in this new area, are not capable of setting goals. Rather, the learners enter into a contract of sorts in which they are "temporarily giving up [their] freedom to choose in favor of being guided, criticized, and tested according to the standards of a discipline of some kind beyond [themselves]."[39] Lawson thus prefers a teacher-centered approach. A student-centered approach is inadequate because it assumes "that the input provided by equals is sufficient . . . for the educational process to begin." It also assumes that

> the members of a group are sufficiently articulate and possess an adequate vocabulary and conceptual framework to enable them to conduct a meaningful discussion. If these conditions are met then the validity of the student-centered approach can perhaps be recognized, but it seems to require a group of "educated" people in order to make it work.[40]

Paterson, recognizing that he is "flying in the face of much recent thinking, in both philosophy and educational theory," also emphasizes "the subject matter of knowledge rather than the procedures."[41] To emphasize procedures rather than the body of knowledge itself "obscures and distorts a great deal more than it clarifies and explains. A body of knowledge is not a creation ex nihilo by a consortium of imaginative methodologists. It is not a cobweb spun by the human mind out of its own resources."[42]

In summary, a curriculum emphasizing liberal studies and a teacher-centered instructional methodology are logical extensions of these two philosophical analysts' view of adult education. The aim, for them, is the development of rationality, which is assisted by the transmission of educationally worthwhile knowledge. Education stands independent of its social context and thus needs no socially relevant purpose. Partly because of its claim of neutrality, and partly because of its liberal studies bias, the view held by Paterson and Lawson has not been widely accepted by American adult educators. Many raise the troubling question of whether any programmatic decision can be neutral or value-free. Likewise, adult education in North America is widely conceived of as encompassing a range of subjects, skills, procedures, practices, aims, and objectives.

While philosophically at the opposite end of the spectrum, Paterson and Lawson have in common with those who advocate radical social change as the goal of education a singular focus and prescribed methods for bringing about their desired ends. The next two sections of this chapter present the schools of educational thought that represent the mainstream of adult educational thinking today.

Individual Self-Actualization

Those who write from an humanistic or an existentialist position focus upon individual self-actualization as the principal aim of adult education. Underlying their approach is the belief that human beings are inherently good and possess the power for achieving the good life. Based upon the assumption of innate goodness and personal freedom in this orientation, the purpose of education becomes the development of persons—persons who are open to change and continued learning, persons who strive for self-actualization, and persons who can live together as fully functioning individuals. The focus is upon the individual learner rather than upon content and upon the affective rather than cognitive aspects of education.

A number of educators, psychologists, and philosophers have written in support of personal development as the major purpose of education. Humanistic psychologists Abraham Maslow and Carl Rogers see education as a means of fostering self-actualizing and fully functioning individuals. The overall goal of education, Maslow states, is "helping the person to become the best he is able to become."[43] Among adult educators, Knowles is a prominent advocate of this goal of adult education. For him the learning process involves the whole being, emotional and psychological as well as intellectual. It is the mission of adult educators, then, to assist adults in developing their full potential. Andragogy, the art and science of helping adults learn, is a methodology for facilitating this end. Knowles's philosophy of education is characterized

> by a concern for the development of persons, a deep conviction as to the worth of every individual, and faith that people will make the right decisions for themselves if given the necessary information and support. It gives precedence to growth of *people* over the accomplishment of *things* when these two values are in conflict. It emphasizes the release of human potential over the control of human behavior.[44]

In an earlier publication Knowles speaks of the aim of adult education as being to help adults become liberated. He speaks of a model of a " 'free man' but this is not a stereotypic model, since each individual defines what he will be when free."[45] All adult educators can rally around this common aim, he feels, because it allows for any type of adult education as long as the individual sees it as liberating. Society does not enter into the process except as a vehicle for providing a full range of choices to a potential participant.

Among the writers who view the purpose of adult education primarily as self-development are those influenced by existential philosophy. They emphasize the educational task of assisting a feeling, suffering, rejoicing free person to fashion his or her essence or character. The primary aim of adult education is to help in the development of responsible selfhood in the face of the complexities and problems of modern life. Broudy sees humanity caught in an *existential* or *cultural predicament*," between the demands of a modern system of mass production and the democratic commitment to individual freedom and development. The aim of adult education, he says, is to make every adult aware of this predicament and his or her role in it. Adults who are sensitive to their predicament will then commit themselves to "self-cultivation."[46]

McKenzie sees the aim of adult education as more than the recognition of one's predicament in modern society. Adult education should also foster a courageous spirit among individual learners. It should, he believes, facilitate the development of a proactive, self-directed adult who will be responsible for the evolution of a more enlightened human existence.[47]

Whether writing from an existentialist or a humanistic orientation, these philosophers see the focus of adult education as upon individual growth and development. This emphasis in turn strongly influences their views of the nature of the curriculum or content of adult education, the roles of teacher and learner, and the instructional process.

The basic philosophic question that underlies content selection is a consideration of the source of knowledge. For those who see the aim of adult education as personal development, the source of knowledge lies in experience itself. The act of learning is highly personal. An individual learns what he or she perceives to be necessary, important, or meaningful. The "knowledge" one gleans from content depends upon one's own experiences, goals, interests, attitudes, and beliefs. Knowles, for example, maintains that the content itself is unimportant; what is crucial is the "effect upon the learner."[48]

For those who place greater emphasis upon the goal of education as the transmission of culture or the passing on of a specified body of knowledge, a liberal arts curriculum is highly valued. Such a curriculum, however, is not necessarily incompatible with the self-development aim of education. Kallen, who views education as a liberating experience, advocates liberal studies as a means of achieving liberation.[49] Simpson and Gray point out that the humanities—philosophy, literature, history, ethics, language, and social studies—"have traditionally been concerned with the person—the individual—and the eternal, existential question of relationships among persons, universes, gods, and dreams."[50] Indeed, specific liberal education curricula such as the Great Books program attempt to assist persons to grow intellectually, morally, and esthetically.

While studying the social, political, religious, and philosophical values of other ages and cultures might contribute to the development of the self, examining one's *own* values, attitudes, and emotions is equally valued. With youth, such an emphasis finds expression in the evaluation of moral dilemmas and in attempts to develop acceptable values and attitudes. In adult education, values clarification workshops, encounter groups, transactional analysis, and human potential workshops exemplify the emphasis.

Teaching of content, then, is not, in this viewpoint, the goal of the educational process. The focus is upon the individual learner rather than upon a body of information. Subject matter, or a curriculum, serves as a vehicle that, if creatively employed, can lead to self-development. According to one writer, "teaching subject matter in a more human way" is one of two foci in this type of education. The second is that of "educating the nonintellectual or affective aspects of the student, that is, developing persons who understand themselves, who understand others, and who can relate to others."[51]

If one accepts personal development as the aim of adult education, then content is secondary to process, the student becomes the center of the experience, the teacher assumes the role of facilitator, and learning occurs through experimentation and discovery. Philosophical assumptions of individual freedom, responsibility, and natural goodness underlie the student-centered aspect of this approach. Arbitrary decisions about curriculum and methodology violate the individual student's ability to identify his or her own learning needs. The responsibility for learning is placed on the student—the student is free to learn what he or she wants to learn in the manner desired.

The role of the teacher is that of facilitator, helper, and partner in the learning process. The teacher does not simply provide information; he or she must create the conditions within which learning can take place. In order to facilitate, one must trust students to assume responsibility for their learning. This is a difficult stance to accept for the traditional teacher, for it necessitates abdicating the authority generally ascribed to the teaching role.

Knowles proposes andragogy, a technology of learning especially suited to adults in which the teacher is a facilitator who aids adults in becoming self-directed learners.[52] For McKenzie, the teacher of adults allows learners to free themselves from historical determinism in order to become liberated and courageous people.[53] The teacher of adults can "facilitate" the process by serving as a resource person, by encouraging students to set their own goals, and by refusing to

> weave a fabric of destiny which controls absolutely the course of events in the learning situation, by refusing to play God in writing a lesson plan that is perceived as a providential design for the learners, by refusing to carve out in stone the rules for the "historical" development of the learning situation.[54]

While group activity is the instructional technique favored in bringing about individual growth, Rogers specifies several other "methods of building freedom" a teacher might employ in encouraging self-directed learning. The facilitator can provide "all kinds of resources which will give his students experiential learning relevant to their needs" and use student contracts, simulation games, and even programmed instruction, especially that which addresses affective as well as cognitive dimensions.[55]

Those who espouse individual self-actualization as the primary aim of adult education are often aware of the constraints involved in transforming this ideal into practice. McKenzie, for example, asks whether "self-directed learning in educational groups" is "always and in every circumstance possible or even desirable."[56] The answer of course is that one must consider factors such as time constraints, organizational expectations, group size, and so on. As McKenzie observes, "I must grapple not only with ideas in the confines of my ivory tower but also with the application of these ideas in a less-than-perfect, and certainly complex, real world."[57] Those who value individual growth and development as the aim of education can, however, guide their practice toward this end by emphasizing process over content, the adult as the center of the experience, teacher as facilitator, and group interaction as the primary vehicle for learning.

Personal and Social Improvement

In contradistinction to those who see the aim of adult education as cultivation of the intellect or personal fulfillment, and those who advocate using education to bring about social change, are the philosophers and educators who emphasize the individual within the social context. In the opinion of one such scholar, the major issue of adult education revolves around the relation of the individual to the groups with which he lives and of which he is a part.[58] Writers who emphasize the personal development aim of education concede that the more self-actualized adults we have, the better our society. But this salutary outcome is a by-product of educating individuals, not a goal in itself. Educators influenced by progressivism, however, see education as having a dual function of promoting individual growth and maintaining and/or promoting the good society.

In analyzing the role of adult education in society, Hallenbeck points out that the individual learner and the society cannot be separated. And while adult education's primary concern might be to help individual adults to grow and develop, "what adults want to learn and are constrained to learn . . . is generated by the social milieu in which they live. Their interests, their needs, their problems, and their ambitions are products of their environment."[59] Broudy underscores this idea with the observation that if the emphasis in education is solely upon individual growth, then "the problem of aims in adult education becomes, so far as the educator is concerned, a problem of means; in short, the problem disappears."[60]

Aside from learning what the social milieu determines they will learn, adults have a responsibility to the society in which they live, according to Hallenbeck. In speaking of an adult learner's responsibility towards society and society's changing circumstances, Hallenbeck has defined what it means to be an adult. This notion of reciprocal responsibility was also pointed out by Lindeman in *The Meaning of Adult Education*. "Knowing-behavior," he says, "is social in two directions: it takes others into account and it calls forth more intelligent responses from others." If adult learners want their "intellectual alertness" to "count for something . . . they will be as eager to improve their collective enterprises, their groups, as they are to improve themselves."[61]

In sketching its historical roles, Hallenbeck observes that society has emphasized adult education in times of social crisis and has turned to it when adjustments to social changes have been necessary. He concludes that the basic aims of adult education are:

> to maintain an adult population up to the standards of competence in the knowledge, wisdom, and skill which society requires; to develop in adults an understanding of the serious problems which interrupt the operations and

progress of their cooperative society and prepare them to participate in the solution of these problems; and to provide all adults with opportunities for their highest possible development in attitudes, understanding, knowledge, and quality of human existence toward the goal of the greater self-fulfillment and realization of each individual human being.[62]

Fifteen years after the above was published, Jerold Apps delineated four purposes of continuing education that again reflect both personal and social dimensions. The overall goal of "enhanc[ing] the quality of human life" more specifically consists of:

1. helping people acquire the tools for physical, psychological, and social survival;
2. helping people discover a sense of meaning in their lives;
3. helping people learn how to learn;
4. helping communities [societies] provide a more humane social, psychological, and physical environment for their members.[63]

The relationship between adult education and social responsibility has been most clearly articulated by Lindeman and Bergevin. These two adult educators were influenced by the progressive education movement and its chief proponent, John Dewey. Their views on the purpose of adult education can be better understood given some familiarity with Dewey and progressive ideals.

The progressive movement attempted to respond to the social changes occurring as a result of mass immigration and industrialization in the early decades of the twentieth century. In the face of severe social, political, and economic upheavals, many people put great faith in the power of education to solve them. Programs from kindergarten through high school, as well as in adult education, were developed to socialize the new immigrants, ameliorate the social ills brought about by rapid urbanization, train workers and leaders needed for the growing industrial society, and contribute to the development of a democracy without corruption. The highest ideal of the progressive movement was education for democracy. Thus, the goals of education the progressives held were both individual and social. Liberating the learner released the potential for the improvement of society and culture.

Dewey felt that education had a role in social reform and reconstruction. He felt that education would flourish if it took place in a democracy, but democracy would develop only if there were true education. He defined democratic societies as intentionally progressive and aimed at a greater variety of mutually shared interests. Since greater freedom was allowed their members there was a need to develop a social consciousness in individuals. Thus, for Dewey, a democratic society was committed to change. A democracy, he wrote, "is more than a form of government; it is primarily a mode of associated living, of conjoint communication experience."[64] Dewey saw the goals of education primarily in social terms. A democratic education, he felt, would produce a society that was constantly in a state of growth and development.

Lindeman's *The Meaning of Adult Education* was strongly influenced by Dewey and the progressivism of the 1920s. While emphasizing individual growth and a situation-approach to learning, Lindeman viewed humans as social beings. Thus, he said, adult education should be aimed at improving the individual's life in society. Education allows adults to cope with and function in a changing social milieu:

> Adult education will become an agency of progress if its short-time goal of self-improvement can be made compatible with a long-time, experimental but resolute policy of changing the social order. Changing individuals in continuous adjustment to changing social functions—this is the bilateral though unified purpose of adult learning.[65]

Lindeman did not merely advocate using education to cope with social change. Adult education, he felt, should also contribute to social action:

> Adult education turns out to be the most reliable instrument for social actionists. If they learn how to educate the adherents of their movement, they can continue to utilize the compelling power of a group and still remain within the scope of democratic behavior. When they substitute something other than intelligence and reason, social action emanates as sheer power and soon degenerates into habits which tend toward an anti-democratic direction. Every social-action group should at the same time be an adult-education group, and I go even so far as to believe that all successful adult education groups sooner or later become social-action groups.[66]

Even more concerned with adult education's duty to promote the democratic way of life is Paul Bergevin. Bergevin sees adult education as essential in contributing to what he calls "the civilizing process." The civilizing process has both an individual and a societal dimension. At the individual level, the civilizing process refers to a person's "maturing" from a "mere survival" state to become a "responsible member of the social order." At the societal level, the civilizing process is a "corporate, social movement involving the whole of society, as it moves from barbarism toward refinement in behavior, tastes, and thought."[67] Adult education, then, consists of

> a consciously elaborated program aiding and reinforcing the civilizing process. The over-all aim of the professional or lay adult educator, then, will be to bring each of us into some kind of constructive relationship with the civilizing process, always remembering that this process should represent those positive elements in environment and society that help us develop mature rationality in our lives and institutions.[68]

For Bergevin, the continuing education of adults is essential in preserving and enhancing a democratic way of life. It is a necessity, a "built-in requirement of a society emerging from control by the few to control by the many."[69] Bergevin recognizes the validity of presenting "the adult the opportunity to advance as a maturing individual," but it should always come within the context of helping him or her to learn "how to contribute his share to the civilizing process."[70] For Bergevin, the individual cannot be separated from the surrounding society. The positive environment behind the individual allows societies to progress. Self-development is important in that it leads to being better members of society.

In exploring the role of education in social change, Blakely, like Bergevin, delineated both an individual and a social dimension to adult education. "Education," Blakely feels, "leads to a better, more fulfilling personal life, while at the same time making a better citizenry and a better world."[71] While Bergevin speaks of the "civilizing process," Blakely sees education as working towards a "homeodynamic" society— that is, a society in which a balance is achieved between cultural components that imitate the past and components that invent the future. Survival of individuals and society depends upon achieving this balance.[72]

When the aim of adult education is individual development within, but having an influence upon, the social context, the curriculum, the role of the teacher and student, and the instructional process function to bring about both individual and social ends. Yet this aim also seems to result in ambivalence on these issues for some of its advocates. Bergevin, for example, at one point emphasizes the need to develop the liberal arts curriculum in order "to show a relationship to the adult's own needs and to show what is meant by such ideas as responsibility for one another, freedom, discipline, and a free society." At another point he says that although sometimes certain "subjects—history, mathematics, arts, etc.—are useful," programs "should be developed around the particular problems and needs of the participants." In yet another place he states that adult educators must be "concerned about the indigenous nature of the learning program" guided by the "*peculiar problems* at hand in terms of the *particular adults* involved."[73] It is difficult to determine whether Bergevin views content as a specific body of knowledge to be transmitted or as that which is established to meet individual needs, or as both. His writing reflects a conflict between the value of having the learner determine content and the value of learning an established body of knowledge that can further the civilizing process.

The determination of appropriate content in adult education relates to basic assumptions about the nature of knowledge. Dewey, Lindeman, and other progressives see knowledge as inseparable from ever-changing experience. Knowledge is equated with experience, experience that is reflected upon and that forms the basis for further learning. Dewey defined education as the reconstruction and reorganization of experience, which increases one's ability to direct the course of subsequent experience. It is both active and passive. That is, education or experience is not just what happens to a person, but also what that person does. It is, more precisely, the interaction of the individual with the environment.[74]

Lindeman echoes the notion of education as both passive and active. "My conception of adult education," he says, "points toward a continuing process of evaluating experiences. . . . Experience is, first of all, doing something; second, doing something that makes a difference; third, knowing what difference it makes."[75] This process of evaluating experience is engaged in by both learner and teacher. The teacher who functions from this perspective is "doing philosophy" in the words of Maxine Greene. "To do philosophy," she states, "is to become highly conscious of the phenomena and events in the world as it presents itself to consciousness." To do educational philosophy is "to become critically conscious of what is involved in the complex business of teaching and learning."[76]

This emphasis upon the critical reflection of experiences can be contrasted to the importance in traditional education of books that report the experiences of other people. The progressives felt that the learners' own experiences were an equally valid basis for education. Lindeman criticizes conventional education in which "knowledge is conceived to be a precipitation, a sediment of the experience of others." It is a brave teacher "who dares to reveal his special subject in the context of the whole of life and learning."[77] Greene also addresses this issue:

> The teacher can no longer simply accept what is transmitted by "experts" and feel he is properly equipped to interpret the world. He cannot even rely on the authority of accumulated knowledge or the conventional wisdom on which so many people depend. He must make decisions of principle, which may make necessary a definition of *new* principles, more relevant norms and rules. Therefore, he must become accustomed to unconventional presentations of situations around him, to ways of talking with which textbooks cannot deal.[78]

The content of education deemed appropriate by a particular school of thought is thus closely linked to how the school conceives knowledge itself. For progressive educators, knowledge is experience which is both reflected and acted upon by the learner. Specific content becomes subordinated to the developing of skills to evaluate experience. The method becomes the focus of the instructional process. In one of his few allusions to specific content, Lindeman does note that to confront "properly" situations one should use as much as possible the "relevant experience of others . . . experience which has been stored away in books and that which comes freshly from researchers and expert knowledge."[79]

Educators who are equally concerned with individual and societal development see education as intimately related to its social context and the learner's everyday life and experiences. All of life becomes the curriculum. Education is thus not restricted to schooling but includes all those incidental and intentional activities that society uses to pass on values, attitudes, knowledge, and skills. Education in this view becomes extensive. It includes the work of many institutions of society: family, work, school, churches, and in fact the entire community. Lawrence Cremin echoes this progressive notion in asserting that "every family has a curriculum . . . every church and synagogue has a curriculum . . . every employer has a curriculum and so forth."[80] Dewey broadly conceived of education as a lifelong experience:

> Education must be reconceived, not as merely a preparation for maturity (whence our absurd idea that it should stop after adolescence) but as a continuous growth of the mind and a continuous illumination of life. In a sense, the school can give us only the instrumentalities of mental growth; the rest depends upon an absorption and interpretation of experience. Real education comes after we leave school and there is no reason why it should stop before death.[81]

The content of education, while secondary to method, was in fact broadened by the progressives to include the practical, pragmatic, and utilitarian. Knowledge of and training in practical skills helps both individuals and society. Curriculum that is both liberal and practical reconciles, in Dewey's words, "liberal nurture with training in social serviceableness, with ability to share effectively and happily in occupations which are productive."[82] Dewey advocated doing away with the dualism in education and establishing a curriculum that reflected the needs of work and leisure, including the humanities and the sciences, the liberal and the pragmatic.

The methodology most favored by educators who stress the interrelationship of the individual and society is the scientific method of arriving at knowledge. Also termed problem solving, project methods, or the activity method, this approach involves several steps. As described by Dewey and others, the process entails the clarification of a problem to be solved, the development of ideas or hypotheses about this problem, and the testing of these hypotheses by an examination of evidence. Progressives felt that this method could be used in most subject areas and that it was based on the natural inclination of the learner to grapple with problems. This experimental method was seen as a vehicle with which to discover the truths about one's world.

Lindeman advocates the situation-approach to learning and states that "the best teaching method is one that emerges from situation experiences."[83] "Every adult person," Lindeman writes, "finds himself in specific situations with respect to his work, his recreation, his family-life, et cetera—situations which call for adjustments. Adult education begins at this point."[84] This approach involves: (1) a recognition of what constitutes the situation; (2) an analysis of the situation as a set of manageable parts or problems; (3) discussion of the problems in light of other people's experiences and available information; (4) use of information and experience to formulate tentative solutions; and, finally, (5) acting upon a solution.[85]

Benne also has proposed an experimental methodology. In arguing the merits of various philosophical approaches to methodology, he concludes that "a broadened method still must be an experimental method, rather than a method of authority, of intuition, of deduction, or of induction." In this experimental view, learning is a "series of experiments with respect to problems encountered and constructed."[86] Benne sees the preferred methodology in adult education as problem solving, for "programs of learning for adults must be adjusted to the learners, to the problems they need solved, to the situations confronting them."[87]

In the experimental, problem solving, or situation approach to learning, the relationship of teacher and student is perhaps best characterized as a partnership. The progressives opposed viewing the teacher as the sole source of knowledge, whose task was to put, or as Freire would have it, "bank,"[88] knowledge into the minds of students. In an educational theory that views the learning of subject matter or academic disciplines as the heart of the educational effort, the "banking" concept is functional. But if education is seen as the progressives viewed it—as the reconstruction of experiences through interactive processes with one's environment—then the traditional view of the teacher-learner relationship is inadequate.

Learning, according to Dewey, is something that students do for themselves. The teacher's responsibility is to organize, stimulate, instigate, and evaluate the highly complex processes of education. The teacher provides a setting that is conducive to learning. In so doing, the teacher also becomes a learner, for the relationships between teacher and learners are reciprocal. Both should plan and learn from each other. The teacher is neither totally directive nor totally passive. Rather, in Dewey's words, "the teacher is a learner, and the learner is, without knowing it, a teacher, and upon the whole the less consciousness there is, on either side, of either giving or receiving instruction, the better."[89] While seeing learning as based in personal experiences of the learner, teachers could also share with learners insights that had come from their own experiences.

Lindeman, obviously influenced by Dewey, stated that in adult education

> the teacher finds a new function. He is no longer the oracle who speaks from the platform of authority, but rather the guide, the pointer-out, who also

participates in learning in proportion to the vitality and relevance of his facts and experiences.[90]

The role of the teacher in progressive thought as helper, consultant, or encourager is, in some ways, similar to the facilitator role in humanistic education. There are, however, subtle differences. When personal development is the primary aim of adult education, the teacher's role is primarily supportive in allowing individuals to unfold, mature, and grow. When individual *and* social action are the goals, the role of teacher involves a more active partnership with the learner. Cognitive, affective, and skill development are stressed equally as they relate to the individual's social context and to the enhancement of the social order in general. Again, Lindeman expresses this notion when he characterizes the adult educational process as

> a cooperative venture in nonauthoritarian, informal learning, the chief purpose of which is to discover the meaning of experience; a quest of the mind which digs down to the roots of the preoccupations which formulate our conduct; a technique of learning for adults which makes education coterminous with life and hence elevates living itself to the level of adventurous experiment.[91]

This active, cooperative role of teacher is also emphasized by Bergevin and Benne. Bergevin advocates treating the adult as a "full partner in the educational enterprise." Through inclusion in every stage of the programming process, adult students learn social skills that will serve to advance the civilizing process. Besides content, participants learn "how to accept and discharge responsibility and how to work with others."[92] For Benne, the role of teacher has three dimensions: the helper who furnishes a model of "learner"; the expert who knows more about that which is being studied than the learner; and the therapist who removes attitudinal blocks to learning. Perhaps the most novel part of Benne's view of the teacher is the role of helper-model in which the learner emulates the helper's evaluative approach to knowledge.[93]

Thus, individual growth in conjunction with social development is for many adult educators the primary function of adult education. While not rejecting what Kohlberg and Mayer term "romanticism"—that is, the unfolding of the inner self—educators such as Dewey, Lindeman, and Bergevin maintain that the individual and the social context are inseparable. Education stimulates the learner's interaction with the environment while society simultaneously influences the learner's needs, desires, and motivation to learn. Improving individuals through education leads to a better society—indeed, the direction of personal development is with the overall social goal in mind. This goal leads to a specific view of the instructional process. Kohlberg and Mayer summarize the natural affiliation between the aim of progressive education and the method:

This aim requires an educational environment that actively stimulates development through the presentation of resolvable but genuine problems or conflicts. . . . Although both the cultural transmission and the progressive views emphasize "knowledge," only the latter sees the acquisition of "knowledge" as *an active change in patterns of thinking* brought about by experiential problem-solving situations.[94]

Social Transformation

The progressive educators view adult education as a means of creating a more desirable society while maintaining basic democratic values. The relationship of adult education to society also is the central concern of the radical philosophers and educators. Their emphasis, however, is on using education to bring about a new social order. Thomas and Harries-Jenkins provide a framework for conceptualizing the different philosophical stances with regard to adult education's role in social change. At one extreme is the view that education "*must* . . . challenge established economic, political, and social assumptions"; at the other extreme is the desire to preserve inherited cultural traditions and protect the status quo.[95] The authors label these two positions as "revolution" and "conservation." Between these two positions are the less extreme views of "reform" and "maintenance."[96]

Clearly, in advocating radical social change as the aim of education, thinkers such as Freire, Illich, Reimer, and Counts fall into Thomas and Harries-Jenkins's category of revolution. The very nature of a radical approach to education involves both criticizing existing practices and advancing visions of a better society. In making its criticisms and presenting its visions, the radical tradition questions the basic values, structures, and practices of society. Every area of social life is touched— family, schooling, work, religion, and economic and political systems. This section will first look at the radicals' criticisms of society and education and then examine their vision of education's role in bringing about a new social order.

With the exception of Freire, the main concern of radicals has been with public schooling. Many of their criticisms and proposals are applicable to adult education, however, especially given the ever-increasing institutionalization of adult education. Ivan Illich, prominent in the radical education movement of the 1960s and 1970s, writes from an anarchist philosophical position. As a social and political philosophy, anarchism raises fundamental questions about the role and nature of authority in society. Moreover, since the eighteenth century its proponents have questioned the very existence of state systems of schooling and the possibility of nonauthoritarian forms of education. The anarchists oppose national systems of education because of their conviction that education in the hands of the state would serve the political interests of those in control. The central concern of the anarchist tradition is to preserve, as much as possible, personal autonomy.

In numerous articles and books Illich has proposed the elimination of schools from society as the necessary condition for freeing people from their addiction to manipulative and oppressive institutions. Illich's criticism and rejection of schooling is based not so much on its failures as an institution, but on its central position in maintaining an overindustrialized and overconsumerized society. "We are all involved in schooling," he writes, "from both the side of production and that of consumption." We are

> superstitiously convinced that good learning can and should be produced in us—and that we can produce it in others. Our attempt to withdraw from the concept of school will reveal the resistance we find in ourselves when we try to renounce limitless consumption and the pervasive presumption that others can be manipulated for their own good. No one is fully exempt from the exploitation of others in the schooling process.[97]

Illich points out that schools are not the only institutions that shape a person's "vision of reality." Family life, health care, professionalism, and the media have hidden curricula that manipulate one's "world-vision, language, and demands." But, he says,

> school enslaves more profoundly and more systematically, since only school is credited with the principal function of forming critical judgement, and, paradoxically, tries to do so by making learning about oneself, about others, and about nature depend on a prepackaged process. School touches us so intimately that none of us can expect to be liberated from it by something else.[98]

Though Illich is principally a radical social critic, his views on education and learning are at the heart of his thinking. The type of learning that Illich espouses is one that promotes human freedom, equality, and close personal relationships. Unfortunately, in Illich's view, "the equal right of each man to exercise his competence to learn and to instruct is now pre-empted by certified teachers."[99] True learning, he says, is learning in which a person freely consents to participate. For Illich, no one has the right to interfere in the learning of another without that person's consent. He contends, in addition, that most learning is not the result of teaching, but rather is gathered incidentally as one participates in life. Teachers "may contribute to certain kinds of learning under certain circumstances. But most people acquire most of their knowledge outside school."[100] The learning that a person cannot gather incidentally from life and things can easily be appropriated from a skill master, a peer, or from books and other learning instruments.

The anarchist influence also can be seen in Ohliger's stance against mandatory adult education and against the professionalization and institutionalization of the field. Ohliger has alleged that, increasingly, adult education institutions define people as inadequate, insufficient, lacking, and incomplete. Over the years he has kept watch over the number of courses that adults are required to take by law, regulation, or social pressure. His enumeration of the groups now involved in compulsory adult education is extensive:

> traffic offenders and judges; parents of delinquents and public school teachers; illiterates on welfare; nurses; pharmacists; physicians; optometrists; nursing home administrators; firemen; policemen; dentists; psychiatrists; dieticians; podiatrists; preachers; veterinarians; many municipal, state, provincial, and federal civil servants; employees of all types pressured into taking courses, classes, joining sensitivity training or organizational development groups; and of course the military, where most, if not all, adult education is compulsory.[101]

The institutionalization of adult education is the chief target of Ohliger's criticism. Compulsory adult education has become pervasive in the health professions. Adult education has become more imbedded in the structure of the schooling establishment. Adult degrees, external degrees, and open learning for adults are means the educational establishment has developed for making education a commodity for thousands of adults. Ohliger echoes Illich when he asks,

> As we seem to be moving toward a society in which adults are told more and more that they must consume official knowledge in lifelong learning, is it any wonder that we say that adult education is becoming an oppressive force that is taking over people's lives?[102]

While Illich and Ohliger find institutions and in particular compulsory education at any level oppressive, Freire speaks more to changing the world view, the mind-set, the consciousness of individuals. In his theory, societal liberation and individual liberation are interdependent. While the anarchist attempts to promote personal freedom and autonomy by removing education from state control, the Marxist-humanist tradition, of which Freire is a part, attempts to produce the free and autonomous person through a revolutionary change from a capitalistic political economy to a socialist state.

For Freire, a society that is dehumanizing and oppressive must be changed. True humanization takes place in the world only when each person becomes conscious of the social force working upon him or her, reflects upon these forces, and acquires the capability to transform the world. To be human is to seek to guide one's own destiny. To be free means knowing one's identity and realizing how one has been shaped by one's social world and environment. The opposite of humanization is dehumanization or oppression. The condition of oppression is what Freire calls the culture of silence, and such silence can come from either ignorance or oppressive education. Oppression for Freire means "any situation in which 'A' objectively exploits 'B' or hinders his pursuit of self-affirmation as a responsible person."[103] Liberation of individuals and societies, in Freire's view, is a two-stage process:

> In the first, the oppressed unveil the world of oppression and through the praxis commit themselves to its transformation. In the second stage, in which the reality of oppression has already been transformed, this pedagogy ceases to belong to the oppressed and becomes a pedagogy of all men in the process of permanent liberation.[104]

Becoming aware of one's oppression, according to Freire, requires a movement through stages of consciousness. As described in his *Education for Critical Consciousness*, the lowest level is intransitive consciousness. This is the culture of silence that exists in the peasant societies of the Third World. Individuals are preoccupied with meeting elementary needs and do not comprehend the forces that have shaped their lives. Semi-intransitivity or magical consciousness is the second level and can be found in emerging societies of the Third World. Here, individuals have internalized the negative values that the dominant culture ascribes to them and are marked by excessive emotional dependence. The third level of consciousness, naive-transitiveness, occurs when people begin to experience reality as a problem and begin to sense that they have some control over their lives. The highest level of consciousness is critical consciousness, marked by depth in the interpretation of problems, self-confidence in discussions, responsibility, and dialogical discourse. Critical consciousness is brought about not through intellectual efforts alone, but through praxis, the authentic union of action and reflection. Education plays a crucial role in its emergence. "It will not appear," Freire says, "as a natural by-product of even major economic changes, but must grow out of a critical educational effort based on favorable historical conditions."[105]

While it is not possible to separate his political philosophy from his educational philosophy, Freire does address the inadequacy of traditional education for bringing about social change. For Freire, traditional education equals "banking education," in which learners receive and store mental deposits. Knowledge is seen as a gift bestowed on learners by the teacher. This type of education offends the freedom and autonomy of the learners. Banking education domesticates students for it emphasizes the transfer of existing knowledge to passive objects who must memorize and repeat this knowledge. Such education is a form of violence, for in imposing facts, ideas, and values it submerges the consciousness of the students. This process alienates consciousness, as students are not involved in a real act of knowing but are given a ready-made view of social reality. Traditional education thus perpetuates individual and social oppression:

> It follows logically from the banking notion of consciousness that the educator's role is to regulate the way the world "enters into" the students. His task is to organize a process which already occurs spontaneously, to "fill" the students by making deposits of information which he considers to constitute true knowledge. And since men "receive" the world as passive entities, education should make them more passive still, and adapt them to the world. . . . Translated into practice, this concept is well suited to the purposes of the oppressors, whose tranquility rests on how well men fit the world the oppressors have created, and how little they question it.[106]

Radicals such as Illich and Freire criticize the educational system because they see it as perpetuating the evils of oppressive society, as dehumanizing, and as stifling individual freedom. Most radicals also offer a plan or alternative methodology that they envision will bring about personal and social liberation.

In rejecting schools as an instrument of education, for example, Illich does not fail to provide alternative arrangements for learning. Planning new educational institutions, he writes, starts not with the question of *what* should be learned but with the consideration of "What kinds of things and people might learners want to be in contact with in order to learn?"[107] To this end he proposes four channels or learning exchanges or networks. Replacing schools, containing all the resources necessary for real learning, and capable of assisting both children and adults, these networks are:

1. reference services to educational objects—which facilitate access to things or processes used for formal learning, such as books, radios, microscopes, and television. These can be stored in libraries, laboratories, theaters, and so on;
2. skill exchanges—which permit persons to list their skills, and the conditions under which they are willing to serve as instructors;
3. peer-matching—a communications network which permits persons to describe the learning activity in which they wish to engage, and find a partner for the inquiry;
4. reference services to educators-at-large—who can be listed in a directory giving addresses and descriptions of services. Such educators could be chosen by consulting former clients.[108]

In place of the traditional banking form of education, Freire offers a dialogic and problem-posing education. Cultural action for freedom, as Freire calls it, is action in which a group of persons, through dialogue, come to be aware of the concrete situation in which they live, the reasons for this situation, and its possible solutions. In order for action to be authentic, the participants must be free to create the curriculum along with the teacher. Freire's problem-posing education is based upon respect, communication, and solidarity. For Freire, the only justifiable content is that which emanates from the learners. Their views or opinions, "impregnated with anxieties, doubts, hopes, or hopelessness, imply significant themes on the basis of which the program content of education can be built."[109] Out of an existential dialogue come what Freire calls generative themes, and "to investigate the generative theme is to investigate man's thinking about reality and man's action upon reality."[110] Materials are prepared based upon these elicited themes, and "the themes which have come from the people return to them—not as contents to be deposited, but as problems to be solved."[111]

Freire is careful to distinguish between problem-solving education and what he calls "problematizing" education. Problem solving is part of banking education and separates the person from the world or the world from the person. Problematizing, on the other hand, does not separate the person from the world, the teacher from the student, or knowing from action:

> Problematization is so much a dialectic process that it would be impossible for anyone to begin it without becoming involved in it. No one can present something to someone else as a problem and at the same time remain a mere spectator of the process. S/he will be problematized even if methodologically speaking, s/he prefers to remain silent after posing the problem, while the educatees capture, analyze, and comprehend it.[112]

Central to Freire's educational revolution is a changed relationship between teacher and student. Insight into the learner's world, into the state of oppression, comes about through the use of dialogue which he defines as "the encounter between men, mediated by the world, in order to name the world."[113] Dialogue presupposes "intense faith in man," for, "founding itself upon love, humility, and faith, dialogue becomes a horizontal relationship of which mutual trust between the dialoguers is the logical consequence." It follows that the roles of the learner and the teacher involve a "horizontal relationship." Teachers and students both teach and learn simultaneously, becoming participants and co-investigators in the dialogue.[114] With dialogical encounter as the method and generic themes as the content, education becomes a task of praxis—combining reflective activity with action.

In terms of the aims and objectives of adult education, Freire's major contribution lies in his marriage of education and political action. For him there is no such thing as neutral education. Education is either for domestication or for liberation. In Western thought, education is often regarded as the public transmission of neutral information about the world. What is taught is presumed to be devoid of ideological content. In Freire's analysis of the relationship between education and culture, it is culture that produces education and uses it for its own self-perpetuation. In fact, the assumptions of the culture are contained in the educational process. Education for Freire is inherently value-laden.

In summary, radical thinkers place great importance on the role of education in bringing about social change. The educational system as it now exists is, however, inadequate as a tool for change. Education must itself be transformed from that which perpetuates the social order and hence oppresses, to that which challenges the social system and thus liberates.

In practice, few educators advocate radical social transformation as the aim of adult education. This perspective does serve, however, to challenge traditional views of educational purpose and method. To the extent that radical social change is not equated with political revolution, the views of Freire and other radical theorists may well receive increasing attention from adult educators in the years ahead.

Organizational Effectiveness

The four emphases so far presented in our conceptualization of the philosophies of adult education around the field's aims and objectives focus either upon the individual, as in the cultivation of the intellect and personal development, or upon the individual in conjunction with society, as with progressive and radical approaches. There exists yet another focus—organizational effectiveness. Adults employed by public and private agencies and organizations are involved in educational programs designed to achieve the organization's goals. In the private sector, organizational and employee development programs are ultimately aimed at realizing greater profit; in the public sector the aim is enhancing service to the public.

Whatever the aim, organizations, Lefebvre points out, "have only two resources with which to accomplish goals and objectives—men and money. . . . The human resource . . . is the source for ideas, technical and professional skills, and know-how. With money we purchase land, buildings, equipment, and other materials needed."[115] The development of human resources for the purposes of enhancing an organization's effectiveness has thus become one of the aims of adult education.

Training, education, and *development* are three terms commonly used in referring to this aspect of adult education. There is little agreement as to whether, or how, these concepts should be differentiated. In a recent book on management development and training, Watson uses *training* and *education* synonymously, stating that "people act as integrated beings, whose knowledge, skills, and attitudes are interrelated and inseparable. To make a distinction between training and education is to ignore these interrelationships."[116] However, he does distinguish between *training* (formal classroom learning activities) and *development* (all learning experiences, both on and off the job, including formal classroom training).[117] Discussing the terms in their broader social context, Patten views *education* as socialization and "thus outside the purview of organizations."[118] *Development* also is too broad a term because it is both a formal and informal process by which individuals learn. Within the organizational context, Patten favors *training*, defined as the "formal procedure which is used to facilitate employee learning so that their resultant behavior contributes to the organization's objectives."[119] Training encompasses a wide range of activities from learning a simple motor skill through "developing attitudes toward intricate and controversial social issues."[120]

The most specific delineation of the three terms is made by Nadler. All three are subsumed under the umbrella of *human resources development*, which he defines as "a series of organized activities, conducted within a specified time and designed to bring about behavioral change."[121] Differentiating among training, education, and development, Nadler injects a time dimension. *Training* thus includes activities "designed to improve performance on the job the employee is presently doing or is being hired to do."[122] *Education* prepares an employee for a place in the organization different from the one now held. While the goals of training and education are clearly specified, *development* activities have the broad goal of producing a flexible work force that can "move with the organization as it develops, changes, and grows."[123]

Regardless of the terms used, learning activities structured by public and private organizations for employees involve billions of dollars and millions of adults each year. As one writer notes, employer-sponsored education has become

> a segment, a significant subsystem of the nation's educational system. It develops its own courses and curricula, employs faculty and nonteaching professional staff, carries on formal instructional activities, evaluates its programs and methods, and often does these in well-designed and equipped facilities that are devoted to them exclusively.[124]

Much of employee education and training draws on the psychology of behaviorism. With organizational effectiveness the goal of this form of adult education, ways must be found to determine or to measure whether the gain in organizational effectiveness justifies the expenditures. Concerned with the most economical and efficient ways to accomplish a task, corporate training often makes use of competency-based concepts and modern instructional technologies. The greatest emphasis in training is placed upon "the importance of thinking through and specifying the desired outcomes of particular learning programs with respect to changes in knowledge, behavior, attitudes, or sensibilities of the learner—and on making reasonable efforts to appraise results and make appropriate modifications."[125]

The impact of behaviorism upon training can be viewed in terms of the overall goals of training as well as of the adaptation of behavioral methods and techniques. Etington, tracing the changes in employee training over the years, presents a "model man" chart in which the outdated "Newtonian" model is contrasted to the present "Einsteinian" man. Trainers are now dealing with an individual who is characterized by modifiable intelligence, a computer brain, potential created through transaction with environment, and development as modifiable in both rate and sequence.[126] Etington's Einsteinian man could, in fact, be "behaviorist man," with its emphasis upon behavior modification and environmental control.

Several other writers define the overall goal of training as behavioral change. Nadler, it might be recalled, writes that human resource development is designed to produce behavioral change.[127] And in a discussion of management training, Watson lists benefits that include changing behavior and developing an awareness of the consequences of one's actions.[128]

To insure for accountability and measurable results, training programs are often structured using a systems approach. The systems approach is one way of looking at the various component parts of an organization or program and how they fit together to bring about a specified end product. Byers writes that

> trainers are being urged to adopt this form of thinking or reasoning in order to be more confident that the development program is truly designed for the purpose of accomplishing organization objectives and to be able to measure with greater assurance the extent to which the development program and activities actually are meeting the goals set.[129]

Whether in dealing on a large scale with the overall training program or with something as specific as a single instructional unit, behavioral and performance objectives are also widely utilized in employee education. Behavioral objectives provide the mechanism by which a change in behavior can be measured. Behavioral objectives contain three components: (1) the relevant conditions or stimuli under which a learner is expected to perform; (2) the behavior a learner is to perform, including a general reference to the product of the behavior; and (3) a description of the criteria by which the behavior will be judged acceptable or unacceptable, successful or unsuccessful. Like behavioral objectives, performance objectives specify the conditions, behavior, and criteria that will be used to evaluate an employee's performance. These objectives are often set by the employee in conjunction with a supervisor. Johnson notes that "to improve productivity, organizations increasingly are turning to programs of formal periodic appraisal of individual performance. A device is developed and a procedure worked out. Standards of performance are used as a basis for measurement."[130]

Behaviorism, with its emphasis upon measurable outcomes, overt behavior, and arranging environmental contingencies to bring about desired behavior, is the orientation underlying much of the employee education sponsored by organizations. Many programs, however, incorporate humanistic philosophical principles and techniques. Sensitivity training, human potential seminars, nondirective counseling, self-guided learning, and so on emphasize personal growth and development, which in turn is important to the overall effectiveness of the organization. One of the philosophical issues in employee training is, in fact, the extent to which individual development is or should be congruent with organizational goals. Argyris, in writing about this issue, looks at the nature of the adult and notes that there is a "basic dilemma between the needs of the individuals aspiring for psychological success and self-esteem and the demands of the pyramidal structure."[131] Argyris's conditions for "optimum personality expression while at work" bring to mind Knowles's assumption of andragogy. Adults in a work setting, Argyris writes, need to have

> jobs which permit them to be more active than passive; more independent than dependent; to have longer rather than shorter time perspectives; to occupy higher positions than their peers; to have control over their world; and to express many of their deeper, more important abilities.[132]

The tension between individual and organizational needs can, he notes, be "the foundation for increasing the degree of effectiveness of both."[133] Argyris and Likert,[134] among others, have suggested ways of integrating individual and employee needs through supportive employee-centered supervision, democratic decision making, group leadership methods, and decentralization of authority.

The concept of organizational development (OD) is an attempt on the part of organizations to match employee development with organizational growth. "A basic assumption of the OD movement," writes Strain, "is that an organization's effectiveness can be increased by a process of integrating the goals of the individual working for an organization with the objectives of the organization."[135] Beck and Hillmar enumerate the types of activities used in OD: team building, job design/enrichment, goal setting, problem solving, decision making, managing differences/conflict, process consultation, diagnosis and feedback, interpersonal skills, values clarification, transactional analysis, managing accountability, helping relationships, Gestalt applications in organizations, open system concepts, and psychological contracting.[136]

As in other adult education settings, philosophical goals determine the role of the teacher/facilitator. The role of the training officer in an organizational setting reflects the contemporary notion that developing effective employees results in more effective organizations. A large-scale study of trainer roles conducted in 1978 by the American Society for Training and Development (ASTD) revealed that trainers are indeed conscious of individual as well as organizational development. Among the role-related tasks identified by over 2500 trainers were: conducting needs analysis and diagnosis, designing and developing appropriate programs, planning and counseling individuals, facilitating group and organizational development, and establishing good relationships with managers.[137] The survey also probed how the training and development activity of organizations had changed within the past five years. The majority of respondents noted that their organization's training and development programs had expanded in that period and were placing more emphasis upon long-range development, career counseling, minority development, and human relations and communications skills.[138] It would appear from the survey that current practice at least to some extent reflects the interrelationship of employee and organizational development.

A wide variety of instructional techniques reflecting several philosophical orientations are used in employee training. Lectures, conference methods, panel discussion, workshops, laboratory or sensitivity training, role playing, case studies, brainstorming, buzz groups, and management games are among the methods used "to effect change in the behavior of trainees."[139] Also prevalent in training is the use of programmed instruction, a technique that allows for self-paced learning.

As with instructional methods, the content of employer-sponsored training varies enormously. Depending upon the needs of the employee and the organization, training might encompass learning administrative and supervisory techniques, developing basic skills, acquiring technical information, or changing attitudes. For the most part, however,

> course content, related as it is to company problems, products, and processes, verges toward the particular and away from the abstract, the utilitarian rather than theoretical. Much of this material is more appropriately taught by operating specialists and managers than by professional educators. The length of company courses tends to be determined by no criterion other than what is needed to convey particular skills or knowledge to specific employees or groups.[140]

In summary, the aim of education sponsored by organizations in the public or private sector is organizational effectiveness. Referred to as training, education, and/or development, employee education is characterized by clearly defined goals and objectives. Behavioral principles and methodologies underlie much of this form of adult education. Measures of accountability, behavioral change, behavioral objectives, systems approaches, and programmed instruction are some of the prevalent manifestations of behaviorism in organization-sponsored education. Techniques and strategies that foster individual growth and development also are incorporated into training curricula. Thus, employee education demonstrates a wide range of content and instructional methods used to advance organizational effectiveness.

CONCLUSION

This chapter has attempted to present an overview of the philosophies of adult education. The differing aims of adult education provided a focus for organizing the diverse philosophical writings. Five emphases were discussed, with their respective views on content, the role of the teacher and learner, and the nature of the instructional process.

The cultivation of the intellect is one objective of adult education. Proponents of this view conceive of adult education as a neutral activity divorced from social action. A curriculum emphasizing liberal studies and a traditional view of the teacher-student interaction characterizes this approach.

Personal development constitutes a second emphasis in adult education. Drawing from humanistic and existential orientations, educators with this bias see adult education as concerned primarily with promoting individual growth and development. A by-product of this emphasis will be benefits to society. Content thus becomes whatever promotes individual growth, the student is the focus of the process, and group interaction is the favored instructional mode.

Perhaps the major proportion of American educational philosophers reflect the progressive view of adult education. Here the aim of adult education is both personal development and social progress. Content is drawn from life situations, the preferred method is problem solving, and teachers and learners are partners in the task of learning.

In direct opposition to the proponents of "neutral knowledge" are those who advocate radical social change through adult education. Here education is viewed as value-laden and never neutral. Content comes from the consciousness of the oppressed and disadvantaged, the teacher is also a learner, and the methodology is a dialogical encounter that leads to praxis—that is, reflective thought and action.

Finally, organizational effectiveness is the aim of a large segment of American adult education. Public and private sector organizations strive to become more efficient deliverers of goods or services. To this end, they may engage their employees in training, education, or development activities characterized by a variety of purposes and instructional methodologies.

While this approach to the philosophies of adult education tends to highlight the differences in aims, content, and instructional process, there are some underlying similarities among the principal schools of thought. Powell and Benne have delineated several beliefs held in common by most adult educators. Most adherents of the positions outlined in this chapter would agree that: (1) adults are different from young people; (2) education is an activity that emphasizes learning rather than teaching; (3) there is some interplay between the intellectual and emotional elements in learning; (4) a primary vehicle of adult learning is the group; and (5) emphasis is placed on the individual as a learner.[141]

Organizing and presenting the various philosophical views on a major issue like the aims and objectives of adult education should shed some light on the practice of adult education. While practicing adult educators may not assume any one particular philosophical stance, it behooves all educators to attempt to identify the philosophical assumptions that necessarily inform and guide their practice.

NOTES

1. Robert S. Blakely, *Adult Education in a Free Society* (Toronto: Guardian Bird, 1967), p. 14.
2. John S. Diekhoff, quoted in *Handbook of Adult Education*, ed. Robert M. Smith, George F. Aker, and J. R. Kidd (New York: Macmillan, 1970), p. 122.
3. Hayden W. Roberts, "Goals, Objectives, and Functions in Adult Education," *Adult Education* 26, no. 2 (1976): 127.
4. Thurman J. White, "Philosophical Considerations," in *Handbook of Adult Education*, ed. Smith, Aker, and Kidd, p. 121.
5. Paul Bergevin, *A Philosophy for Adult Education* (New York: Seabury Press, 1967), p. 3.
6. Jerold W. Apps, *Toward a Working Philosophy of Adult Education* (Syracuse, N.Y.: Syracuse University Publications in Continuing Education, 1973), pp. 3–5.
7. Charles Silberman, *Crisis in the Classroom* (New York: Random House, 1970), p. 11.
8. Maxine Greene, *Teacher as Stranger* (Belmont, Calif.: Wadsworth, 1973), pp. 10–11.
9. Israel Scheffler, *The Language of Education* (Boston: Allyn & Bacon, 1960), p. 5.
10. K. H. Lawson, *Philosophical Concepts and Values in Adult Education* (Nottingham, England: Barnes and Humby, 1975), p. 14.
11. Ibid.
12. Winthrop D. Jordan, "Searching for Adulthood in America," in *Adulthood*, ed. Erik Erickson (New York: Norton, 1978).
13. Ibid., p. 189.
14. R. W. K. Paterson, *Values, Education, and the Adult* (London: Routledge & Kegan Paul, 1979), p. 10.

15. Ibid., p. 13.
16. Greene, *Teacher as Stranger*, p. 53.
17. Cyril Houle, *The Design of Education* (San Francisco: Jossey-Bass, 1972).
18. Lawson, *Philosophical Concepts and Values in Adult Education*, p. 92.
19. R. W. K. Paterson, "Social Change as an Educative Aim," *Adult Education* (British) 45, no. 6 (1973): 356.
20. Jack Mezirow, "Perspective Transformation," *Adult Education* 28, no. 2 (1978): 100–110.
21. Lawrence Kohlberg and Rochelle Meyer, "Development as the Aim of Education," *Harvard Educational Review* 42, no. 4 (1972): 449.
22. Mary L. Ely, ed., *Adult Education in Action* (New York: American Association for Adult Education, 1936).
23. Kohlberg and Meyer, "Development as the Aim of Education," pp. 451–454.
24. Apps, *Toward a Working Philosophy of Adult Education*, pp. 21–24.
25. John Elias and Sharan Merriam, *Philosophical Foundations of Adult Education* (New York: Kreiger, 1980).
26. Harry S. Broudy, *Aims in Adult Education: A Realist's View* (Chicago: Center for the Study of Liberal Education for Adults, 1960), p. 7.
27. Paterson, "Social Change as an Educative Aim," p. 357.
28. Paterson, *Values, Education, and the Adult*, pp. 256, 258.
29. Ibid., p. 259.
30. Lawson, *Philosophical Concepts and Values in Adult Education*, p. 8.
31. Paterson, "Social Change as an Educative Aim," p. 356.
32. Paterson, *Values, Education, and the Adult*, p. 94.
33. Ibid., p. 84.
34. Lawson, *Philosophical Concepts and Values in Adult Education*, p. 8.
35. Ibid
36. Ibid., p. 40.
37. Ibid., p. 67.
38. Ibid., p. 22.
39. Ibid., p. 83.
40. Ibid., p. 22.
41. Paterson, *Values, Education, and the Adult*, p. 80.
42. Ibid.
43. Abraham Maslow, "Education and Peak Experience," in *The Person in Education: A Humanistic Approach*, ed. Courtney D. Schlosser (New York: Macmillan, 1976), p. 120.
44. Malcolm Knowles, *The Modern Practice of Adult Education*, rev. edition (Chicago: Association Press/Follett, 1980), p. 67.
45. Malcolm Knowles, "Philosophical Issues That Confront Adult Educators," *Adult Education* 7 (1957): 238.
46. Broudy, *Aims in Adult Education*, p. 11.
47. Leon McKenzie, *Adult Education and the Burden of the Future* (Washington, D.C.: University Press of America, 1978).
48. Knowles, "Philosophical Issues That Confront Adult Educators," p. 239.
49. Horace M. Kallen, *Philosophical Issues in Adult Education* (Springfield: Thomas, 1962).

50. Elizabeth Simpson and Mary Anne Gray, *Humanist Education: An Interpretation* (Cambridge, Mass.: Ballinger, 1976), ·p. 26.
51. C. H. Patterson, *Humanistic Education* (Englewood Cliffs, N.J.: Prentice-Hall, 1973), p. *x*.
52. Knowles, *Modern Practice of Adult Education*.
53. McKenzie, *Adult Education and the Burden of the Future*.
54. Ibid., p. 72.
55. Carl Rogers, *Freedom to Learn* (Columbus, Ohio: Merrill, 1969), pp. 129–144.
56. McKenzie, *Adult Education and the Burden of the Future*, p. 73.
57. Ibid., pp. 74–75.
58. Paul H. Sheats, "What is Adult Education," *Adult Education* 5, no. 3 (1955).
59. Wilbur C. Hallenbeck, "The Role of Adult Education in Society," in *Adult Education: Outlines of an Emerging Field of University Study*, ed. Gale Jensen, A. A. Liveright, and Wilbur Hallenbeck (Chicago: Adult Education Association of the U.S.A., 1964), p. 5.
60. Broudy, *Aims in Adult Education*, p. 11.
61. Eduard Lindeman, *The Meaning of Adult Education* (Montreal: Harvest House, 1961), p. 104.
62. Hallenbeck, "Role of Adult Education in Society," p. 7.
63. Jerold W. Apps, *Problems in Continuing Education* (New York: McGraw-Hill, 1979), pp. 91–99.
64. John Dewey, *Democracy and Education* (New York: Macmillan, 1916), p. 90.
65. Lindeman, *Meaning of Adult Education*, p. 105.
66. Eduard Lindeman, quoted in J. R. Kidd, *How Adults Learn*, rev. ed. (New York: Association Press, 1973), p. 154.
67. Bergevin, *Philosophy for Adult Education*, pp. 7–8.
68. Ibid., pp. 9–10.
69. Ibid., p. 35.
70. Ibid., pp. 4, 114.
71. Blakely, *Adult Education in a Free Society*.
72. Robert Blakely, *Toward A Homeodynamic Society* (Boston: Center for the Study of Liberal Education for Adults, 1965), p. 54.
73. Bergevin, *Philosophy for Adult Education*, pp. 12, 13, 125.
74. John Dewey, *Experience and Education* (New York: Macmillan, 1938), p. 42.
75. Lindeman, *Meaning of Adult Education*, pp. 85, 87.
76. Greene, *Teacher as Stranger*, p. 7.
77. Lindeman, *Meaning of Adult Education*, p. 111.
78. Greene, *Teacher as Stranger*, p: 8.
79. Lindeman, *Meaning of Adult Education*, p. 115.
80. Lawrence Cremin, "Public Education and the Education of the Public," *Teachers College Record* 77, no. 1 (1975): 5.
81. Dewey, *Democracy and Education*, p. 25.
82. Ibid., p. 260.
83. Lindeman, *Meaning of Adult Education*, p. 115.
84. Ibid., p. 6.

85. Ibid., p. 122.
86. Kenneth Benne, "Some Philosophical Issues in Adult Education," *Adult Education* 7 (1957): 79.
87. Ibid., p. 149.
88. Paulo Freire, *Pedagogy of the Oppressed* (New York: Herder and Herder, 1970).
89. Dewey, *Democracy and Education*, p. 160.
90. Eduard Lindeman, *The Democratic Man: Selected Writings of Eduard Lindeman*, ed. Robert Messner (Boston: Beacon Press, 1956), p. 160.
91. Ibid.
92. Bergevin, *Philosophy for Adult Education*, p. 168.
93. Benne, "Some Philosophical Issues in Adult Education," p. 79.
94. Kohlberg and Meyer, "Development as the Aim of Education," pp. 454–455.
95. J. E. Thomas and G. Harries-Jenkins, "Adult Education and Social Change," *Studies in Adult Education* 7, no. 1 (1975): 2.
96. Ibid., p. 3
97. Ivan Illich, *Deschooling Society* (New York: Harper & Row, 1970), p. 48.
98. Ibid., p. 47.
99. Ibid., p. 22.
100. Ibid., p. 12.
101. John Ohliger, "Is Lifelong Education a Guarantee of Permanent Inadequacy?" (Paper delivered at Saskatoon, Saskatchewan, March 1974), p. 2.
102. Ibid., p. 9.
103. Freire, *Pedagogy of the Oppressed*, p. 40.
104. Ibid.
105. Paulo Freire, *Education for Critical Consciousness* (New York: Seabury Press, 1973), pp. 17–19.
106. Freire, *Pedagogy of the Oppressed*, pp. 62–63.
107. Illich, *Deschooling Society*, p. 78.
108. Ibid., pp. 78–79.
109. Freire, *Pedagogy of the Oppressed*, p. 82.
110. Ibid., p. 97.
111. Ibid., p. 116.
112. Freire, *Education for Critical Consciousness*, p. 153.
113. Freire, *Pedagogy of the Oppressed*, p. 76.
114. Ibid., pp. 79–80.
115. Leon J. Lefebvre, "Elements of the Development Policies and Plans," in *Employee Training and Development in the Public Sector*, ed. Kenneth T. Byers (Chicago: International Personnel Management Association, 1970), p. 71.
116. Charles Watson, *Management Development Through Training* (Reading, Mass.: Addison-Wesley, 1979), pp. 4–5.
117. Ibid., p. 5.
118. Thomas H. Patten, Jr., *Manpower Planning and the Development of Human Resources* (New York: Wiley, 1971), p. 16.
119. Ibid., p. 18.
120. Ibid.

121. Leonard Nadler, *Developing Human Resources* (Houston: Gulf, 1970), p. 40.
122. Ibid.
123. Ibid., p. 88.
124. Seymour Lusterman, "Education in Industry," in *Yearbook of Adult and Continuing Education, 1978-79* (Chicago: Marquis Academic Media, 1978), p. 478.
125. Ibid.
126. Julius E. Etington, "The Training Function—Current and Future Directions," in *Employee Training and Development*, ed. Byers.
127. Nadler, *Developing Human Resources*, p. 40.
128. Watson, *Management Development Through Training*, pp. 9–11.
129. Kenneth T. Byers, "Developing Effective Employees and Organizations," in *Employee Training and Development*, ed. Byers, p. 14.
130. Richard B. Johnson, "Determining Training Needs," in *Training and Development Handbook*, ed. Robert Craig and Lester Bittel (New York: McGraw-Hill, 1969), p. 19.
131. Chris Argyris, *Integrating the Individual and the Organization* (New York: Wiley, 1964), p. 58.
132. Chris Argyris, *Personality and Organization* (New York: Harper & Row, 1957), p. 53.
133. Argyris, *Ingegrating the Individual and the Organization*, p. 7.
134. Rensis Likert, *The Human Organization* (New York: McGraw-Hill, 1967).
135. Andrew C. Strain, "Organization Development," in *Employee Training and Development*, ed. Byers, pp. 59–60.
136. A. C. Beck, Jr. and Ellis Hillmar, *Making MBO/R Work* (Reading, Mass.: Addison-Wesley, 1976), p. 4.
137. Patrick R. Pinto and James W. Walker, "What Do Training and Development Professionals Really Do?" *Training and Development Journal* 32, no. 7 (1978): 58–64.
138. Ronald W. Clement, James W. Walker, and Patrick R. Pinto, "Changing Demands on the Training Professional," *Training and Development Journal* 33, no. 3 (1979): 3–7.
139. Norman R. Smith, "Employee Development Methods" in *Employee Training and Development*, ed. Byers, p. 145.
140. Lusterman, "Education in Industry," *Yearbook of Adult and Continuing Education*, p. 478.
141. John Walker Powell and Kenneth Benne, "Philosophies of Adult Education," in *Handbook of Adult Education in the United States*, ed. Malcolm S. Knowles (Washington, D.C.: Adult Education Association of the U.S.A., 1960), pp. 50–52.

Chapter 3
Adults as Learners

The differences between children and adults as learners have profound implications for educational practice. One can assume, for example, that most children in a group of fourth graders are approximately 9 years old, are at one particular stage in their social and physical development, are capable of certain learning tasks, and have had limited life experiences. On the other hand, those in a group of adult learners might range in age from 18 to 80, be at different stages of psychosocial and physical development, be able to employ complex problem-solving strategies, and have had rich and varied life experiences. Indeed, the diversity so characteristic of the field of adult education is as true of the learners as it is of institutions, programs, and philosophies. For as individual adults function in society, age, and accumulate experience, they become more and more differentiated from one another. A group of 44-year-olds will be less like each other than a group of 20-year-olds. Similarly, any group of adults who come together for an educational purpose is likely to be more diverse than a class of children.

Facilitating the learning experience for adults thus necessitates an understanding of adulthood in conjunction with the learning process. The adult's ability to acquire new information may have more to do with lifestyle, social roles, and attitudes than with an innate ability to learn. Likewise, an older adult's success in processing information may be hampered by physiological impairments. It would seem that few generalizations can be made about adults as learners without considering the interrelatedness of cognitive, biological, and psychosocial factors. This chapter attempts to present a holistic view of adults as learners through a consideration of the complex nature of adulthood as it affects and is affected by learning.

Contrasting adult learning with childhood learning offers one means for exploring the unique characteristics of adult learners. As previously discussed, Malcolm Knowles has proposed adoption of the term *andragogy*, the "art and science of helping adults learn,"[1] to be distinguished from *pedagogy*, the instruction of children. Andragogy is grounded on four assumptions that pinpoint some of the salient features of adulthood:

1. As a person matures his or her self-concept moves from one of a dependent personality toward one of a self-directing human being;
2. An adult accumulates a growing reservoir of experience, a rich resource for learning. For an adult, personal experiences establish self-identity and so are highly valued;
3. The readiness of an adult to learn is closely related to the developmental tasks of his or her social role; and
4. There is a change in time perspective as individuals mature, from one of future application of knowledge to immediacy of application; thus an adult is more problem-centered than subject-centered in learning.[2]

These assumptions encapsulate much that is important about adult learning and development. The first two—that adults are independent beings and have forged their identities from unique personal experiences—are drawn from humanistic philosophy and psychology and readily generate implications for adult learning. The third and fourth assumptions, dealing with the adult's readiness and orientation to learning, provide the links to understanding adult learning from a psychosocial developmental perspective. Some knowledge of both the humanist and developmental orientations, when combined with principles related to the learning process itself, can offer the adult educator an understanding of the complex interrelationship between adulthood and learning.

THE ADULT AS SELF-DIRECTED LEARNER

In our society, chronological age does not provide a reliable indicator for differentiating adults from children. More central to the concept of adulthood is the notion of independence. Those who have assumed responsibility for managing their lives are society's adults. Young children are dependent upon others for their well-being; adolescents exhibit patterns of both dependent and independent behavior. The adult, however, can be distinguished from a child or adolescent by his or her acceptance of the social roles and functions that define adulthood. The roles of wage earner, marriage partner, parent, decision maker, and citizen all denote the independence characteristic of adulthood. Johnstone and Rivera used this notion of adulthood along with chronological age in their study of participation in adult education. They defined an adult as a person who was married, head of a household, or over 21 years of age.[3]

Educational practice reflects the difference between children, who are learning to be independent social beings, and adults, who have assumed independent decision-making roles. The main function of childhood education is to prepare young people to function as adults. For the most part, society, through the educational system, decides what knowledge, skills, and attitudes a child must acquire to be equipped for participation in the adult world. Even institutions of higher education are basically preparatory. That is, students are "prepared" to become economically, socially, and psychologically independent.

Adult education, on the other hand, assumes that students are already functioning as adults in society. Thus, its mission is not preparatory so much as it is one of assistance—helping adults to realize their potential, make good decisions, and, in general, better carry out the duties and responsibilities inherent in the adult role. The differences between children and adults have ramifications for all aspects of the instructional setting. Adults who have had many and varied experiences and who daily make decisions affecting their lives and the lives of their dependents are capable as well of participating in the planning and implementation of their own learning. They also are the ones who can most accurately judge the value of a learning activity and its relevance to their own lives. Often the teacher of adults functions most appropriately as a resource person who views the learning situation as a cooperative endeavor. That is not to say that the adult student possesses knowledge equal to that of the teacher in any given area. Rather, the teacher respects and values the experiences and expertise of the adult students and shares with them his or her own base of competency.

The shift in emphasis from preparatory education to the enhancement of adult living warrants approaching adult learners as individuals. For, as Knowles's first two assumptions suggest, adults are self-directing in their own growth and development and have accumulated experiences that set them apart from others. Facilitating learning experiences thus requires knowledge of the goals and needs of the individuals involved.

This focus upon individual growth and development is the main tenet of humanistic philosophy and psychology. Born out of a dissatisfaction with a purely behavioristic-mechanistic orientation to behavior and learning, humanistic psychology seeks to understand the affective as well as intellectual dimension of individuals. That feelings and emotions play an important part in any learning activity cannot be denied. For example, adults feel independent, feel unique, and feel they can make contributions based on their experiences. A teacher who does not recognize these feelings will most likely miss many opportunities to facilitate learning. Further, it would also seem likely that an adult who returns to a structured learning situation with painful memories of earlier schooling will feel insecure, fearful, and inadequately equipped to handle the learning tasks. Such emotions may interfere with learning unless the teacher establishes a climate of encouragement and understanding.

Knowles's andragogical approach emanates from humanistic assumptions. The primary concern of humanists is, as Charlotte Buhler simply stated, "man in his wholeness."[4] Rather than merely seeking to describe the human experience, humanists ask how it might be "extended, enriched, or made more meaningful"; an effort is made to help people "to grow and evolve more fully in realization of their potential."[5] The challenge set down by humanists has found expression in adult education through andragogy.

Humanism draws on phenomenology, which emphasizes a person's perceptions that grow out of experience, and existentialism, which stresses individual responsibility for becoming what one wants to become. Since an adult has accumulated more life experiences than a child and has assumed responsibility for his or her own life, a humanistic approach to adult learning seems particularly appropriate. The following four tenets of the Association for Humanistic Psychology succinctly express the foundation for an andragogical approach to adult learners:

A centering of attention on the experiencing *person* and thus a focus on experience as the primary phenomenon in the study of man.

An emphasis on such distinctively human qualities as choice, creativity, valuation, and self-realization, as opposed to thinking about human beings in mechanistic and reductionistic terms.

An allegiance to meaningfulness in the selection of problems for study and of research procedures, and an opposition to a primary emphasis on objectivity at the expense of significance.

An ultimate concern with and valuing of the dignity and worth of man and interest in the development of the potential inherent in every person. Central in this view is the person as he discovers his own being and relates to other persons and to social groups.[6]

Abraham Maslow

While there is general agreement on these four elements, there also exists within the humanistic orientation a diversity of opinion and approaches. Abraham Maslow is generally considered to be the major theoretician of the humanist psychology movement in America. Although trained as a behaviorist, Maslow eventually embraced a more comprehensive view of human behavior. Maslow's contributions on motivation, self-actualizing individuals, and peak experiences have had an impact on all levels of education.

In *Motivation and Personality,* first published in 1954, Maslow offers a theory of human motivation based on a hierarchy of needs. The needs at the lowest level of the hierarchy are physiological, such as hunger and thirst, and must be attended to before a person can cope with safety needs—those related, for example, to security and protection. The next three levels on Maslow's hierarchy are belongingness and love needs, esteem needs (to feel that one is useful and one's life has worth), and, finally, the need for self-actualization. The need for self-actualization manifests itself in a desire for self-fulfillment, for becoming what one has the potential to become. These needs are hierarchical, but "people who are normal are partially satisfied in all their basic needs and partially unsatisfied in all their basic needs at the same time."[7]

Maslow's studies of extraordinary individuals such as Lincoln, Beethoven, and Schweitzer led him to identify 15 basic personality characteristics typical of the self-actualized person. It is interesting to note, and especially relevant to adult educators, that Maslow felt that self-actualization was only possible in adulthood:

> Self-actualization does not occur in young people. In our culture, at least, youngsters have not yet achieved identity, or autonomy, nor have they had time enough to experience an enduring, loyal, post-romantic love relationship. . . . Nor have they worked out their *own* system of values; nor have they had experience enough (responsibility for others, tragedy, failure, achievement, success) to shed perfectionistic illusions and become realistic; nor have they generally made their peace with death; nor have they learned to be patient; nor have they learned enough about evil in themselves and others to be compassionate; nor have they had time to become post-ambivalent about parents and elders, power and authority.[8]

What Maslow is speaking of here is the accumulation of experience that not only serves to define the individual person, but also can, as Knowles has pointed out, be used as a resource for learning activities. The self-concept of an adult, more independent than that of a child, has evolved from more experience, which in turn can be used to assist adults toward even greater self-direction or self-actualization. According to

Maslow, self-actualizing individuals exhibit more of the following characteristics than do other people:

1. They are realistically oriented.
2. They accept themselves, other people, and the natural world for what they are.
3. They are spontaneous in thinking, emotions, and behavior.
4. They are problem-centered rather than self-centered in the sense of being able to devote their attention to a task, duty, or mission that seems peculiarly cut out for them.
5. They have a need for privacy and even seek it out on occasion, needing it for periods of intense concentration on subjects of interest to them.
6. They are autonomous, independent, and able to remain true to themselves in the face of rejection or unpopularity.
7. They have a continuous freshness of appreciation and capacity to stand in awe again and again of the basic goods of life, a sunset, a flower, a baby, a melody, a person.
8. They have frequent "mystic" or "oceanic" experiences, although not necessarily religious in character.
9. They feel a sense of identification with mankind as a whole in the sense of being concerned not only with the lot of their own immediate families, but with the welfare of the world as a whole.
10. Their intimate relationships with a few especially loved people are profound and deeply emotional rather than superficial.
11. They have democratic character structures in the sense of judging people and being friendly not on the basis of race, status, religion, but rather on the basis of who other people are as individuals.
12. They have a highly developed sense of ethics.
13. They have unhostile senses of humor.
14. They have a great fund of creativeness.
15. They resist total conformity to culture.[9]

Maslow had much to say about the implications of humanistic philosophy for education. Simply stated, according to Maslow, the goal of education is self-actualization, or "helping the person to become the best that he is able to become." Educators should think in terms of bringing about intrinsic rather than extrinsic learning— "that is, learning to be a human being in general, and, second, learning to be *this* particular human being."[10] The educative process should provide peak experiences in which insight and learning occur. The goals of education at any level, Maslow says, should be the "discovery of identity" and "the discovery of vocation." "Finding one's identity," he says, "is almost synonymous with finding one's career."[11]

Maslow, then, the "spiritual father" of psychological humanism in America, also was responsible for promulgating the view of the person as a self-actualizing learner. Similar to Maslow's self-actualizing person is the "fully functioning person" postulated by Carl Rogers, another psychologist who has made a significant contribution to humanistic psychology and education.

Carl Rogers

In Rogers's theory of the self the principal conceptual elements are: "(1) the *organism,* which is the total person; (2) the *phenomenal field,* which is the totality of experiences; and (3) the *self,* which is a differentiated portion of the . . . field."[12] The self has its own characteristics, which include striving for consistency, and change as a result of maturation and learning. Rogers also feels there is a real self and an ideal self, that which the person would like to be. The discrepancy between the two can provide a stimulus for learning as well as the potential for unhealthy tension-relieving behaviors.

Seeing therapy and education as similar processes, Rogers attempts to answer the question "If education were as complete as we could wish it to be in promoting personal growth and development, what sort of person would emerge?" His answer is:

> [The person who] is able to experience all of his feelings, and is afraid of none of his feelings; he is his own sifter of evidence, but is open to evidence from all sources; he is completely engaged in the process of being and becoming himself, and thus discovers that he is soundly and realistically social; he lives completely in this moment, but learns that this is the soundest living for all time. He is a fully functioning organism, and because of the awareness of himself which flows freely in and through his experiences, he is a fully functioning person.[13]

Rogers also has described what the process of learning consists of as one strives towards becoming "fully actualized." There is a continuum of meaning involved in learning ranging from nonsense and meaningless memorizing to "significant, meaningful, experiential learning." Rogers delineated the qualities of experiential learning necessary for developing fully functioning individuals:

1. personal involvement—the affective and cognitive aspects of a person should be involved in the learning event;
2. self-initiated—a sense of discovery needs to come from within;
3. pervasive—the learning makes impact on the behavior, attitudes, or personality of the learner;
4. evaluated by the learner—the learner can best evaluate if the experience is meeting a need;

5. essence is meaning—when experiential learning takes place, its meaning to the learner becomes incorporated into his total experience.[14]

Rogers's emphasis upon self-initiated learning is relevant to the learner, and his idea of student participation in planning and evaluating learning has served as a model for adult educators. For if being an adult presupposes some measure of independence and self-responsibility, adult students then also are capable of participating in the structuring of their own learning.

The encounter group was one mechanism Rogers developed for assisting individuals to grow and develop. Like client-centered therapy, in which an individual can grow by removing artificial restraints, recognizing the real self, and then experiencing and interacting with other people, an encounter group provides an atmosphere in which public masks are unveiled. The encounter group "seeks to enable the participants to become experiencing persons capable of choice, creativity, valuation, and self-actualization."[15]

Groups, of course, are not new to adult education. Since colonial times they have provided a format for information exchange, problem solving, and personal development. Rogers introduced the notion of using group processes to facilitate emotional and psychological maturity of individual persons. Encounter groups, training groups (T-groups), and sensitivity groups achieved great popularity in the late 1960s. Rogers is not unmindful of the possible drawbacks of using groups for personal development: behavior changes that occur in the group are not necessarily lasting; a person may "become deeply involved in revealing himself and then be left with problems which are not worked through"; marital tensions may surface; and complications may develop related to liaisons between group members.[16] Aside from these possible disadvantages, group process is a real force, Rogers feels, for rehumanizing human relationships and assisting individuals to "live life fully in the here and now."[17]

Rogers's goal of a fully functioning person is predicated upon humanistic assumptions quite at odds with those of the behaviorists. Scientific investigation into human behavior should have as its major purpose to release rather than control the individual. "We can choose to use the behavioral sciences," he says,

in ways which will free rather than control; which will bring about constructive variability, not conformity; which will develop creativity, not contentment; which will facilitate each person in his self-directed process of becoming; which will aid individuals, groups, and even the concept of science to become self-transcending in freshly adaptive ways of meeting life and its problems.[18]

Other Humanists

In addition to Rogers and Maslow, scholars such as Buhler, Allport, Fromm, Sullivan, G. H. Mead, Frankl, May, Adler, Lewin, and Jourard have made significant contributions to the andragogical approach to adult learning.

Sidney Jourard, for example, has postulated that one of our basic needs is to make ourselves known to others. Self-disclosure in a dynamic relationship is akin to a learning experience. Through self-disclosure, "we can learn wherein we are identical with our fellow man and wherein we differ. Such knowledge," Jourard states, "provides us with the basis of action which can either destroy man or meet his needs for more abundant human living."[19]

Psychologist Gordon Allport spent a lifetime researching and writing about human nature. He too took issue with the behaviorists. "The secret of man," he wrote, "will not be found in a reductive analysis of his *being*, but only by tracing coherently the course of his *becoming*."[20] Allport studied what he called "mature adults" in order to determine what motivated human actions and what characterized maturity. While he did not specifically address education's role in forming the mature person, implications can be drawn from the way he characterized such a person. According to Allport there are seven criteria of the mature personality:

1. extension of the sense of self—psychologically healthy persons are those who are able to become actively involved with activities, people, or ideas;
2. warm relating of self to others—the capacity for intimacy and the capacity for compassion;
3. emotional security—self-acceptance, control of emotions, and a tolerance for frustration are qualities of emotional security;
4. realistic perception—the ability to view the world objectively;
5. skills and assignments—the development of one's skills and the full commitment of one's self to work;
6. self-objectification—knowledge and understanding of oneself;
7. a unifying philosophy of life—healthy persons are characterized by directedness, that is, guided towards the future, towards long-range goals and plans.[21]

Allport's model complements the view of the adult as a self-actualizing learner. Education can be seen as one way to assist an individual in becoming a "mature personality." Active involvement with others or with ideas, the development of work skills, and self-understanding all can be fostered in educational settings.

Similar to Allport's mature personality or Maslow's self-actualizing person is Erich Fromm's productive personality. For Fromm, personality is determined by specific social forces in childhood as well as by the nature of society. The healthy person is a productive one, where "being productive means using all of one's powers and potentialities. . . . Productivity is synonymous with full functioning, self-actualizing, loving, openness, and experiencing."[22] A productive person is capable of productive love and productive thinking; happiness and a humanistic conscience are other defining characteristics. The conscience guides a person to behavior that "produce[s] a feeling of internal approval and happiness. . . . Thus, the productive, healthy personality is self-directed and self-regulated."[23]

Other theoretical contributions such as Adler's "life plan," Frankl's self-transcendent person, and G. H. Mead's socially formed self also are relevant in understanding the adult as learner. However, the purpose of this section is merely to offer a glimpse of a few personality theorists and suggest how work such as theirs illuminates our understanding of the adult as a self-actualizing, self-directing learner.

The drive toward self-actualization in adult learning has been documented in the research of Allen Tough. He found that a great number of adults are engaged in individual learning projects. Tough estimates that probably 90 percent of the adult population conducts at least one major learning effort per year and 73 percent of the projects are self-planned.[24]

Especially intriguing are the "high learners"—those who spend perhaps 2000 hours a year at systematic learning and complete 15 or 20 projects in one year. "In their lives," Tough says, "learning is a central activity; such individuals are marked by extraordinary growth." The learners are characterized by curiosity and the "confidence and courage to reveal their real self. . . . They strive to achieve certain major goals, are spurred on rather than blocked by obstacles, and are productive and successful."[25] McLeish has made the observation that Tough's high learners portray "characteristics common to Carl Rogers's 'fully functioning' persons" and have "close analogies with Maslow's 'self-actualized' people."[26]

It is clear from Tough's research that most adults are indeed self-directed and independent. An adult educator who operates from this premise is able to differentiate between child and adult learning. "Ego-involvement," Knowles asserts, "lies at the heart of the adult educator's art. . . . The main thrust of modern adult educational technology is in the direction of inventing techniques for involving adults in ever-deeper processes of self-diagnosis of their own needs for continued learning, in formulating their own objectives for learning, in sharing responsibility for designing and carrying out their learning activities, and in evaluating their progress toward their objective."[27]

In applying the principles of humanistic psychology to education,

Carl Weinberg extracted five principles of learning that are particularly applicable to adult education:

1. Persons learn in a free environment: "the kind of environment that is free allows the person full exposure to his human potential." The learning environment should permit and encourage self-determination and self-expression.
2. One learns by relating the world to one's experiences. This principle draws upon John Dewey's notion of learning by doing, and "the experience of doing must be selected by the learner in line with his own theory of what he needs to do."
3. Persons learn cooperatively, although learning cooperatively, Weinberg notes, does not necessarily mean in a group. Rather, it refers to "relying upon others to support the learning experience rather than retard it." It includes constructive feedback in a noncompetitive environment.
4. Persons learn from the inside out: the learning that has the most meaning is that which is constructed from within the individual, rather than drawn from some outside force.
5. Persons learn in relation to their human qualities.[28]

There are certain "irreducible" qualities related to being human, such as the fact that a human being is unique, is part of the human experience, is a social and political being, and is a sentient being. Human feelings—or what has been called the affective domain—must be recognized. "We have the responsibility," Weinberg states, "not only to permit students to feel, but to develop that capacity that is at the heart of the creative process."[29]

A commitment to this approach to adult learning has ramifications for all educational settings. One must constantly be concerned, notes Laudon, with "creating awareness, understanding, and facilitation of growth, regardless of the relationship, institution, agency, or circumstance."[30] Facilitating individual growth and development regardless of the circumstances is not, however, always an easy task. Often institutional or program goals are not congruent with those of individual learners, nor is there always enough time available for assessing needs and planning individual learning activities. Agencies involved in training, and businesses and industries that invest time and money in employee education, are more likely to be concerned with production-related skills than personal development.

There are other possible drawbacks to approaching the adult as an independent self-directed learner. Because a person has assumed some of the responsibilities and duties a society considers to be "adult" does not necessarily mean that the person handles the role in a mature manner. Nor can it be assumed that an adult always is able to identify what he or she wants to know or needs to learn. Identifying, verbalizing, and translating needs into a planned learning program can be time-consuming and frustrating. And satisfying an identified need may not achieve an adult's long-range goals. The training for a teacher or lawyer, for example, may not lead to a job in today's labor market. So while adults are capable of directing their own learning, it is the responsibility of educators to guide learners within a realistic framework of possibilities.

That an adult has had many experiences that can provide a reservoir for learning cannot be denied. These same experiences, however, can be an impediment to growth if they have caused the individual to become rigid and closed to new experiences, values, and attitudes. One task of the adult educator is to assist the learner in going beyond what he or she has already experienced.

In summary, institutional constraints, difficulties in determining real needs, and immaturity or the ossification of personal experiences can impede a humanistic-andragogical approach to adult learning. All adults, however, are growing, changing beings, who are in different phases of personal development and capable of moving towards greater independence, self-direction, and self-actualization. It is the challenge of overcoming artificial constraints, identifying needs, and helping adults to live more fulfilling lives to which andragogy responds.

ADULT READINESS AND ORIENTATION TO LEARNING

In contrast to those of children, adults' self-concepts are more independent, are more self-directed, and are defined by an accumulation of life experiences. Adult learning also is affected by developmental tasks related to social roles and an orientation to learning that seeks an immediate application of new knowledge. These two latter assumptions underlying andragogy provide a link for viewing the adult in a psychosocial developmental context. Understanding the adult as he or she fits into a developmental framework provides the educator with additional insights into differences between adult and childhood learning and a greater understanding of the qualities of adult learners.

Exploring the adult's readiness and orientation to learning from a psychosocial developmental perspective also serves to mitigate some of the criticism leveled at a totally humanistic approach to learning. Facilitating individual growth and development overemphasizes, some believe, a person's experiences, feelings, and emotions at the expense of intellectual development. Critics charge that working toward "self-actualization" or attempting to become a "fully functioning self" develops into a preoccupation with the self. What is needed is a view of the self within a social framework. Considered in a learning context, one's growth and development are to some extent a function of interaction with others who also are attempting to maximize their individual potential.

Children as well as adults learn within a social context. The emphasis in childhood is upon socialization—learning to live with others in ways deemed desirable by the larger society and culture. The "teachable moment" for a child depends to a great extent upon his or her physiological development and what is learned either forms the basis for more knowledge or is stored for future use. Indeed, most childhood learning relates to the acquisition of knowledge, skills, or attitudes necessary for entering the adult world.

The adult, however, has assumed certain roles, each having behavioral norms and functions deemed appropriate by society. Effective education for adults assists them with managing the roles in which they are engaged. As adults age, their social roles change and education can be a means of facilitating the necessary adjustments. The "teachable moment" for an adult depends not upon physiological maturation, but in large measure upon the immediate problems or tasks associated with social roles and functions. In a discussion of the themes of work and love in adulthood, Smelser further illuminates the orientation of adults:

> The adult years mark the development and integration of cognitive and instrumental capacities that enable people to reach whatever heights of purposeful, organized mastery of the world they are capable of reaching. Too, the adult years are those in which people are able to reach their maximum of mutually gratifying attachments to other individuals.[31]

Positing the adult learner in a developmental context necessitates viewing adult learning as more than a striving towards self-fulfillment or a mechanistic response to a learning stimulus. Adult learning becomes a complex phenomenon involving interaction with biological, psychological, and social environmental factors. Such an orientation to the adult learner draws on developmental psychology, which focuses upon the *process* of development. That is, there is less concern with defining the particular capabilities of adults at a certain age than with charting the patterns of change and stability over the entire life span. Adult educators who are cognizant of the patterns of adult change and development can facilitate more meaningful learning experiences, which in turn will bring about further growth and development.

Adulthood is no longer thought of as merely a plateau between adolescence and old age. There is increasing evidence that adulthood is a changing, fluctuating, developmental phenomenon. What is of concern to researchers in adult development are questions about the existence and universality of stages of development, the nature and sequences of development, and the directionality of development. Time is the key element in adult development research. Three types of time that affect human development have been distinguished by Neugarten and Datan: *life time*, or chronological age, is the most frequently used index of change, although it fails to be a meaningful predictor of much social and psychological behavior; *social time* refers to the age-grade system of a particular society—that is, culture determines the appropriate time for certain behaviors and different societies have different sets of age expectations not necessarily related to chronological age; and *historical time* "shapes the social system, and the social system, in turn, creates a changing set of age norms and a changing age-grade system which shapes the individual life cycle."[32] Historical time refers to what writers call long-term processes, such as industrialization, as well as specific historical events. With the various dimensions of time in mind, Neugarten and Datan present the essence of developmental psychology: "to study sequences of change for the purpose of determining *which ones* are primarily developmental (in the sense of being tied to maturational change), and *which ones* are primarily situational—if indeed, this distinction can be made at all."[33]

The concept of development itself has been defined differently by various writers. Some see development as the process "whereby the individual goes from a less differentiated to a more differentiated state, from a less complex to a more complex organism, from a lower or early stage to a higher or later stage of an ability, skill, or trait."[34] Neugarten avoids the connotations of "less" and "more" or "lower" and "higher" by defining development as those processes in which the organism is "changed or transformed by interaction with the environment."[35]

Inherent in both these definitions of development is that the process takes place in conjunction with other variables in the adult's environment. An adult becomes "changed" or "transformed" or even "differentiated" as he or she encounters the social, physical, and psychological tasks that are part of daily living. Charting the changes likely to occur from a person's interaction with life tasks is further complicated by the individual's personal history and the collective history of the generational cohort of which he or she is a member. All these factors contribute to individual differences among persons at any particular age. While developmental psychologists do appreciate individual differences, they are particularly interested in identifying the commonalities of human experience.

Learning in adulthood occurs as very different individuals react to the commonalities of human experience over the life span. This in fact is the foundation for much of Bernice Neugarten's research. Neugarten speaks of the "normal expectable life cycle." The existence of regularities of change through the life cycle have biological, social, and psychological dimensions. It is these regularities that make the life cycle "expectable" and "predictable."[36] Neugarten underscores the importance of the individual within a particular social context with a discussion of the "outer" and "inner" sources of regularity in the life cycle. The outer sources of regularity are those related to age norms and age-appropriate behavior. Every culture has a prescribed pattern of behavior for each age group.

Yet, while there is an expected series of life events (such as marrying, raising children, working, retiring), Neugarten now sees them as age-irrelevant. That is, "chronological age is becoming a poorer and poorer predictor of the way people live. . . . Lives are more fluid."[37] Such norms and expectations, however, do provide incentives for learning. They act as "prods and brakes upon behavior, in some instances hastening an event, in others, delaying it." The "social clock" becomes internalized and regulates an individual's movement through the events of a life cycle.[38]

Examples of the "inner" sources of regulation are intrinsic psychological changes that occur with age, such as a changed time perspective, increased interiority, and personalization of death. "As a result of accumulative adaptations to both biological and social events," Neugarten notes, "there is a continuously changing basis within the individual for perceiving and responding to new events in the outer world. It is in this sense that orderly and predictable changes occur within the personality as well as in the social environment."[39] In understanding and charting the "normal expectable life cycle," Neugarten feels one must look to social events as being the "major punctuation marks in the adult life line."[40]

Adult development is a function of the individual's interaction with the social system. It is also a function of historical time. Troll describes this as the generation effect, and it can be viewed from an individual perspective of moving from one life stage (or generation) to the next or in the context of the family or an age cohort within a social group:

> As people move from early to middle adulthood, their parents are simultaneously moving from middle adulthood to middle age, and their children are moving from childhood to adolescence. What is more, as their age cohort moves from youth to established adulthood, their parents may still be in the social position of established adulthood, also, but perhaps with another set of values, while a new age cohort is already replacing them in their earlier social niche. While all this is going on, the society as a whole is changing. Any attempt to understand development, particularly in adulthood, must recognize the complex effects of the intertwining of these different kinds of generations.[41]

Thus, a developmental perspective on adulthood must take into account historical factors, social and cultural norms, and individual differences. Developmental psychology attempts to determine the commonalities that exist for all human beings moving through the life cycle, while at the same time keeping sight of the uniqueness of each individual in his or her responses to life's events or tasks. The developmental approach also considers the adult as a learning organism, for the intellectual or cognitive dimension of adulthood is one of the factors that determines an individual's adaptation to the tasks and events of the life cycle. The investigation of adult development is of necessity most often approached from one dimension, such as cognitive change. Patterns of development have also been charted in terms of career, family, physical, and personality dimensions.

Within a developmental context, adult learning to a large extent consists of accumulated experiences that influence problem solving strategies, coping mechanisms, and adaptations to the tasks salient to different stages of adulthood. Knowledge of the general patterns of development enhances the possibility of facilitating adult learning. Developmental tasks offer one means of conceptualizing the different phases of the life span, each with its own typical concerns. Robert Havighurst defines a developmental task as "a task which arises at or about a certain period in the life of the individual, successful achievement of which leads to his happiness and to success with later tasks, while failure leads to unhappiness in the individual, disapproval by society, and difficulty with later tasks."[42]

The concept of developmental tasks can be used to position the individual adult in a social context. The age norms and age-related behavior of which Neugarten speaks can be interpreted in terms of the broadly defined tasks with which each age level must deal. These tasks describe the "demands, constraints, and opportunities provided by the social environment" and successful coping with the tasks is a learning process that "results in the development of competence and differentiation of skills and personality."[43] Thus, the individual grows or becomes more "self-actualized" in response to the pattern of social demands.

Robert Havighurst has delineated developmental tasks for the stages of adulthood as well as for childhood. These tasks may be related to physical maturation, cultural pressure of society, or the personal values and aspirations of the individual. In most cases, the needs for the tasks arise "from combinations of these factors acting together" and offer to the educator a "teachable moment."[44] Developmental tasks for the three periods of adulthood are as follows:

Early adulthood: selecting a mate, learning to live with a marriage partner, starting a family, bringing up young children, managing a home, getting started in an occupation, taking on civic responsibilities, finding a congenial social group.

Middle age: achieving adult civic and social responsibilities, establishing and maintaining an economic standard of living, assisting one's children to become adults, developing durable leisure-time activities, relating to one's marriage partner as a person, accepting and adjusting to physical changes, adjusting to one's aging parents.

Late maturity: adjusting to decreasing physical strength and to death, adjusting to retirement and to reduced income, adjusting to death of one's marriage partner, establishing an explicit affiliation with one's age group, meeting social and civic obligations, establishing satisfactory physical living arrangements in the light of physical infirmities.[45]

It is interesting to note that the tasks of adulthood relate primarily to societal expectations and pressures. The developmental tasks of childhood, however, have more to do with physical maturation: learning to walk, getting ready to read, learning physical skills necessary for ordinary games, etc. Childhood developmental tasks, as well as those of adolescence, also are nearly all preparatory in nature. Most of the tasks require "learning," "developing" concepts and skills, and "preparing" for future adult roles. A shift in emphasis occurs with the tasks of young adulthood. Adulthood tasks are less preparatory than aimed at functioning well in the adult role: "starting" a family and career, "establishing and maintaining a standard of living," "assisting one's children," and "adjusting" to the changing demands of adult life. The differences between the tasks of childhood and those of adulthood further illuminate the differences between childhood and adult learning. The preparatory nature of childhood developmental tasks suggests an educational thrust that prepares children for adulthood; likewise, the adulthood tasks suggest education to assist adults to perform better the roles and functions that they have already assumed.

These developmental tasks change according to the various roles one plays in life. Havighurst feels adult development can be viewed as the interaction between the tasks for different ages and the "social role construct."[46] Within the broad categories of family, work, and community are more specific social roles of worker, parent, spouse, homemaker, citizen, neighbor, friend, club or association member, and church member. These roles are of particular interest to adult educators, as "educational programs can be conceived to help people improve their performance of [such] roles."[47] Role participation has been studied with reference to socioeconomic status, sex, and age variables and, in general, "participation and performance in a given role have an age pattern."[48] Thus, age-related patterns of development can be seen in terms of both tasks and roles.

Similar to developmental tasks are Kimmel's milestones in human development. "The notion of milestones in human development is an appropriate concept," he says, "because when we think of the life cycle we mark it off with developmental milestones, and in fact, often celebrate these milestones (such as graduation, marriage, or retirement)."[49] These age-related milestones incur role shifts central to adult development. Milestones are largely social events, and it is the individual's response to them that brings about development. A person learns from his or her interaction with others, and the accumulated knowledge and experience of each individual then influences his or her future development. Kimmel speaks of three types of accumulated experiences that affect development and that involve learning. The first is *situation experience*, in which a "person gains a greater range of past situations from which he can draw possible responses for the present situation." Through *interaction experience*, the person "becomes increasingly adept at seeing himself from the point of view of the other." Finally, *self-experience* involves the person's becoming "adept at seeing himself from the point of view of the other and at integrating this awareness in the present moment with the memories of this awareness in past situations."[50]

The interactive effect of development and experience described by Kimmel underscores the importance of understanding adult development, especially when planning learning experiences designed to bring about *further* growth and development. The accumulation of experience, divided by Kimmel into situational, interactive, and self-experience, is one of the defining characteristics of adulthood and forms a basis for the andragogical approach to learning. Thus the accumulated experiences of an adult in interaction with developmental tasks serve to differentiate the adult learner from the child learner; they also provide a foundation for educational planning.

Adulthood is characterized by periods of stability and periods of change. Events or tasks that stimulate change offer the greatest potential for continued adult growth and development and the changes in a person's life that are most likely to result in systematic learning experiences. Alan Knox makes a case for viewing both adult development and adult learning in terms of "change events." Change events occur at different times in the life cycle; in different contexts such as those of family, occupation, or community; and may "entail a gain, a loss, or a combination of gains and losses in role relationships."[51] Events such as leaving home, getting married, having children, or retiring can be plotted on an adulthood time line in terms of the age at which they typically occur, providing a generally predictable pattern of adult development. Other change events, such as the death of a friend, a health problem, or a new job, are not so predictable but still provide stimuli for an educative experience:

> When a change event occurs, the need for some adaptation produces, for some adults at least, a heightened readiness to engage in educative activity. The resulting educative activity may be directly or indirectly related to the change event, and the relation may or may not be recognized by the individual. This period of heightened readiness has been referred to as a teachable moment. The educative activity may include all types of informal information seeking such as reading and talking with others, as well as more formal participation in part-time, externally sponsored educational programs.[52]

Change events follow a patterned sequence consisting of five stages: prestructure—the period of stability before the change event; anticipation—when the individual becomes aware that a change event will occur; actual change event (such as moving, marriage); disorganization period—between the change event and reestablishment of a stable pattern of participation; and poststructure—stability that reflects reorganization.[53] Adults respond to change events, some of which are self-imposed and some of which are externally imposed or inevitable, by adopting a strategy to deal with each event. One such strategy is participation in an educative undertaking "characterized by purposeful efforts to alter one's own competence by means of systematic and sustained learning activities."[54] Interestingly, the notion that adults seek learning activities in order to deal with change events has been borne out by a recent study of over 1500 adults aged 25 years and older. Among the learners in the sample, 83 percent named some transition, some identifiable event (such as getting fired or promoted, becoming a parent, reentering the job market), as the cause of their learning.[55]

Knox's concept of change events involves more than the accomplishment of developmental tasks at different stages of the life span. Change events affect the adult's structure of participation in family, occupational, political, religious, and leisure activities. "When a major activity or role relationship is added, changed, or lost, there must be some alteration of the individual's time use, usually to make way for the new relationship or to fill in the time released because a relationship is lost."[56] Each individual has his or her own unique structure of participation which is dependent upon many factors, including personality, social class, age, and opportunity. While individual differences in the pattern of participation are recognized, adult educators can plan around the commonality of experiences of adults attempting to cope with change events—whatever they might be and at whatever age they occur. As Knox notes, "when practitioners help adults adapt to change, the specific instances are unique but the process is generalizable."[57]

Knox, Kimmel, Neugarten, and Havighurst emphasize the development of the adult within a social context. It is in fact dealing with the functions and tasks of social roles that results in experiences leading to growth and development. Learning in either a systematic or incidental manner is a function of adapting to or coping with the milestones, developmental tasks, or change events that challenge adults as they move through the life cycle.

Other Stage Theories

Identifying developmental tasks and social functions likely to occur at various ages is one approach to adult development. Other stage models of development emphasize the psychological dimension of growth and change. Tasks to be grappled with are more intrapsychic and ego-centered.[58] Birren's discussion of the differences between sociological and psychological age is helpful for differentiating between socially oriented and psychologically oriented stage models:

> Psychological age should be expected to be closely related to measures of adaptive capacity, and the task consists of identifying and measuring those aspects of adaptive capacity which show a change with chronological age. In comparison with psychological age, social age has the additional criterion of the extent to which the individual has acquired or performs the various social roles which his society and his immediate social group expect of a person of his age. The emphasis in psychological age is on the *capacity* to adapt, whereas in social age the emphasis is on the *social output,* or *performance* of the individual in relation to others. . . . Viewing the individual in terms of his social age, we are faced with an organization of habit patterns which may be judged according to their appropriateness in some group. The individual may be simultaneously viewed in terms of psychological age or the processes by which he acquires, maintains, and modifies the habit patterns.[59]

Vaillant's in-depth longitudinal study of 95 Harvard graduates is a good example of a psychological charting of adult development. Vaillant focused on the subjects' adaptation to life's demands and found that adaptive style matures with age. Besides biological and cognitive maturation, he found that the development of mature psychological defenses also requires "close relationships with benign individuals, who [can] serve both as models and as positive objects for identification."[60]

Erikson, Jung, and Peck have proposed psychological models of adult development that emphasize the individual's inner capacity to adapt to the tasks of each stage of life. These ego-centered models can also be viewed in terms of the larger social context. Progression through the life cycle does not happen in a vacuum. The growth of the self occurs in response to or in interaction with other people, groups, or social-cultural norms and expectations. This can be seen in an analysis of the stages of development proposed by Erikson, Jung, and Peck with regard to young adulthood, middle age, and old age.

Young adulthood, according to Erikson, is a time for developing the capacity for intimacy. "The young adult, emerging from the search for and the insistence on identity, is eager and willing to fuse his identity with that of others." This period of self-development occurs, paradoxically, "in situations which call for self-abandon: in the solidarity of close affiliations, in orgasms and sexual unions, in close friendships and in physical combat, in experiences of inspiration by teachers and of intuition from the recesses of the self."[61] Avoiding intimate relationships results in isolation. Thus Erikson's sixth stage—intimacy versus isolation—establishes the critical issue of ego development in young adulthood as one that necessitates relationships with others.

Erikson's stages are maturational, sequential and "epigenetic"—that is "each stage has a modifying influence on all later stages," and the study of a particular stage must "be pursued always with the total configuration of stages in mind."[62] In postulating the negative and positive dimension of each stage, Erikson cautions against making an "achievement scale" out of the stages. Rather, one strives for a "favorable ratio" of the positive over the negative at each juncture.[63]

Similarities can be drawn between Erikson's young adulthood stage and Jung's. For Jung, movement through the life cycle is viewed in terms of intrapsychic occurrences and a widening of one's consciousness. In young adulthood a wider consciousness occurs as one gives up childhood illusions and comes to terms with inner conflicts caused by the sexual instinct and feelings of inferiority. Intimacy cannot be achieved by avoiding encounters with others; neither can there be an expansion of consciousness if one clings to childhood and resists "the fateful forces in and around us which would involve us in the world."[64]

For Erikson, Jung, and Peck, middle age is a stage of life in which ego development is very much associated with social interaction. Erikson defines this stage as generativity versus stagnation. Movement into this stage is a function of individual readiness, societal encouragement, and the successful negotiation of earlier stages. Generativity is a concern for and interest in guiding the next generation. Erikson defines generativity to mean not only parenthood, but "everything that is generated from generation to generation: children, products, ideas, and works of art."[65]

Production and the basic virtue of care characterize this stage. Erikson defines care as "the widening concern for what has been generated by love, necessity, or accident; it overcomes the ambivalence adhering to irreversible obligations."[66] Failure of the adult to embrace his or her generative function and emerge a caring individual results in self-absorption, which Erikson calls a "mental deformation" with which the individual "becomes his own infant and pet."[67]

Generativity, production, care—these require the individual to reach out. Reaching out is part of the widening consciousness of middle age. Jung compares extension of oneself in middle age to the rising sun, which looks upon the world "in an expanse that steadily widens the higher it climbs in the firmament. In this extension of its field of action caused by its own rising, the sun will discover its significance; it will see the attainment of the greatest possible height, and the widest possible dissemination of its blessings, as its goal."[68]

Peck has proposed a set of critical issues for middle age that incorporate the notions of generativity and expansion. For the most part, he says, the self develops through a restructuring of values and attitudes. His issues of middle age are: (1) valuing wisdom versus valuing physical powers—mental resources must be seen as primary not dependence upon physical powers; (2) socializing versus sexualizing in human relationships—people take on a new value for one another as "individual personalities, rather than primarily as sex-objects"; (3) cathectic flexibility versus cathectic impoverishment—this is "the capacity to shift emotional investments from one person to another." The opportunity for achieving this in middle age is perhaps greater than at any other time in the life cycle for it is at this time that adults "have the widest circle of acquaintances in their community and vocational worlds"; (4) mental flexibility versus mental rigidity—this is close to Jung's idea of a widening consciousness. One must remain open to new experiences and resist becoming locked into a set of inflexible attitudes and behaviors.[69]

Peck's tasks for the ego in old age can be viewed as adaptive strategies for dealing with the social, biological, and psychological changes inherent in this stage of the life cycle. Ego differentiation versus work-role preoccupation allows one to cope with retirement from work and family roles through participation in other meaningful activities. Body transcendence versus body preoccupation requires one to focus away from a deteriorating body, toward activities and interaction with others. Finally, ego transcendence versus ego preoccupation results in one's sensing the worth and significance of one's life. One is thus freed from a preoccupation with death.[70]

Similar to Peck's concept of ego transcendence versus ego preoccupation is Erikson's last stage of life, which he calls integrity versus despair. The task here is to be able to affirm the meaningfulness of one's life, to realize that "an individual life is the accidental coincidence of but one life cycle with but one segment of history; and that for him all human integrity stands or falls with the one style of integrity of which he partakes." Erikson goes on to state that "the lack or loss of this accrued ego integration is signified by fear of death" and, hence, despair.[71]

For Jung also, death must be reckoned with if old age is to be lived to its fullest. The task of the ego in old age is to resist looking back, to set future goals, and "to think of death as only a transition, as part of a life process whose extent and direction are beyond our knowledge."[72]

The stage models presented by Erikson, Jung, and Peck offer frameworks for better understanding adulthood. They are psychological in emphasis, yet there is inherent in each the social context within which an individual grapples with the issues of each stage. Gould, who has also delineated stages of adult development, expresses the phenomenon of the development of self in a social context as follows: stages, he says, "are best thought of as a description of a sequence of process fluctuations that define the posturing of the self to its inner and outer world over time. The fluctuations are time-dominated [and] take place within the context of a total personality, life-style, and subculture."[73]

Levinson's psychological model of male development is dependent on individual/societal interaction. Origins of his phases "lie both in the nature of the individual as a biological and biopsychological organism and in the nature of society as an enduring multigenerational form of collective life."[74]

His stages or periods are closely linked to age-related developmental tasks and social roles: leaving the family; getting into the adult world; age 30 transition; settling down; midlife transition; and restabilization—entry into middle adulthood. The tasks that men grapple with and the periods they move through are all in the service of forming what Levinson calls the "life structure." Adult development thus consists of periods of stability, structure building, transitions, and structure changing.[75]

In contrast to Levinson's socially oriented phases Lawrence Kohlberg's stages of moral development are both maturational and structural. Drawing upon Piaget's research, Kohlberg describes developmental stages as follows:

1. Stages imply distance or qualitative differences in structure.
2. These different structures form an invariant sequence, order, or succession in individual development. While cultural factors may speed up, slow down, or stop development, they do not change its sequence.
3. Each of these different and sequential modes forms a structured whole.
4. Stages are hierarchical integrations, . . . higher stages displace (or, rather, reintegrate) the structure found at lower stages.[76]

Kohlberg's moral stages are loosely comparable to Erikson's ego states and Piaget's logical-cognitive stages. The bulk of moral stage development occurs in childhood and adolescence and reflects biological and cognitive development. These earlier stages are "conventional" in contrast to the "principled" moral stages that occur in adulthood. Kohlberg's stage five, which reflects a responsibility toward others in one's moral decisions, and stage six, which involves decisions oriented toward universal and abstract ethical principles, require the added dimension of adult experience. It is only through the integration of cognitive reflection and personal experiences of choice exercised in adulthood that the highest stages of moral development are obtainable. And the acting out of a truly ethical perspective (stage six) may not develop until middle age, if at all.[77]

Studies by Kohlberg and others seem to suggest that movement through the conventional stages of moral development can be facilitated through structured discussion groups and vicarious experiences of role taking. The highest levels of moral development, however, require the integration of personal experiences of adulthood. Kohlberg feels that the capacity and the preference for the higher stages "can develop relatively speedily in a cognitively and socially rich environment."[78] Likewise, it would seem that the learning that occurs as adults make decisions, resolve conflicts, and cope with the tasks of adulthood works toward achievement of the higher moral stages.

Stage theories or models stress the universality of orderly sequences of change throughout the life span. The existence of such stages, whether dependent upon biological maturation, age-related developmental tasks and social roles, or psychosocial growth, has been debated. Some feel that the complexity and "increasing diversification of environmental inputs" working upon the adult make it difficult to extract true stages of development. Likewise, "it is difficult to make a strong case for a universal set of experiences in adult development."[79]

On the other hand, Ausubel argues that stages of development can be viewed as "identifiable sequential phases in an orderly progression of development that are *qualitatively* discriminable from adjacent phases and generally characteristic of most members of a broadly defined age range." Ausubel also addresses the question of universality of stages. "As long as a given stage occupies the same sequential position in all individuals and cultures whenever it occurs," he says, "it is perfectly compatible with intraindividual, interindividual, and intercultural differences."[80]

Stage models relating to human development can be used by adult educators to gain insights into the nature of the adult as learner. Such constructs, McKenzie points out,

> have helped adult educators impose a degree of order and intelligibility upon the data relating to adult behaviors, adult needs, and the demands made upon adults by society. These lifespan paradigms furnish the adult educator with a gestalt or overarching structure for diagnosing adult learning needs, for planning educational programs, and for selecting appropriate strategies for the teaching-learning situation.[81]

Whether concerned with moral issues, psychological development, or socially oriented tasks and roles unique to adulthood, stage theories are relevant to adult educators. Although varying in their emphasis upon the self and the social context, stage models are useful for the insight each provides into human development over the life span. The tasks to be grappled with, the conflicts to be resolved, the growth to be accomplished at each stage or juncture all involve some form of learning.

Educators are only beginning to incorporate such insights into practice. The newness of research into adulthood, the ambiguity of some of the findings, and the lack of a simple explanation of the link between learning and development have contributed to the cautious programmatic response of most adult educators. A clearer conceptualization of the relationship between adults as learners and adults as changing, developing beings is needed to aid practitioners in translating this knowledge into practice. K. Patricia Cross has taken a step in this direction by advancing a tentative framework for understanding adult learners.[82] Called CAL (Characteristics of Adults as Learners), Cross's model consists of two variables: situational characteristics which describe conditions under which learning takes place, and personal characteristics which describe the learners. The situational characteristics differentiate adults from children in that adults are usually part-time, rather than full-time learners, and voluntary, rather than compulsory learners. Interwoven with the situational variables are three personal variables: physical, sociocultural (which she equates with the life phase models of Levinson, Neugarten, Sheehy and Lowenthal), and psychological (equated with the life stage theories of Erikson, Loevinger, Kohlberg). For each of these three personal variables Cross proposes different educator responses. With regard to physical aging, educators should *compensate* for losses and *capitalize* on those attributes which improve with age. In helping learners negotiate the transitions between life phases, the educator's stance is one of *adjustment*. Finally, the educator's response to the psychological dimension wherein adults move toward higher or more integrative stages of development is one of *challenge*.[83] This model's usefulness to educators for explaining the physical, psychological, and sociocultural dimensions of adulthood and learning has yet to be tested. It is, however, an example of what needs to be done in order for educators to understand more fully an adult's readiness and orientation to learning.

THE LEARNING PROCESS

The assumptions underlying an andragogical approach to adult learning help to define the unique qualities of the adult learner. As independent and self-directed beings, most adults are capable of assisting in the planning, execution, and evaluation of their own learning activities. The adult's readiness and orientation to learning are a function of a developmental context different from that of a child. To a large extent, performing the roles and tasks inherent in adulthood determines what is to be learned, and results as well in immediate, rather than future, application of newly acquired knowledge. The necessity of dealing with the challenges inherent in adult living can form a basis for many adult education programs. Understanding the learning process itself also can enhance the practice of adult education.

Various principles of learning have been derived from controlled experiments with animals, children, and adults. Some of the research has not attempted to separate children from adult subjects and the findings are considered applicable to learners of any age. Other investigations have explored changes in learning ability as a function of age and have particular relevance to adult education. The contributions to knowledge about the learning process made by behaviorists, Gestalt psychologists, and cognitive theorists are applicable to both children and adults.

Behaviorists and Gestalt Psychologists

Although the nature of mental processes has been the subject of speculation for many centuries, it was not until the late nineteenth and early twentieth centuries that learning was investigated systematically. Expanding upon the work of his German and Russian predecessors, John B. Watson's research, writings, and lectures established behaviorism as the predominant school of psychology in the early twentieth century. E. L. Thorndike, a psychologist and contemporary of Watson, investigated the measurement of mental ability and educational achievement and experimentally derived theories of learning. Using animals in controlled laboratory experiments, Thorndike explained learning as a process of association. An organism presented with a stimulus, he said, found a connection or bond with a response. Hence, his findings became known as "connectionism" or the "S-R" theory of learning. Thorndike's laws of learning were major contributions to the psychology of learning. According to Thorndike, learners will acquire and remember those responses that lead to satisfying aftereffects (law of effect); repetition in itself does not establish a connection, but repetition of a meaningful bond will strengthen the learning (law of exercise); and a pleasurable bond, hence maximized learning, occurs if the organism is ready (law of readiness).[84] In terms of an instructional setting, Thorndike advocated the arrangement of situations to facilitate establishing pleasurable connections. "Put together," he stated, "what should go together and keep apart what should not go together. . . . Reward desirable connections and make undesirable connections produce discomfort."[85]

Thorndike's experimental work was further advanced by Tolman, Guthrie, Hull, Skinner, and others. Edward Tolman introduced the notion that learning occurs in relation to purpose or goals and that there are intervening variables between a stimulus and a response.[86] Hull and his colleague, Spence, sought to expand Tolman's concept of intervening variables. A response to a stimulus, they felt, depended upon habit, strength, drive, and motivation. The work of Hull, Spence, and Edwin Guthrie on stimulus reception and attention elaborated upon the S-R theory as well as anticipated the research of later cognitive theorists.[87]

The work of B. F. Skinner is most often associated with behaviorism. Skinner's major theoretical contribution has been to distinguish between classical and operant or instrumental conditioning. As differentiated from a reflex response in classical conditioning, operant conditioning postulates that a response operates or is instrumental in obtaining reinforcement. A reinforced response serves to solidify the bond to the stimulus.[88] Skinner's research on rats, pigeons, monkeys, and humans has focused on positive and negative reinforcement schedules, manipulation of rewards, and an analysis of avoidance learning. Behavior, according to Skinner, is learned and therefore can be modified if certain environmental factors are shaped in a predetermined way. Thus, "the generic bases of behavior vis-à-vis biological, social, or self-determinism are less important than arranging contingencies of reinforcement in the organism's immediate environment so that the probability of a given response is heightened."[89] In summing up Skinner's position, Poppen and Wandersman point out that "Skinner prefers to deal with the properties of behavior and avoids mental constructs such as habit, ability, motive, needs, and cognition. . . . A small number of learning concepts such as reinforcement, extinction, and counterconditioning can account for complex human behavior."[90]

Although there are some differences in emphasis among the proponents of behaviorism, "the common point of reference for all behaviorists is the attempt to explain phenomena, particularly those of learning and motivation, in terms of the connection between physical stimuli . . . and observable responses."[91] Beginning with Thorndike's experiments, behaviorists have sought to discover general principles that explain human learning. Through controlled laboratory experiments behaviorists observe an organism's overt behavior and attempt to explain it in terms of external environmental contingencies rather than internal causes of action.

In 1929, Thorndike's approach was challenged by Bode, who introduced Gestalt psychology to America. "The fundamental difficulty with Thorndike, as with the behaviorists," Bode stated, "is that he depends too exclusively upon the nervous system. The environment does nothing except to press the buttons which release the reflexes."[92] Gestalt psychology, he noted, allowed one "to see life steadily and see it whole, in terms of the circumstances and opportunities of the modern age."[93] Gestalt (a German word meaning pattern or shape) theorists proposed looking at the whole rather than individual parts, and at the total structure of learning rather than at isolated incidents.

By the mid-twentieth century, the major proponents of Gestalt psychology, Köhler, Koffka, and Wertheimer, rivaled the behaviorists in influence on educational thought. The general assumptions of Gestalt psychology have had a significant impact on learning theory. To begin with, the total phenomenon of human experience is thought by the Gestaltists to be greater than the sum of the parts. Therefore, they believe, by studying a stimulus and a response one does not achieve a full understanding of the incident. Perception of the environment is not an isolated experience, but occurs in relation to the total configuration of the environment. When an individual perceives the environment his or her behavior is dependent upon the meaning a given situation establishes for the incident. This behavior has a purpose; the individual sets goals on the basis of his or her insight into the meaning of a situation. In Gestalt theory, insight and motivation are key elements in learning. Learning involves the development of insight and of more effective ways to use the elements of a given situation to achieve a goal. Learning necessitates the reorganization of experiences into systematic and meaningful patterns. Thus, the Gestaltists broadened the investigation of learning to include notions of understanding, insight, and problem solving.

Cognitive Theorists

Cognitive theorists are closer to Gestalt psychologists than to behaviorists in their focus on perception and thinking as they relate to conscious experience. Cognitivists seek to understand mental processes, thinking, concept-formation, and the acquisition of knowledge. Many of their findings have direct application to educational settings.

One of the most influential cognitive theorists in terms of educational practice has been Jean Piaget. Piaget was influenced by both behaviorist and Gestalt schools of thought. From Gestalt theory Piaget derived the proposition that perceptions and thoughts could be understood only in reference to the wholes in which they were organized. From the behaviorists Piaget derived the ideas of operant conditioning and "the sequence of more and more complex behavior patterns" depicted "as outgrowths of simple reflexes and habits."[94]

Although focused on children, Piaget's work is important for the psychology of adult learning because he identifies, "at least tentatively, significant changes in cognitive capacities, processes, and phenomena as a function of age, experience, and intellectual sophistication."[95] Piaget's explanation of the movement from the sensorimotor intelligence of infants and young children to the concrete intelligence of mid-childhood to the formal operational intelligence of adulthood involves concepts of special relevance to understanding adult learning. For progression through the stages of intellectual development depends not only upon physical and neural maturation, but also upon experiences, social context, and self-regulation.[96] A person's intellectual growth, then, is very much interrelated with other growth dimensions. The maximization of intellectual development takes into account the individual's experiences, social setting, and decision-making ability.[97] As noted earlier, these factors are particularly distinct in adulthood.

Other cognitive theorists have explored mental processes as separate phenomena which are age-related insofar as years of accumulated experience may facilitate the integration of new knowledge. Ausubel, for example, differentiates between meaningful and rote learning. The acquisition of new information is meaningful when it can be related to existing concepts in a person's cognitive structure. "As new material enters the cognitive field," Ausubel states, "it interacts with and is appropriately subsumed under a relevant and more inclusive conceptual system."[98] The "principal factor influencing the learning and retention of meaningful new material," according to Ausubel, is

> an individual's organization, stability, and clarity of knowledge in a particular subject matter field at any given time. . . . If the existing cognitive structure is clear, stable, and suitably organized, it facilitates the learning and retention of new subject matter. If it is unstable, ambiguous, disorganized, or chaotically

organized, it inhibits learning and retention. Hence it is largely by strengthening relevant aspects of cognitive structure that new learning and retention can be facilitated.[99]

Implications for adult education are clear. "When we deliberately attempt to influence cognitive structure so as to manage meaningful learning and retention," Ausubel states, "we come to the heart of the educative process."[100]

Knowledge learned by rote does not become integrated within one's cognitive structure and so is more easily forgotten. Ausubel also distinguishes between reception and discovery learning. In reception learning, an individual internalizes material that is presented. What is internalized can be rote or meaningful learning. In discovery learning, the content is not given to a learner but is discovered and then internalized by the learner. Ausubel feels that after elementary school "verbal reception learning constitutes the most efficient method of meaningfully assimilating the substantive content of a discipline." Discovery learning, which he equates with concept formation and inductive problem solving, is "useful for communicating certain insights" but should not be "overemphasized" in educational settings because it is "too time-consuming."[101]

In contrast to Ausubel, Jerome Bruner contends that learning through discovery is necessary for the retention of knowledge and has several benefits. Discovery is "in its essence a matter of rearranging or transforming evidence in such a way that one is enabled to go beyond the evidence so reassembled to additional new insights."[102] An increase in intellectual potency is the first benefit one derives from learning through discovery. Practice in discovery teaches one to acquire information in ways that make problem solving easier. Through repeated exercises in discovery one learns how to process information for later use and to avoid "information drift." A second benefit of discovery learning involves bringing about a shift from extrinsic to intrinsic motivation. Rather than learning for external rewards, the individual sees discovery as a reward in itself and is thus motivated to further learning. Third, through "the exercise of problem solving and the effort of discovery" one learns how to discover and can "improve in the art and technique of inquiry." Finally, discovery learning facilitates remembering. The "process of memory," Bruner says, "is also a process of problem solving: how can material be 'placed' in memory so that it can be got on demand?"[103]

Cognitive theorist Robert Gagne has made a conscious effort to separate the twin factors of growth and learning in the overall development of an individual. Growth and development are genetically determined and so are largely unalterable. Learning, on the other hand, is dependent upon environmental circumstances that can be scientifically studied, altered, and controlled. Influenced by the associationists and behaviorists,

Gagne breaks down a learning event into three elements: the learner, in whom the senses, central nervous system, and muscles are the most important parts; the stimulus, or stimulus situation; and the response. Learning has taken place if there is an observable change in performance that is "not simply ascribable to the process of growth."[104]

Gagne's assumption that "learning is not simply an event that happens naturally; it is also an event that happens under certain observable conditions"[105] implies that one can bring about learning by manipulating environmental factors. Gagne goes a step further in suggesting that the specific arrangements of conditions can produce different varieties of learning. He has distinguished eight sets of conditions that produce eight types of learning. The learning ranges in complexity from signal learning, in which the individual makes a response to a signal, to problem solving, which requires thinking in concepts.[106]

Gagne, as well as Bruner, Ausubel, and Piaget, offers an approach to human learning that has relevance for understanding adults as learners. While there are differences in emphases, the major theorists seem to agree in their view of the learner in an educational setting. The "major long-term objective of education," according to Ausubel, is "the learner's acquisition of clear, stable, and organized bodies of knowledge." Ausubel goes on to point out that

> these bodies of knowledge, once acquired, constitute in their own right the
> most significant *independent variable* influencing the meaningful learning and
> retention of new subject-matter material. Hence control over meaningful
> learning can be exercised most effectively by identifying and manipulating
> significant cognitive structure variables. This can be done in two ways: (a)
> substantively, by showing concern for the "structure" of a discipline . . . ; and
> (b) programmatically, by employing suitable principles of ordering the
> sequence of subject matter, constructing its internal logic and organization,
> and arranging practice trials.[107]

Indeed, Ausubel's argument that the previous accumulation of knowledge is the most significant variable influencing future learning suggests that adults who have accumulated more knowledge than children are in a better position to learn new things, and, barring physiological impairments, learning potential increases with age.

The behaviorists, Gestalt psychologists, and cognitive theorists have sought to understand and explain the learning process. Their investigations have focused upon the individual components of the learning act and the delineation of various types of learning. Their findings, for the most part, are applicable to both children and adults. To the extent that experience or accumulated knowledge or maturational factors influence learning, adult learning can be differentiated, in a hierarchical sense at least, from childhood learning. Research that emphasizes learning as a function of aging provides additional insights into the nature of adult learning.

Intelligence, Learning, and Aging

In exploring learning in conjunction with aging, theorists have emphasized charting the changes that occur in intelligence, memory, thinking, and creativity as adults grow older. Unfortunately, much of the research has "followed the orientation of our culture in focusing on the debilitating aspects of aging. . . . Rarely, of course, is there an indication that aging may be associated with growth or improved functioning in some areas."[108] The following discussion on intellectual functioning and aging presents a somewhat more optimistic view—that knowledge of which abilities are maintained and which decline can be used to assist adults in accommodating and adapting to any such changes.

Historically, researchers have investigated learning and aging by mapping changes in intellectual functioning. Attempts to measure adult intelligence, however, have suffered from a lack of consensus as to just what is being measured. Birren points out that the meaning of intelligence may not, in fact, be constant over the life span. For children, "intelligence is that variable which governs the upper limit of mastery or the rate of mastery of the school curriculum." Effective adult functioning, however, might be "the skill with which relationships with other people are managed, usually with the effective use of words." Birren goes on to speculate that "if 'social intelligence' is to be emphasized as a criterion of adult intelligence, then the measures of verbal comprehension might be weighted more heavily than measures of perceptual function."[109]

The first significant work on adult intelligence was published by E. L. Thorndike in 1928. His systematic inquiry into an adult's ability to learn demonstrated that, contrary to popular thought, adults could learn and that intelligence did not drop significantly with age. Such an optimistic evaluation evolved in spite of the fact that his experiments did include factors that have since been shown to contribute to a negative picture of learning and aging. That is, his studies were cross-sectional, testing a young cohort against an older cohort, most of the results were based on timed and/or motor tasks, and the tasks selected were not particularly meaningful to the participants (learning to write with the left hand or memorizing an artificial language, for example).

What is more interesting, especially for adult educators, is Thorndike's suggestion that factors other than intelligence might significantly affect adult learning. Thorndike identified general health and energy, interest in learning, and opportunity as factors that might influence the amount of adult learning.[110] He also noted that "adults learn much less than they might partly because of unpleasant attention and comment."[111] McLeish has noted how perceptive Thorndike was with regard to adult learning:

> *Adult Learning* is a kind of Universal Declaration of Adult Rights to Learn. Thorndike calls for a society in which there will be a redistribution of the

formal hours of learning experience—so that these might be spread into and through adult life. He notes how usually inadequate both content and teaching strategies are for adult learners. He cites the need for the availability of counseling for adults—the mature counseling by peers for those whose hesitation on the brink of learning, or discouragement many times in the course of it, hinders their learning adventures. He urges a more sensible approach to the "dropout" from adult classes—perhaps the adult happens to know what he needs and does not need, or perhaps there is a message for the instructor and the institution. . . . And Thorndike deplores people who apply to adults tests validated and standardized for child and school use.[112]

Thorndike's objection to using IQ tests designed for children on adults was scarcely heeded for the first half of the century. When Binet developed his tests for atypical children, it was assumed that intelligence was genetically predetermined and relatively fixed by the early teen years. Hence, it mattered little what test was administered to which age groups. It was thought the IQ could be determined at any age. Working from this assumption in 1930, Jones and Conrad administered the Army Alpha test to the residents of a New Hampshire village who were between the ages of 10 and 60 years. They found that 18- to 21-year-olds scored the highest and that after 21, IQ steadily declined.[113] A later study of the educational levels of the participants, however, revealed a correlation with the distribution of IQ scores. Nevertheless, it was not until longitudinal studies of intelligence began to appear after 1950 that the notion of significant intellectual decline associated with aging began to be challenged.

The Wechsler Adult Intelligence Scale (WAIS) designed by David Wechsler in the early 1930s has been the most commonly used test of adult intelligence. The WAIS is standardized for each adult age group and consists of 11 subtests, each tapping a different component of intellectual functioning. A Verbal Intelligence Score based on general information, short-term memory, and socially based reasoning, and a Performance Intelligence Score based mainly on abstract reasoning and ability to manipulate objects are combined to yield an overall score. Wechsler himself is convinced that intellectual functioning declines with increasing age.[114] Numerous longitudinal studies, however, tend to support the idea that different components of intelligence (as differentiated by the 11 subtests of the WAIS) show different age-related trends. In a review of longitudinal studies, Jarvik concludes that the "one common thread leading toward a cohesive pattern of intellectual functioning in the later years of life" is the "remarkable stability of verbal scores—whenever health has been preserved—accompanied by a relentlessly progressive decline in performance on speeded tasks."[115]

Roughly equivalent to Wechsler's Performance IQ and Verbal IQ is Catell's theory of "fluid" and "crystallized" intelligence. Catell's model is both flexible and developmental and offers an interesting perspective on the complexity of human intelligence. Fluid intelligence is genetically based, neurophysiologically bound, and independent of education or life experience. Fluid intelligence peaks during late adolescence and then gradually declines during adulthood. This decline is reflected on the performance subtests of the WAIS. Crystallized intelligence, however, increases with age. This type of intelligence is dependent upon experience, accumulated knowledge, and the interplay between the organism and the social environment. The decrease in fluid and the increase in crystallized intelligence serve as equalizers with the end effect of a fairly stable overall IQ measure throughout adulthood.[116]

A parallel can be drawn between Catell's model of intelligence and creativity in adulthood. Investigations of the relationship between creative output and age seem to support the notion that the "more a creative act depends on accumulated development . . . the more likely it is to occur in the later years of life." In reviewing the research in this area Troll notes that "a mathematician's or artist's creative act may involve a heavier proportion of fluid intelligence, and a novelist's or philosopher's creative act a heavier proportion of crystallized intelligence."[117]

Intelligence has been one focus of investigation into learning and aging; cognitive functioning, which includes learning, memory, and problem solving, has been another. As with intelligence testing, studies of cognitive processes in adults have drawn heavily upon the behaviorist and cognitive theorist orientations. That is, most researchers have placed the adult in an experiment in a laboratory setting, provided a stimulus situation, and observed the results. Differences in performance between older and younger adult subjects have often been construed as age-related changes. The definition of cognition presented by Arenberg reflects the orientation of much of the research: "the processes of registering, storing, and retrieving information and manipulating that information to solve problems."[118]

Verbal learning as one aspect of cognitive functioning is focused on attention and set, practice, speed of performance, and learning strategies. "Evidence that has been accumulating on both animal and human learning suggests," Birren writes, "that changes with age in the primary ability to learn are small under most circumstances." The differences that do appear are "more readily attributed to processes of perception, set, attention, motivation, and the physiological state of the organism . . . than to a change in the primary capacity to learn."[119] Arenberg also notes that studies in verbal learning have included other variables (pacing being the most potent) that affect age differences in performance.[120] Overall, older adults seem to make more errors of omission than of commission. That is, they may not respond at all, rather than answer erroneously. Allowing self-pacing of the learning task reduces errors of omission. Eisdorfer has made an interesting discovery with regard to pacing and learning. Older subjects under test conditions may experience a high arousal state (as measured by free fatty acids in blood), which inhibits responses. Eisdorfer demonstrated that this response could be controlled, with a result in improved performance, by administering a drug that suppresses arousal.[121] His studies add credence to the position that changes in verbal learning ability may be more related to context variables than to changes in the capacity to learn.

Memory is another aspect of cognitive functioning that has been studied with reference to age. Separating memory from learning is not easily done, for "changes in memory with age are likely to affect learning; and changes in learning with age are likely to affect recent memories."[122] Nevertheless, researchers have distinguished between long-term and short-term memory and have postulated an information-processing model as a framework for investigation. In this model, memory consists of input (acquisition or reception), storage, and output (recall or retrieval). Most studies have found that there is little change with age in long-term memory or in the storage of information. Age-related decrements occur in the acquisition of short-term memory, perhaps because of sensory impairments. What is to be remembered must first be processed through the senses, and all five senses, especially sight and hearing, decline with age. Information that has been registered and stored may not be as easily retrieved as one ages. Studies suggest that it takes older adults longer to search for stored information. Other factors that might contribute to problems with retrieval are disuse, interference, neurochemical activity, and physiological functioning.[123]

The problem-solving, thinking dimension of cognitive processes and aging has been less explored than either memory or learning. Arenberg remarks that this is perhaps related to "the difficulties in measuring performance." After reviewing the work done on problem solving and aging, Arenberg concludes:

> In general, the findings from the studies of problem solving demonstrated age differences just as were found in many of the studies of verbal learning and memory. Studies that provided opportunities for the subjects to elicit information showed that the aged make more inquiries, especially noninformative inquiries. In addition, the old make less effective use of the information that they have requested or that has been presented by the experimenter. Both analysis (obtaining information) and synthesis (processing information to arrive at a solution) seem to be impaired with age.[124]

Knox has identified at least five factors that would seem to contribute to the decrement of problem solving abilities and that reflect the interrelatedness of learning and memory and problem solving strategies. They are: decline in short-term memory capacity, increased difficulty in organizing complex material, greater interference from previous learning, more difficulty in disregarding irrelevant aspects in a learning situation, and reduced ability to discriminate between stimuli.[125]

In attempting to respond to the question of whether or not learning deteriorates with advancing age, Botwinick concludes that it is not readily answerable because of the interrelationship of cognitive and noncognitive variables on performance. Noncognitive factors may hinder or facilitate a person's performance in a learning task but are not related to inherent learning ability. Among these noncognitive factors are: (1) pacing (speed)—the time a person has to examine a problem or to respond to a situation; (2) meaningfulness—how personally relevant or familiar material is makes a difference in learning; and (3) motivation—the extent to which an adult is motivated affects learning. The cognitive variables are associated with competence or "true learning ability." Botwinick distinguishes three: (1) organization—the ability to organize material into manageable units; (2) mediation—the ability to relate two or more elements of a learning activity; and (3) rigidity and cautiousness—a multidimensional concept that refers to the amount of flexibility a person has to make appropriate cognitive responses.[126]

While not identifying them as noncognitive variables, researchers have noted the presence of other factors that affect learning as well as account for a wide range of individual differences at any specified age. Birren noted motivation, speed, interference, and set or expectancy as unrelated to intrinsic learning ability.[127] Physical condition; social class, including educational level; and personality also might account for age trends in observed learning ability.[128] And, according to Eisdorfer, the "paramount importance" of physical health must be taken into account when making generalizations about cognitive and intellectual behavior.[129]

As many researchers have suggested, investigations into learning in conjunction with aging are beset by difficulties in separating learning ability from a host of confounding variables. And while intelligence and cognitive processes have been investigated independently, there is little consensus as to how one component can be distinguished from another. After reviewing the research on adult learning and aging, Baltes and Labouvie conclude that its relevance lies in applying what is known to a larger social context. Their conclusion is significant for adult educators: "Major aspects of educational reform should consist of *redistributing educational programs throughout the life-span*."[130]

In summarizing, it is obvious that many approaches have been subsumed under this section on the learning process. There are major differences between the behaviorists and Gestaltists, and between the cognitive theorists and those investigating adult learning in conjunction with aging. What permits these approaches to be combined is the common view of learning as a phenomenon evidenced by a change in behavior. Such change can be controlled to a large extent by manipulation of environmental variables. From the connectionists who produced a response to a specific stimulus, to the researchers in adulthood and aging who can achieve predictable results by varying the pacing of a task, emphasis has been upon experimental laboratory settings in which the learning process itself has been studied. Research on the learning process has made valuable contributions toward understanding the nature of learning, mental processes, and age-related changes in intelligence and cognitive functioning. Principles of learning relevant to adult education can be derived from the theories of behaviorists, Gestaltists, and cognitive theorists. The following list is not meant to be exhaustive; rather, it presents a sample of some of the findings from learning process research which can serve as guidelines for educational practice:

1. An adult's readiness to learn depends upon the amount of previous learning. The more knowledge a person has accumulated the better able he or she is to absorb new information and engage in complex modes of thinking. The variety of past educational experiences characteristic of a group of adult learners underscores the diversity of starting points for any educational activity.

2. Intrinsic motivation produces more pervasive and permanent learning. When needs are directly satisified by the learning itself, what is learned becomes an integral part of the learner. Extrinsic motivation may produce learning but the learning is not as effective as that which is intrinsically motivated. Building an educational activity around the adult learner's needs thus insures more permanent learning.

3. Positive (reward) reinforcement of learning is more effective than negative (punishment) reinforcement. As many adults are insecure and fearful because of negative experiences in earlier schooling, feelings of success in adult learning are essential for continued learning and participation.

4. To maximize learning, information should be presented in some organized fashion. Material can be arranged to proceed from simple to complex or can be organized around related concepts. The starting point for organizing a body of material for adults is related to the adults' past experiences and knowledge.

5. Learning, especially with regard to skill development, is enhanced by repetition, preferably spaced systematically over a period of time.

6. Meaningful material and tasks are more easily learned and longer remembered than nonmeaningful or nonsensical material. This is especially true for older adult learners. Any information or task has the potential of being meaningful or not. The challenge to a

facilitator of adult learning is to find ways in which material can be significantly related to the experiences and needs of the learners.

7. Active rather than passive participation in the learning activity enhances learning. Adults who are personally involved, who "discover" relationships, concepts, meanings on their own are rewarded by the learning itself. Adult educators who allow for active participation help bring about more meaningful and permanent learning.

8. Environmental factors affect learning. Tangible stimuli such as noise, crowded seating, temperature, lighting, etc., can interfere with the learning process. Other factors such as tension, derision, pressure, fatigue, and poor health also can impede learning. Older adults' learning performances are especially affected by environmental factors.

CONCLUSION

The preceding list of principles drawn from the research on the process of learning is helpful as a set of guidelines for an instructional setting. It does not, however, offer a great deal of insight into what differentiates adult learners from children. Most of the guidelines can, in fact, be applied to children as well as adults. Only through using the findings related to the learning process in conjunction with an understanding of the unique qualities of adulthood can one begin to comprehend the nature of adult learning.

The psychosocial developmental context provides a framework for understanding the adult's readiness and orientation to learning. Such an approach necessitates seeing the adult as a changing, developing being responding to and having an impact upon psychological, physical, and social environmental variables. While recognizing the uniqueness of individuals, this perspective involves attempts to delineate regularities of experience over the life span. Familiarity with patterns of adult psychosocial development provides insights into the differences between adult and pre-adult learners, helps explain the systematic and incidental learning that does take place in adulthood, and provides guidelines for structuring meaningful educational activities.

Humanistic philosophy and psychology also have contributed to an understanding of the adult learner. Independent and self-directed, adults can guide and promote their own growth and development. Whether one is striving toward self-actualization, greater maturity, or being fully functioning, the emphasis is upon continued self-improvement through learning. Knowles's andragogical approach to adult learning is based on humanistic assumptions.

Adult learning is a complex phenomenon. While it shares commonalities with childhood learning, there are at the same time substantial differences that necessitate approaching adult students differently from school children. The adult's independent self-concept, ability to be a self-directed learner, readiness, and orientation to learning are interactive factors that help explain not only the great diversity among adult learners, but also many of the commonalities.

NOTES

1. Malcolm Knowles, *The Modern Practice of Adult Education*, Revised Ed. (Chicago: Association Press/Follett, 1980), p. 43.
2. Ibid., pp. 44–45.
3. John W. C. Johnstone and Ramon Rivera, *Volunteers for Learning: A Study of the Educational Pursuits of American Adults* (Chicago: Aldine, 1965).
4. Charlotte Buhler, "Human Life as a Whole as a Central Subject of Humanistic Psychology," in *Challenges of Humanistic Psychology*, ed. James F. T. Bugental (New York: McGraw-Hill, 1967), p. 83.
5. James F. T. Bugental, ed., *Challenges of Humanistic Psychology* (New York: McGraw-Hill, 1967), p. 8.
6. Henry K. Misiak and Virginia Standt Sexton, *Phenomenological, Existential, and Humanistic Psychologies: A Historical Survey* (New York: Grune & Stratton, 1973), p. 116.
7. Abraham Maslow, *Motivation and Personality* (New York: Harper & Row, 1954), p. 54.
8. Abraham Maslow, quoted in John A. B. McLeish, *The Ulyssean Adult: Creativity in the Middle and Later Years* (New York: McGraw-Hill, 1976), pp. 87–88.
9. Maslow, *Motivation and Personality*, pp. 149–180.
10. Abraham Maslow, "Education and Peak Experiences," in *The Person in Education: A Humanistic Approach*, ed. Courtney D. Schlosser (New York: Macmillan, 1976), pp. 120–121.
11. Abraham Maslow, "Goals and Implications of Humanistic Education," in *Person in Education*, ed. Schlosser, p. 133.
12. Donald E. Hamachek, *Encounters with the Self* (New York: Holt, Rinehart and Winston, 1971), p. 54.
13. Carl Rogers, *Freedom to Learn* (Columbus, Ohio: Merrill, 1969), p. 288.
14. Ibid., p. 5.
15. Misiak and Sexton, *Phenomenological, Existential, and Humanistic Psychologies*, p. 121.
16. Carl Rogers, "The Process of the Basic Encounter Group," in *Challenges of Humanistic Psychology*, ed. Bugental, pp. 272–274.
17. Ibid.
18. Carl Rogers, "The Place of the Person in the New World of the Behavioral Sciences," in *Humanistic Viewpoints in Psychology*, ed. Frank T. Severin (New York: McGraw-Hill, 1965), p. 396.
19. Sidney M. Jourard, "Self-Disclosure and the Mystery of the Other Man," in

Bridges Not Walls, ed. John Stewart (Reading, Mass.: Addison-Wesley, 1977), p. 177.

20. Gordon W. Allport, "The Person in Psychology," in *Humanistic Viewpoints in Psychology*, ed. Severin, p. 41.

21. Gordon Allport, quoted in Duane Schultz, *Growth Psychology* (New York: Van Nostrand Reinhold, 1977), pp. 16–20.

22. Schultz, *Growth Psychology*, p. 47.

23. Ibid., p. 49.

24. Allen Tough, "Major Learning Efforts: Recent Research and Future Directions," *Adult Education* 28, no. 4 (1978): 250–263.

25. Allen Tough, *The Adult's Learning Projects* (Toronto: Ontario Institute for Studies in Education, 1971), p. 28.

26. McLeish, *The Ulyssean Adult*, p. 176.

27. Knowles, *Modern Practice of Adult Education*, p. 56.

28. Carl Weinberg and Philip Reidford, "Humanistic Educational Psychology," in *Humanistic Foundations of Education*, ed. Carl Weinberg (Englewood Cliffs, N.J.: Prentice-Hall, 1972), pp. 118–125.

29. Ibid.

30. Steven Laudon, "Actualization Education: A Human Potential Program in Action," *Sightings: Essays in Humanistic Psychology*, ed. Fred Richards and I. David Welch (Boulder, Colo.: Shields, 1973), p. 83.

31. Neil J. Smelser, "Issues in the Study of Work and Love in Adulthood," in *Themes of Work and Love in Adulthood*, ed. Neil Smelser and Erik Erikson (Cambridge, Mass.: Harvard University Press, 1980), p. 4.

32. Bernice L. Neugarten and Nancy Datan, "Sociological Perspectives on the Life Cycle," in *Life Span Developmental Psychology: Personality and Socialization*, ed. Paul Baltes and K. W. Schaie (New York: Academic Press, 1973), p. 57.

33. Ibid., p. 69.

34. James E. Birren and Diana S. Woodruff, "Human Development Over the Life Span through Education," in *Life Span Developmental Psychology*, ed. Baltes and Schaie, p. 307.

35. Bernice Neugarten, "Personality Change in Late Life: A Developmental Perspective," in *The Psychology of Adult Development and Aging*, ed. Carl Eisdorfer and M. Powell Lawton (Washington, D.C.: American Psychological Association, 1973), p. 312.

36. Bernice Neugarten, "Adaptation and the Life Cycle," in *Counseling Adults*, ed. Nancy K. Schlossberg and Alan D. Entine (Monterey, Calif.: Brooks/Cole, 1977), p. 39.

37. Elizabeth Hall, "Acting One's Age: New Rules For Old (Bernice Neugarten Interviewed)," *Psychology Today* (April 1980): 66.

38. Bernice Neugarten, "Adult Personality: Toward a Psychology of the Life Cycle," in *Middle Age and Aging*, ed. Neugarten (University of Chicago Press, 1968), p. 143.

39. Neugarten, "Adaptation and the Life Cycle," p. 37.

40. Neugarten, "Adult Personality," p. 146.

41. Lillian Troll, *Early and Middle Adulthood* (Monterey, Calif.: Brooks/Cole, 1975), p. 13.

42. Robert J. Havighurst, *Developmental Tasks and Education* (New York: McKay, 1952), p. 2.
43. Birren and Woodruff, "Human Development," p. 332.
44. Havighurst, *Developmental Tasks*, pp. 4—5.
45. Ibid., pp. 72—97.
46. Robert J. Havighurst, "Social Roles, Work, Leisure, and Education," in *Psychology of Adult Development and Aging*, ed. Eisdorfer and Lawton, p. 598.
47. Robert J. Havighurst, "Changing Status and Roles During the Adult Life Cycle: Significance for Adult Education," in *Sociological Backgrounds of Adult Education*, ed. Hobert W. Burns, reprint ed., (Syracuse, N.Y.: Syracuse University Publications in Continuing Education, 1970), p. 19.
48. Havighurst, "Social Roles, Work, Leisure, and Education," p. 599.
49. Douglas Kimmel, *Adulthood and Aging* (New York: Wiley, 1974), pp. 11—12.
50. Ibid., p. 57.
51. Alan B. Knox, *Adult Development and Learning* (San Francisco: Jossey-Bass, 1977), p. 514.
52. Ibid., p. 539.
53. Ibid., p. 537.
54. Ibid., p. 538.
55. Carol B. Aslanian and Henry M. Brickell, *Americans in Transition* (New York: College Board, 1980).
56. Ibid., p. 519.
57. Ibid., p. 543.
58. See, for example, Jane Loevinger, *Measuring Ego Development* (San Francisco: Jossey-Bass, 1970).
59. James E. Birren, "Principles of Research on Aging," in *Middle Age and Aging*, ed. Neugarten, p. 548.
60. George Vaillant, *Adaptation to Life* (Boston: Little, Brown, 1977), p. 339.
61. Erik H. Erikson, *Childhood and Society*, 2d ed. (New York: Norton, 1963), p. 264.
62. Ibid., p. 272.
63. Ibid., p. 274.
64. Carl Jung, "The Stages of Life," in *The Portable Jung*, ed. Joseph Campbell (New York: Viking, 1971), p. 9.
65. Richard I. Evans, *Dialogue with Erik Erikson* (New York: Harper & Row, 1967), p. 51.
66. Erik Erikson, *Insight and Responsibility* (New York: Norton, 1964), p. 131.
67. Ibid., p. 130.
68. Jung, "Stages of Life," pp. 14—15.
69. Robert C. Peck, "Psychological Developments in the Second Half of Life," in *Middle Age and Aging*, ed. Neugarten, pp. 88—90.
70. Ibid., pp. 90—92.
71. Erikson, *Childhood and Society*, p. 268.
72. Jung, "Stages of Life," p. 21.
73. Robert L. Gould, "The Phases of Adult Life: A Study in Developmental Psychology," *American Journal of Psychiatry* (November 1972): 531.

74. Daniel J. Levinson et al., "Periods in the Adult Development of Men: Ages 18 to 45," in *Counseling Adults*, ed. Schlossberg and Entine, p. 47.

75. Daniel J. Levinson et al., *The Seasons of a Man's Life* (New York: Knopf, 1978).

76. Lawrence Kohlberg, "Continuities in Childhood and Adult Moral Development Revisited," in *Life Span Developmental Psychology*, ed. Baltes and Schaie, pp. 181–182.

77. Ibid.

78. Ibid., p. 194.

79. Paul B. Baltes and Gisela V. Labouvie, "Adult Development of Intellectual Performance: Description, Exploration, and Modification," in *Psychology of Adult Development and Aging*, ed. Eisdorfer and Lawton, p. 179.

80. David P. Ausubel, *The Psychology of Meaningful Verbal Learning* (New York: Grune & Stratton, 1963), p. 113.

81. Leon McKenzie, "Analysis of *Bildungsroman* Literature as a Research Modality in Adult Education: An Inquiry," *Adult Education* 25, no. 4 (1975): 213.

82. K. Patricia Cross, *Adults as Learners* (San Francisco: Jossey-Bass, 1981).

83. Ibid., pp. 239–240.

84. E. L. Thorndike, *The Fundamentals of Learning* (New York: Teachers College, Columbia University), 1932.

85. E. L. Thorndike, *Educational Psychology*, vol. 2, *The Psychology of Learning* (New York: Teachers College, Columbia University, 1913), p. 4.

86. E. C. Tolman, *Purposive Behavior in Animals and Man* (New York: Appelton-Century-Crofts, 1932).

87. W. F. Hill, "Contemporary Developments Within Stimulus-Response Learning Theory," in *Theories of Learning & Instruction*, ed. Ernest Hilgard (Chicago: University of Chicago Press, 1964), p. 34.

88. R. Evans, *B. F. Skinner: The Man & His Ideas* (New York: Dutton, 1968).

89. Ibid., p. 129.

90. Abraham Wandersman, Paul Poppen, and David Ricks, eds. *Humanism and Behaviorism: Dialogue and Growth* (New York: Pergamon Press, 1976), p. 7.

91. Hill, "Contemporary Developments Within Stimulus-Response Learning Theory," p. 19.

92. Boyd Henry Bode, *Conflicting Psychologies of Learning* (New York: Heath, 1929), p. 190.

93. Ibid., p. 302.

94. Richard C. Anderson and David P. Ausubel, eds., *Readings in the Psychology of Cognition* (New York: Holt, Rinehart and Winston, 1965), p. 5.

95. Ibid., p. 13.

96. J. R. Kidd, *How Adults Learn* (New York: Association Press, 1973).

97. Jean Piaget, "Intellectual Evolution from Adolescence to Adulthood," *Human Development* 15 (1972): 1–12.

98. David P. Ausubel, "Cognitive Structure and the Facilitation of Meaningful Verbal Learning," in *Readings in the Psychology of Cognition*, ed. Anderson and Ausubel, p. 5.

99. Ibid., p. 103.

100. Ibid.
101. Ausubel, "In Defense of Verbal Learning," in *Readings in the Psychology of Cognition*, ed. Anderson and Ausubel, pp. 101–102.
102. Jerome Bruner, "The Act of Discovery," in *Readings in the Psychology of Cognition*, ed. Anderson and Ausubel, pp. 607–608.
103. Ibid., pp. 609–620.
104. Robert M. Gagne, *The Conditions of Learning* (New York: Holt, Rinehart and Winston, 1965), pp. 3–5.
105. Ibid., p. 2.
106. Gagne, *Conditions of Learning*, pp. 33–57.
107. Ausubel and Anderson, *Readings in The Psychology of Cognition*, pp. 9–10.
108. Samuel Granick and Alfred S. Friendman, "Educational Experience and the Maintenance of Intellectual Functioning by the Aged: An Overview," in *Intellectual Functioning in Adults*, ed. Lissy Jarvik, Carl Eisdofer, and June Blum (New York: Springer, 1973), p. 59.
109. James E. Birren, *The Psychology of Aging* (Englewood Cliffs, N.J.: Prentice-Hall, 1964) p. 182.
110. Edward L. Thorndike, *Adult Learning* (New York: Macmillan, 1928), p. 147.
111. Ibid., p. 125.
112. McLeish, *Ulyssean Adult*, p. 135.
113. Troll, *Early and Middle Adulthood*, p. 31.
114. McLeish, *Ulyssean Adult*, p. 139.
115. Lissy F. Jarvik, "Discussion: Patterns of Intellectual Functioning in the Later Years," in *Intellectual Functioning in Adults* ed. Jarvik, Eisdorfer, and Blum, p. 65.
116. J. L. Horn, "Organization of Data in Life-Span Development of Human Abilities," in *Life Span Developmental Psychology*, ed. Goulet and Baltes.
117. Troll, *Early and Middle Adulthood*, p. 39.
118. Arenberg, "Cognition and Aging: Verbal Learning, Memory, and Problem-Solving," in *Psychology of Adult Development and Aging*, ed. Eisdorfer and Lawton, p. 74.
119. Birren, *Psychology of Aging*, p. 169.
120. Arenberg, "Cognition and Aging," p. 76.
121. Carl Eisdorfer, "Arousal and Performance: Experiments in Verbal Learning and a Tentative Theory," in *Human Aging and Behavior*, ed. G. A. Tallard (New York: Academic Press, 1968).
122. Kimmel, *Adulthood and Aging*, p. 379.
123. Jack Botwinick, *Cognitive Processes in Maturity and Old Age* (New York: Springer, 1967).
124. Arenberg, "Cognition and Aging," pp. 89, 93–94.
125. Knox, *Adult Development*, p. 454.
126. Jack Botwinick, *Aging and Behavior* (New York: Springer, 1973).
127. Birren, *Psychology of Aging*, pp. 1158–1160.
128. Knox, *Adult Development*, p. 422.
129. Carl Eisdorfer, "Discussion: Mind and Body," in *Intellectual Functioning in Adults*, ed. Jarvik, Eisdorfer, and Blum, p. 125.
130. Baltes and Labouvie, "Adult Development of Intellectual Performance," p. 202.

Chapter 4
Participation

Who participates in adult education? What subjects are most frequently studied? Where do adults learn and what methods do they most frequently employ? What are the underlying motivations for engaging in educative activity and what are the barriers to broader participation, especially by the disadvantaged? These and related questions form the basis for the present chapter, which provides an overview of the many dimensions of participation in educative activity by adults.

Why place so much emphasis on participation? Research on elementary and secondary education has largely ignored the topic and in the higher education arena it has seldom been considered of major importance. Yet participation is central to theory and practice in adult education because the great majority of adults are voluntary learners. This of course is not the case with children and youth in the schools, and even in colleges and universities the extent of voluntariness is questionable. Moreover, in higher education what young people study (and why, how, where, and when) is less variable than in adult education. More to the point is the general concern of adult education with meeting individual needs and with adapting its programs and practices to the unique requirements and preferences of an adult clientele. Adult educators do not usually have a captive audience, nor in most cases is a steady supply of learners assured. Thus in adult education the effectiveness and often the survival of educational programs depends on a thorough understanding of the needs, problems, attitudes, and preferences of its clienteles and potential clienteles. In this sense, participation research in adult education is analogous to market research in the business sector, and equally as important to organizational effectiveness. Participation research is also important for public policy reasons. If equality of educational opportunity for persons of all ages is to become a reality, an understanding of the forces that affect educational participation by adults is essential for the design of effective policies and programs to promote opportunity for disadvantaged groups such as the old and the poor. Consequently, the questions and issues that fall under the general rubric of participation are of considerable importance.

As noted in the first chapter, there is no universally accepted definition of adult education. Whatever the definition one chooses to employ, there will always be some ambiguity (particularly in the degree-credit higher education sector) about what is adult education and what is not. The matter of who is an adult probably poses fewer problems than the question of what constitutes education. Most of the major studies of participation have adopted the social role definition of adulthood employed in this volume. The crucial distinction in this approach to defining adulthood has to do with the primacy of the student role. Persons who have completed or left school or college and are no longer full-time students are considered adults on the grounds that they have assumed the productive social roles that characterize adult status. This conception of adulthood is useful when applied to young adults, but after the age of 25 or 30 it has some shortcomings. A 35-year-old mother who is a "full-time student" is obviously an adult, and because her role as student is probably secondary to her other social roles, she could be considered engaged in adult education. Nonetheless, such individuals are excluded from most of the research on participation in adult education and therefore of necessity from most of the analysis and discussion in this chapter.

Another problematic and controversial issue is how to define education. A crucial question is whether self-education qualifies. The position taken here (as discussed at some length in the first chapter) is that it does. In the first major study of participation, conducted by Johnstone and Rivera in 1962, self-education was included in the analysis along with participation in organized or institutional adult education.[1] A similar national survey conducted by the Educational Testing Service a decade later also employed an encompassing definition of adult education.[2] Unfortunately, both of these studies are now dated. However, they are still valuable resources for students of participation. The more current national statistics on participation, based on data collected every three years (since 1969) by the Census Bureau, are those tabulated and published by the National Center for Education Statistics. Between 1969 and 1975 these surveys employed uniform definitions and items, thus enabling analysis of participation trends over time. However, in the 1978 survey certain changes were made that altered the population base; as a result, reliable comparisons with earlier statistics can no longer be made.[3] In contrast to the Johnstone and Rivera and the Educational Testing Service studies, the National Center for Education Statistics (NCES) tends to collect mostly factual information and to avoid probing learners' attitudes and perceptions. Perhaps the most important difference is that the NCES surveys exclude self-education.

The pages that follow draw on all of these studies, and many others, in an effort to illuminate as fully as possible why and under what conditions adults participate in education. Because they are more current and permit analysis of participation trends between 1969 and 1975, NCES figures will generally be cited in addressing factual questions.

WHO PARTICIPATES?

How many people participate in adult education in any given year? This is not easy to answer. A national survey conducted by the Educational Testing Service found that nearly one out of every three adults between the ages of 18 and 60 participated in some form of adult education, including self-education, in 1972.[4] That would put the total figure in that year at about 32 million. Presumably, it would be considerably higher today. If we take the more conservative figures provided by NCES, which do not take into account self-education, about one adult in 9 (11.8%) participated in organized adult education in 1978, for a total of 18,197,000 participants. The NCES figures almost certainly underestimate the actual rate of participation, even in organized adult education settings. The difficulty in determining a firm figure increases if we turn to the "clinical," in-depth studies of "learning projects." Research by Tough, and others who have replicated his work, suggests that as many as 9 of every 10 adults engage every year in one or more "highly deliberate" efforts to learn, most of which are self-directed.[5] Thus if we emphasize any purposeful and sustained learning, including that which is self-planned or self-directed, it is probable that the majority of adults are continuously engaged in adult education. On the other hand, if we emphasize the more conventional conception of education, then in any one year most adults are nonparticipants. Nonetheless, even the most conservative estimate of one out of 9 adults, or 18 million people, is an impressive figure. It is more than twice the number of full-time college students and nearly two-fifths of the total number of children and young people enrolled in the public schools of the United States.[6] Moreover, while school and full-time college enrollments have declined, participation in organized adult education grew by 38 percent between 1969 and 1978.[7]

How might the average or typical participant in adult education be described? It could be said that the typical participant is not very different from the average American adult or from the average nonparticipant. That is, the typical participant is white and middle class, has completed high school, is married. But to say this is to overlook some important distinctions between adults who participate and those who do not. Furthermore, adult education takes so many forms and is so varied in its settings and purposes, that to talk about the "average participant" using aggregate national statistics can be very misleading. Adults who take part in literacy or job-training programs are very different from those who engage in part-time study in universities, and those in both groups are very distinct from the average or statistically typical participant. However, when we consider participants in general, and compare them to nonparticipants, we find differences in such characteristics as amount of previous schooling, age, sex, occupation, race, place of residence, income, and employment status.[8] Many of these differences are slight, but those related to amount of schooling (educational attainment) and age are significant and will be discussed in some detail. Table 4.1 shows participation rates (proportion of participants to "eligibles") according to several of the basic characteristics noted above. In interpreting the data in Table 4.1 it is important to remember that persons engaged in self-education are excluded and that the overall or benchmark participation rate for 1975 was 11.6 percent of the adult population.

The pattern in Table 4.1 is fairly clear. In general, participants in contrast to nonparticipants tend to be younger, white, better educated, and more affluent. Sex differences, however, are negligible. Further analyses of the NCES data by Anderson and Darkenwald revealed that participants are also more likely than nonparticipants to enjoy higher occupational status, to work in human services fields (health, education, welfare, and religion), to be employed full-time, to be eligible for veterans' benefits, to live in suburban communities, and to reside in one of the Western states.[9]

A shortcoming of simple descriptive statistics such as those in Table 4.1 is that they fail to provide answers to fundamental questions concerning the relative weight of such factors as age, income, race, and schooling in predicting participation in adult education. Consider, for example, the effects on participation of income, occupation, and educational attainment, which taken together can be considered a measure of socioeconomic status (SES). We could simply say that high SES adults are more likely to participate than low SES adults. But which of the three components of SES has the greatest association with participation in adult education? The problem in answering this question is that income,

Table 4.1 Participation Rates in Adult Education by Selected Learner Characteristics, 1975

CHARACTERISTIC	PARTICIPATION RATE IN PERCENT
AGE	
17−34	15.0
35−54	12.7
55+	4.0
SEX	
Male	11.7
Female	11.6
RACE	
Black	6.9
White	12.1
SCHOOLING	
0−11 Yrs.	3.3
12 Yrs.	11.9
1−3 Yrs. College	17.6
4 Yrs. College or more	28.3
FAMILY INCOME	
Under $10,000	7.4
$10,000−$14,999	12.9
$15,000−$24,999	15.9
$25,000 & over	17.7

SOURCE: National Center for Education Statistics, *Participation in Adult Education: Final Report, 1975* (Washington, D.C.: Government Printing Office, 1978).

occupational status, and educational attainment are interrelated. They are also associated with race and age. Thus the separate or independent effects of each of these factors in relation to participation cannot be ascertained without resorting to complex statistical analyses.

To put it simply, affluent, well-educated, white professionals are more likely to participate in adult education than others. Do all of these characteristics predict participation equally well or is, for example, income the only potent predictor? Recent research has provided some answers. Income and race, in and of themselves, bear only a slight relationship to participation. The most potent factor is educational attainment and the next most potent is occupational status. Furthermore, other things being equal (such as educational attainment), black adults are slightly more likely than whites to participate in adult education. Thus while black Americans as a group are underrepresented among participants, the explanation probably lies in the fact that black adults as a group have less formal schooling than whites. On the other hand, being old, in and of itself, has a pronounced negative association with participation.[10]

In brief, the weight of the evidence suggests that amount of formal schooling and age are the most important sociodemographic factors in predicting participation, a conclusion that may be distressing but not surprising. Those who succeeded in school in their early years, who feel comfortable in the learner role, and who value education are those one would expect to participate in organized adult education. Likewise, it is hardly cause for wonder that older people, particularly those past retirement age, are less likely than younger adults to participate in organized adult education. Some of the barriers to participation by older people are obvious: acceptance by many of the elderly themselves of age-related stereotypes about learning ability; physical infirmity; lack of mobility; and insufficient financial resources. A less obvious and probably more significant problem is that adult education in general is oriented to the developmental needs and interests of young adulthood and middle age. Relatively few providers of education attempt to address the particular needs and concerns of older adults, although in recent years there has been improvement in this regard. Nonetheless, much of adult education is in one way or another work-related or geared toward achievement of degrees and diplomas and consequently irrelevant to the concerns of many older people. Educational opportunities geared to the social roles, developmental tasks, or life concerns of later maturity—for example, retirement planning, use of leisure time, health and nutrition, living alone, relating to grown-up children—are not found in abundance. Under these circumstances, it is far from puzzling that older adults fail to engage in educational activities in proportion to their numbers in the population.

Trends

Participation in adult education, as already noted, grew rapidly in the 1970s. Of course, part of that increase can be attributed to the aging of the American population. There were more adults over age 17 in 1975 than in 1969, and this aging of the population is expected to continue for many decades to come. Nonetheless, participation increased 38 percent between 1969 and 1978 while the number of adults over 17 in the population increased only 19 percent. Thus the actual rate of participation independent of the number of adults in the population climbed dramatically.

The great surge in participation in adult education in recent years can be attributed in large part to increases in the numbers of women and older people returning to classrooms. Given the rapidly changing roles of women and older people in our society, such a trend is hardly surprising and indeed can itself be viewed as a significant indicator of social change. Between 1969 and 1975, participation in adult education by women increased 45 percent, compared to an 18 percent increase for men.* Less

*Participation trends discussed here and subsequently are necessarily limited to the period 1969–1975. Changes in the 1978 NCES survey preclude using the more recent data for detailed comparison purposes.

than a third of this increase can be attributed to growth in the number of adult women in the population. The increase in the actual rate of participation can be put at approximately 33 percent. Participation by adults 55 and older has grown even more rapidly, climbing by 55 percent between 1969 and 1975. The population of older people during the same time period increased by only 11.5 percent; therefore, the actual rate of increase has been on the order of 44 percent.[11] Despite this enormous jump in participation by older people, the participation rate for young adults is still nearly four times as great as that for persons 55 and over.

Will participation in adult education continue to increase in the 1980s and 1990s? The answer appears to be yes, but at a somewhat slower rate. Projections by O'Keefe show that if the rate of participation continues at approximately 11.6 percent, growth in the number of adults participating in education will slow to 1.2 percent annually by the mid-1980s and continue to ease off very slightly through the 1990s.[12] However, the assumption of no increase in the *rate* of participation seems excessively cautious, and, as O'Keefe himself points out, fails to take into account rising levels of educational attainment and the entry of the baby boom cohort into young and middle adulthood in the 1980s. Calculations that include the positive effects of these factors show a maximum participation rate of 17.5 percent and an annual growth rate of 2.1 percent in the 1980s.[13] One thing is certain, and that is that demographics alone will not shape the future growth of adult education. If deep-rooted technological and social changes continue to transform modern societies through the end of the century, the future of adult education will surely be one of continued growth.

WHAT ADULTS LEARN

Adults are not only volunteers in the learning process, but the subjects or skills they learn are by and large voluntarily chosen. This freedom of choice in regard to what is learned is a characteristic of adult education that sets it apart from the schooling of children and young people. There are in fact no limits to the "curriculum" of adult education.

While we may say that the curriculum of adult education is infinite and always changing, this does not mean that it lacks any coherence. We can in fact categorize and describe the content of adult education (although somewhat crudely and arbitrarily) in terms of functions or purposes that connect to adult life roles such as worker, citizen, user of leisure time, parent, and spouse. Moreover, a good deal of what adults learn (especially for credits and credentials) is similar to the academic and occupational learning that occurs in schools and colleges.

In the first major survey of adult learning activities, conducted in 1962, Johnstone and Rivera concluded:

It was quite clear from the results of our study that the major emphasis in adult learning is on the practical rather than on the academic; on the applied rather than the theoretical; and on skills rather than on knowledge and information. Subject matter directly useful in the performance of everyday tasks and obligations accounted for the most significant block of the total activities recorded.[14]

This intimate relationship between learning and living is in our view the hallmark of adult education, the quality that most distinguishes it from the schooling of children and young people, and the source of its enduring vitality. It should be recognized in this regard that much adult education is liberal and liberating and speaks to the needs of adult life that transcend everyday "tasks and obligations." That adult education is largely nonacademic is to be expected, although it is a reality that is often not accepted by traditional educators.

If the curriculum of adult education is intimately connected to real life, one would expect to find substantial differences in what people learn as a function of individual personal characteristics and social roles. In schools and colleges, males and females, the socially advantaged and the disadvantaged, racial minorities and the racial majority all tend by and large to study similar subjects. Of course, there are variations and some choice exists. In the wider realm of adult education, the variations and choices in what people learn are substantial. Marital status, sex, age, occupation, income, race, and many other personal characteristics predict to a considerable extent what adults study—and to a lesser extent where and how they study. Many of these relationships of course are easily explained. It is not surprising, for example, that older adults are more likely to engage in leisure-related education and blue-collar workers more likely to participate in work-related education. Table 4.2 presents a summary of courses taken by a national sample of adult education participants that relates differences in what people study to two important characteristics, sex and race.*

The figures for the total adult population in Table 4.2 exemplify the conclusions Johnstone and Rivera reached in 1962. If we examine the five general subject matter categories, it is clear that work-related education (occupational training), with 48.7 percent of all participants, plays a dominant role in American adult education. General or academic education, with 20.6 percent of participants, ranks second, followed by social life and recreation, personal and family living, and community issues.

Differences in subjects studied in relation to sex and race are in some instances pronounced and generally predictable. Particularly notable is the fact that participation by black women is almost totally confined to

---

*Here and in Table 4.3 we present 1975 rather than 1978 statistics because the latter are less valid for our purposes. The 1978 NCES survey included as participants full-time students who engaged in organized education outside their regular course of study.

Table 4.2 Content of Courses Taken by Adult Education Participants in 1975 by Race and Sex of Participants, in Percentages

COURSE CATEGORIES	ALL ADULTS	WHITE		BLACK	
		MALE	FEMALE	MALE	FEMALE
GENERAL EDUCATION	(20.6)	(17.2)	(21.6)	(27.6)	(43.8)
Adult Basic Ed.	3.9	2.4	3.9	6.1	15.7
Citizenship Training	0.3	0.3	0.2	0.0	0.4
H.S. & College Credit	16.7	14.7	17.7	21.5	27.5
OCCUPATIONAL TRAINING	(48.7)	(62.4)	(36.3)	(54.7)	(43.9)
Technical/Vocational	22.4	29.2	15.6	32.1	23.6
Managerial	7.0	12.0	2.8	10.8	2.6
Professional	21.3	24.5	19.0	12.3	19.1
COMMUNITY ISSUES	(10.0)	(10.2)	(10.5)	(6.3)	(4.9)
Civic & Public Affairs	3.0	3.0	3.3	1.6	1.6
Religion	4.7	3.9	5.8	3.8	2.4
Safety	2.4	3.5	1.7	1.0	1.0
PERSONAL/FAMILY LIVING	(14.8)	(10.3)	(19.7)	(10.2)	(8.9)
Home & Family Life	3.9	2.0	5.9	0.0	2.9
Personal Improvement	11.3	8.5	14.4	10.2	6.2
SOCIAL LIFE & RECREATION	(15.9)	(8.3)	(24.2)	(3.8)	(3.4)
Hobbies & Handicrafts	11.4	4.8	18.5	2.9	2.5
Sports & Recreation	5.1	3.7	6.8	0.8	1.3
OTHER/NOT REPORTED	(3.2)	(2.9)	(3.5)	(2.6)	(3.2)
Totals	113.2%	111.3%	115.8%	105.2%	108.1%

Note: Because some participants took more than one course, percentages may not add to column totals and sub-totals.
SOURCE: National Center for Education Statistics, *Participation in Adult Education*, p. 59.

academic and occupational education. White women, in contrast, are disproportionately represented in the categories of personal and family living and social life and recreation. The socioeconomic factors that underlie such differences are fairly obvious. The heavy concentration of white men in professional and managerial training is also notable, as is their underrepresentation in courses categorized as general education—especially adult basic education. In short, the statistics on the kinds of subjects adults study reflect to a considerable extent the social structure of American society.

Social change can be discerned in participation statistics when trends over time are examined, particularly in regard to sex roles. Especially significant are changes in the proportion of women enrolled in occupational training. Male participation in occupational training remained steady at 29 percent from 1969 to 1975, whereas female participation increased about 25 percent in the same time period.[15] Thus the gap between women and men in work-related adult education is narrowing and in all likelihood will continue to do so.

The statistics in Table 4.2 do not include subjects people study on their own. In addressing this question, Johnstone and Rivera in their 1962 survey noted that adults tend not to study vocational subjects, religion, or public affairs on their own. The researchers went on to conclude:

> Learning efforts in the home and family life area, on the other hand, were undertaken independently more often than with instruction. . . . A number of subjects people had studied on their own were in areas influenced by changes in patterns of leisure-time use, by recent innovations in teaching methodology, or by entry of commercial interests into the field of adult instruction. Eighty percent of those who had studied gardening had done so without formal instruction; this was also true of 61 percent who had studied a foreign language, 50 percent who had studied music, and 44 percent who had taken a course in speed reading.[16]

Johnstone and Rivera's findings suggest that what adults study on their own is influenced heavily by the feasibility and convenience of self-instruction as an alternative method of learning. Certain subjects are well suited to self-study, particularly when commercially produced materials are readily available (as in such areas as gardening and home repair).

LOCATIONS FOR LEARNING

Diversity characterizes not only what adults learn but where they learn. It is no exaggeration to say that wherever adults congregate for one reason or another, purposeful learning is likely to be found. Adults take classes on commuter trains, submarines, and luxury liners; they study in hotels, museums, libraries, factories, churches and synagogues, their own homes or other people's homes, hospitals, office buildings, community centers, stores, and a host of other settings. Of course, a great many adults also study in school buildings and at colleges and universities.

There is of course some correspondence between what adults study and where they study, but it is not as great as might be expected. Occupational or technical skills are seldom acquired in churches or museums and likewise religion and the arts are not often studied in factories or office buildings. Nonetheless, even subjects closely associated with preparatory schooling, such as adult basic education or college courses in the humanities, are not always studied in school buildings or college classrooms. Adult basic education or literacy instruction can be found in churches, factories, libraries, and community storefronts as well as in schools, and college credit courses, although sponsored by colleges, are offered on commuter trains and in office buildings and can be pursued in the home via television, newspaper, or correspondence study.

While much of adult education takes place in nonformal or nontraditional settings, if we exclude self-education from statistical tabulations it appears that about half of all learning activities take place in school or college classrooms. Table 4.3 provides a percentage breakdown of locations for learning reported by a national sample of adult education participants in 1975.

It is particularly interesting to note in Table 4.3 that 6.7 percent of all organized learning activities, not including self-education, take place in private homes. Undoubtedly a large proportion of these activities involves private tutoring or correspondence instruction. A smaller proportion probably involves informal group learning such as Great Books discussion clubs and childbirth preparation classes. The relatively large proportion of courses located in hotels and other commercial buildings is also noteworthy and probably reflects the growing popularity of short-term workshops, seminars, and conferences sponsored by professional and trade associations as well as by private entrepreneurs, in areas as diverse as management training and speed-reading. Other data provided by NCES show that differences in where adults study are related to race and sex. Men are much less likely than women to study in community centers, libraries, or museums, and white men are less likely than others to study in school buildings and more likely to study in the workplace.[17] These differences, of course, are related to the race and sex variations discussed earlier in regard to the subjects adults study.

Other studies show that age and level of educational attainment are also linked to locations for learning. The 1972 Educational Testing Service survey found that use of educational institutions declines with age and that older adults 55 to 60 are much more likely than younger adults to study with a private tutor or in a community social center.[18] All the major surveys show that adults with little formal schooling are less likely to study or want to study in formal educational settings, especially colleges and universities. Anderson and Darkenwald found that two-thirds of all part-time adult learners at four-year colleges and universities in 1975 already possessed at least a bachelor's degree.[19]

Table 4.3   Location of Courses Taken by Adult Education Participants in the United States in 1975, in Percent

LOCATIONS	PERCENT OF PARTICIPANTS
School Bldg.	25.1
College/Univ. Bldg.	30.4
Community Center, Library, or Museum	4.6
Church, Other Religious Property	4.9
Place of Work	8.3
Private Home	6.7
Hotel or Other Commercial Bldg.	11.4
Other or Not Reported	8.6

SOURCE: National Center for Education Statistics, *Participation in Adult Education*, p. 75.

Where adults study, consequently, is related not only to what they study but also, as we might expect, to personal characteristics. Interestingly, there is some discrepancy between the locations adults prefer for learning and the locations adults actually use. In contrasting the locations preferred by "would-be learners" (nonparticipants who indicated interest in learning something) with the locations actually used by participants, Carp, Peterson, and Roelfs found that public high schools and public two-year colleges were disproportionately preferred (compared with actual use) and the home and the workplace disproportionately shunned (again compared with actual use).[20] It may be that stereotypes about where learning normally takes place or should take place are reflected in the preferences adults voice in regard to locations for study.

METHODS OF LEARNING

The methods that adults employ to learn a subject or skill vary greatly, presenting a sharp contrast to the relatively uniform techniques used in the schooling of children and young people. Methods that are employed almost solely in adult education include correspondence study, on-the-job training, and short-term conferences, institutes and workshops.

Most adults, nonetheless, do learn in group settings and very often in a formal classroom environment. The 1975 NCES survey, which asked participants to report all teaching methods used for each course taken, found that 61 percent of all learning activities involved the presence of a classroom teacher.[21] Nonetheless, it is striking that nearly two-fifths of all adult education activities occur in the absence of a classroom teacher.

Table 4.4 contrasts the actual learning methods used by participants in adult education with the methods preferred by "would-be learners." The data are taken from the 1972 Educational Testing Service survey and include as participants persons engaged in deliberate self-education.[22]

As Table 4.4 shows, the lecture or class is preferred by only 28 percent of would-be learners but actually used by some 35 percent of participants. Similarly, self-study is preferred by only 7 percent but actually employed as a learning method by 17 percent of the learners surveyed. On the other hand, on-the-job training is preferred by more adults than actually use this method of learning, as are short-term conferences and workshops, informal discussion or study groups, and private instruction.

Perhaps the most startling figures in Table 4.4 are those that pertain to the use of the electronic media and various technological devices for learning. Not only do very few adults actually employ television, radio, or cassettes for learning but, even more surprisingly, only a small fraction of would-be learners indicate a preference for such methods. Johnstone and Rivera reported similar findings a decade earlier.[23] Part of the explanation

Table 4.4   Learning Methods Preferred by Would-Be Learners and Methods Used by Participants in Adult Education in 1972, in Percent (N = 1893)

METHOD	PREFERRED BY WOULD-BE LEARNERS	USED BY PARTICIPANTS
Lectures or Classes	28	35
On-the-Job Training, Internship	21	14
Conferences, Institutes, or Workshops	13	8
Individual Lessons	8	6
Discussion Groups, Book Club, Study Group	8	4
Self-Study, No Formal Instruction	7	17
Correspondence	3	5
Group Action Project	3	2
Travel-Study Program	2	*
TV or Video Cassettes	1	*
Radio, Records, or Audio Cassettes	1	*
Other Method	*	2
No Response	4	8
Totals	100%	100%

*Less than 1 percent.
SOURCE: K. Patricia Cross and John Valley, eds., *Planning Non-Traditional Programs* (San Francisco: Jossey-Bass, 1974), p. 30. Reprinted by permission.

may be that educational programming through the media is so limited that most adults do not see such learning as a meaningful option.

While the traditional class or lecture is the one method most preferred and most used, it would be inaccurate to conclude that adults generally prefer passive and traditional approaches to learning. If we group together all the methods that require active individual or group participation, such as on-the-job training, self-study, short-term workshops, discussion groups, and so on, it is clear that active, less formal learning methods are more often preferred and used by adult learners.

There are, however, differences in preferences associated with individual characteristics such as age, race, and educational attainment. Participation studies have consistently found that older adults, minorities, and adults with little formal schooling often dislike and avoid traditional classroom instruction. On the other hand, younger, better-educated adults of higher socioeconomic status often prefer formal classroom instruction, no doubt in part because they are familiar and comfortable with traditional educational methods.[24]

Finally, it should be recognized that the methods adults use to learn, and those that they prefer, are closely related to their particular educational needs and interests—to what is studied, why, and where. Some subjects or skills are most appropriately learned on the job, others in discussion groups, and others through self-study. Still, there are alternative ways of learning most things and adults can and do exercise a large measure of choice in determining how they will learn.

REASONS FOR LEARNING

The question of why adults engage in educational activities is at once very simple and very complex. Many adults, as we have seen, engage in education that is work-related and many others in courses and self-study geared to various aspects of family living. It seems reasonable to infer motives for participation from the kinds of learning activities, such as these, in which adults engage. Thus we might conclude that two major motivations for adult learning are to improve occupational performance or prospects and to enhance competence or satisfaction in the roles of parent and spouse. While this kind of simple reasoning has some validity, it obscures the fact that reasons for participation are usually multiple and interrelated in complex ways.

Why adults participate in education is a question that can be addressed in at least three ways. First, as noted above, we can inquire into the reasons adults give for participating in a particular learning activity or in adult education generally. Second, we can probe the nature of underlying or generalized orientations to participation. Put another way, we can ask if there are different "types" of adult learners or motivational categories we can use to classify participants. In essence, the issue here is whether there exists some underlying order or structure to the dozens of reasons adults commonly give for participating in educational activities. Finally, we can address the most basic and encompassing issue, which has to do not with reasons for taking a course or generalized motivational orientations but with the decision to participate or not participate. Viewed from this perspective, the question of why adults participate or do not participate is exceedingly complex. This last question, which demands explanatory models or theories of participation, will be discussed in the final pages of this chapter. For the present, the focus will be on the reasons adults give for participation in educational activities and on attempts by researchers to impose some order or structure on these reasons.

Reasons for Participation

If one wants to know why a person is engaged in some activity, an obvious place to start is by asking for a reason or explanation. "Why did you take this course?" has been asked of adult learners by educators and researchers innumerable times. The answers, of course, vary depending on the exact phrasing of the question, who is asked, and who asks it. Despite variations, large-scale national surveys have yielded a considerable amount of useful information about reasons for engaging in adult education.

Table 4.5 compares the reasons for learning given by actual participants with reasons considered "very important" by would-be learners. The statistics are based on the Educational Testing Service survey of adults aged 18 through 60 conducted in 1972.[25]

Table 4.5 Reasons for Learning Checked "Very Important" by Would-Be Learners and Reasons Checked as Applicable by Actual Learners in 1972, in Percent (N = 1893)

REASONS	VERY IMPORTANT TO WOULD-BE LEARNERS	CHECKED BY ACTUAL LEARNERS
KNOWLEDGE GOALS		
Become better informed	56	55
Satisfy curiosity	35	32
PERSONAL GOALS		
Get new job	25	18
Advance in current job	17	25
Get certificate, license	27	14
Attain degree	21	9
COMMUNITY GOALS		
Understand community problems	17	9
Become better citizen	26	11
Work for solutions to problems	16	9
RELIGIOUS GOALS		
Serve church	12	10
Further spiritual well-being	19	13
SOCIAL GOALS		
Meet new people	19	18
Feel sense of belonging	20	9
ESCAPE GOALS		
Get away from routine	19	19
Get away from personal problems	11	7
OBLIGATION FULFILLMENT		
Meet educational standards	13	4
Satisfy employer	24	27
PERSONAL FULFILLMENT		
Be better parent, spouse	30	19
Become happier person	37	26
CULTURAL KNOWLEDGE		
Study own culture	14	8
OTHER REASONS, OTHER		
Response or no response	18	5

Note: Columns do not total 100 because respondents gave multiple reasons.
SOURCE: Cross and Valley, *Planning Non-Traditional Programs*, p. 42.
Reprinted by permission.

What strikes one immediately in Table 4.5 is the variety of reasons for learning that adults consider important. The average would-be learner in fact checked approximately five reasons from the list as "very important." Another striking characteristic of these figures is the high degree of correspondence between actual and potential participants regarding the importance of different reasons for learning. Discrepancies between the groups indicate that would-be learners tend to give more emphasis to learning related to family and community roles (become a better citizen, be a better parent or spouse) and to credentialing (get certificate or license, attain degree). The fact that about half of all learners and would-be learners checked "to become better informed" as an important reason for learning implies a good deal of interest in noninstrumental reasons for participation. Also notable are social and escape goals such as "meet new people" and "get away from routine," which were considered important by about one respondent in five.

As would be expected, reasons for learning are related to personal characteristics such as age, sex, race, and socioeconomic status. Among actual participants, men were more likely than women to stress work-related reasons for learning and women more likely to stress reasons related to personal fulfillment, curiosity, religion, and escape from routine. Curiosity, as might be predicted, was more often given as a reason by learners over 55, while younger adults more frequently cited job-related reasons or getting a degree as important. Black learners were much more likely than whites to stress work-related reasons, including certification and licensing, and community goals and "learning about [their] own background and culture."[26]

It is important to keep in mind that the figures in Table 4.5 are based on questions that allowed respondents to give more than one reason for engaging in a learning activity. When adults have been asked to give the single most important reason for their enrolling in a course or other activity, work-related motives emerged as dominant. For example, the 1975 NCES survey asked participants to give their "main reason" for taking a particular course. Of all the reasons, 41.8 percent chose the response "to improve or advance in current job"; 27.7 said "personal or family interests"; 13.7 percent, "for general information"; 11.5 percent, getting a "new job"; and less than 10 percent, "social or recreational interests" and "community activity."[27]

In conclusion, adults typically engage in education—including a single educational activity—for multiple reasons, some of which may not be related to traditional educational goals (for example, "to escape from routine"). However, when forced to give a single, dominant reason for participation about half of all adults cite improving occupational competence or getting ahead in the world of work. It seems appropriate then that roughly half of all organized adult education activities are concerned with work-related learning.

Motivational Orientations

As noted earlier, attempts have been made to discern order or structure in the enormous variety of reasons that adults give for participating in education. The first major effort of this kind, which had enormous impact on subsequent investigations, was undertaken by Houle in the early 1960s. On the basis of in-depth interviews with 22 particularly active continuing learners, Houle formulated a typology that identified three "types" of adult learner, which he described as follows:

> The first, or, as they will be called, the *goal-oriented*, are those who use education as a means of accomplishing fairly clear-cut objectives. The second, the *activity-oriented*, are those who take part because they find in the circumstances of learning a meaning which has no necessary connection, and often no connection at all, with the content or announced purposes of the activity. The third, the *learning-oriented*, seek knowledge for its own sake.[28]

Houle's provocative study led to a burgeoning of research activity concerned with motivational orientations. Most of the subsequent research has attempted to test and refine Houle's basic concepts. The best research has employed carefully developed measuring instruments and the statistical technique of factor analysis to probe the underlying structure of reasons for participation. In a comprehensive review, Boshier described 14 motivational orientation studies which employed factor analysis.[29]

The most extensive recent studies have yielded remarkably similar findings for different populations of adult learners in the United States, New Zealand, and Canada. The population for the U.S. study was made up of 611 adults enrolled in a variety of evening credit courses at Glassboro State College in New Jersey.[30] The New Zealand study was based on responses from 233 adults in a variety of programs sponsored by three different institutions.[31] The Canadian study population consisted of 242 participants in noncredit evening classes conducted by two public school systems and by the University of British Columbia.[32] All three studies used the Education Participation Scale (EPS), a highly reliable instrument developed by Boshier.

Before turning to the findings, it is important to understand the nature of factor analysis. This is a complex statistical procedure, a basic technical definition of which follows:

> Given an array of correlation coefficients for a set of variables, factor analytic techniques enable us to see whether some underlying pattern of relationships exists such that the data may be "re-arranged" or "reduced" to a smaller set of factors or components that may be taken as source variables accounting for the observed interrelations in the data.[33]

Put more simply, factor analysis is a way of clustering related scale items so as to yield separate, independent constructs that reflect the underlying structure of responses to the instrument. The clusters, of course, are called factors. The factor names or labels are determined by the content of the items that cluster together in each separate factor.

As noted above, there is a striking degree of similarity in the findings of factor analytic studies of motivational orientations. However, inasmuch as there are some variations among studies, the discussion of findings will be based mainly on the results obtained by Morstain and Smart in the United States.

Morstain and Smart identified six factors, which they labelled Social Relationships, External Expectations, Social Welfare, Professional Advancement, Escape/Stimulation, and Cognitive Interest. The Social Relationships factor reflects a desire to develop or improve one's relationships with other people. Individuals who score high on this factor want to make new friends, participate in group activities, or improve their social functioning.

External Expectations reflects a degree of external compulsion or pressure toward participation in educational activities. The scale items suggest that the individual is complying with the requirements or suggestions of someone else or of some agency or organization. Social Welfare is indicative of an altruistic concern for other people, community betterment, or for humanity. Persons who score high on this factor see education as preparing them for service to others or for participation in community affairs. Professional Advancement is strongly associated with improving occupational performance and status. The items reflect a concern for acquiring useful knowledge, credentials, and job-related skills.

The Escape/Stimulation factor comprises two related dimensions—a need to escape from routine, boring, or frustrating situations and a desire to find intellectual stimulation—to "stop myself from becoming a vegetable" as one scale item puts it. Those whose responses indicated Cognitive Interest are identical to Houle's learning-oriented participants. High scorers value knowledge for its own sake rather than for instrumental purposes. For such people, learning is an integral part of living.

While the motivational orientation literature has focused mainly on identifying the general underlying structure of motivations, some attempts have been made to correlate motivational factors with participant and program characteristics. Yet these correlations reveal very little. In general, individual characteristics such as sex, age, and socioeconomic status are only weakly associated with motivational orientation factors. In other words, each of the six orientations seems to be equally important for both men and women, younger adults and older adults, and people of low as well as high socioeconomic status. There are, however, a few interesting variations.

First, however, it should be noted that adult learners in general place the most importance on reasons related to Cognitive Interest and

Professional Advancement. Escape/Stimulation and Social Relationsips tend to be rated least important.[34] Interestingly, the mean importance scores for all factors, including Cognitive Interest and Professional Advancement, are rather low, ranging for example from 2.6 to 5.8 on a 9-point scale.[35] One logical interpretation is that most people have mixed motives for participation, which would tend in general to depress the importance ratings for individual scale items and factors.

Morstain and Smart examined the relationships between sex and age and mean importance scores for each of their six motivational factors. They found that younger participants had somewhat higher mean scores on the Social Relationships factor and that men scored slightly higher than women on the External Expectations dimension. There was a slight tendency for women to place more importance on Cognitive Interest items.[36]

Boshier reported factor score correlations for a random sample of 76 noncredit evening class participants. Among other things, he found a slight tendency for younger adults to enroll for External Expectations reasons and for older people to enroll for Cognitive Interest. In addition, people with less formal education and lower occupational status were more likely to enroll for Professional Advancement reasons.[37]

While these differences in motivation are statistically significant, they are not great enough to have much practical significance for program planners. It is worth noting that the data do not support common assumptions based on sex-role stereotyping. For example, women and men are equally likely to enroll for Professional Advancement as well as for Social Welfare and Social Relationships reasons.

It is difficult to judge whether or not the studies based on factor analysis support Houle's original typology. The Professional Advancement factor can be seen as reflecting "goal-oriented" motivation, the Cognitive Interest factor is identical to Houle's "learning-oriented" category, and the Social Relationships and Escape/Stimulation factors could be construed as dimensions of "activity-orientation." In any event, the factor analytic findings as well as Houle's typology should not be accepted as definitive or universally valid. The Education Participation Scale and other such instruments were designed to study what might be described as typical adult learners in typical school- or college-sponsored programs. The motivational orientations of distinctive subpopulations of adults, such as the disadvantaged or health professionals, might well differ from those of the general public.

Despite its limitations, the motivational orientation research does suggest that there is an underlying structure to the diverse reasons adults give for participating in education. Perhaps the most important conclusion to be drawn from this work is that reasons for participation cannot always be inferred from the content or ostensible purposes of the learning activities in which adults are engaged. That is, underlying motivations are typically multiple and often not obvious or "rational." Thus adults may engage in learning activities not principally or even at all because they want to learn some subject or skill, but to conform to some requirement (e.g., mandatory continuing education for certain professional groups); to obtain some sort of certification, diploma, or degree; to escape from daily routine; or to satisfy needs for human contact. As an illustration, consider a young mother forced by economic need to drop out of high school. She may enroll in an adult high-school completion program because she always liked learning (cognitive interest), because she would like a diploma to qualify for a better job (professional advancement), because she feels stifled by the routine of housework and child care (escape/stimulation), and because she has few friends in the community to which she recently moved (social relationships). She might not be aware of, or be able to articulate, all the underlying motivations for her action. Nonetheless, like those of most adult learners, her reasons for continuing her education are multiple, interrelated, closely connected to life roles, and highly personal.

Motivation for adult learning seems to consist of a mosaic or configuration of diverse needs and purposes. Perhaps this complexity is self-evident, yet adult educators sometimes lose sight of its implications for the educational process. Particularly important, it would seem, is sensitivity to the less obvious components of motivation, such as the need for social contact, which cannot be ignored if learning is to be truly satisfying for all involved.

BARRIERS TO PARTICIPATION

The barriers to participation in educational activities most frequently cited by adults are lack of time and cost. Busy schedules, home responsibilities, job responsibilities, and similar time-related obstacles were cited as important barriers to participation by 30 to 40 percent of potential learners in both the Johnstone and Rivera and the Educational Testing Service surveys.[38] Financial barriers were more formidable, with 43 percent of potential learners in 1962 and 53 percent in 1972 citing cost as a major impediment.[39] While there is little doubt that lack of time and money can be significant obstacles to participation, there is also little doubt that their importance is easily exaggerated. As Cross has noted, adults tend to give socially acceptable responses to questions concerned with reasons for nonparticipation.[40] It is less demeaning to give lack of time or high cost as reasons for not engaging in education than to say one lacks self-confidence or interest. In regard to cost, moreover, there is reason to believe that many adults simply have no information, or only inaccurate information, about actual costs and cost options.[41]

Obstacles to participation can be classified into four general categories: situational, institutional, informational, and psychosocial.

Situational barriers relate to an individual's life context at a particular time, that is, the realities of one's social and physical environment. Cost and lack of time are examples. Other situational barriers of consequence include lack of transportation, lack of child care, and geographical isolation. Institutional barriers, to use Cross's words, are those "erected by learning institutions or agencies that exclude or discourage certain groups of learners because of such things as inconvenient schedules, full-time fees for part-time study, restrictive locations, and the like."[42] Other significant institutional barriers are lack of attractive or appropriate courses and institutional policies and practices that impose inconvenience, confusion, or frustration on adult learners. The category of informational barrier is sometimes construed simply to mean institutional failure in communicating information on learning opportunities to adults, but the problem is more fundamental than this. It involves as well the failure of many adults, particularly the least educated and poorest, to seek out or use the information that is available. Finally, psychosocial barriers (sometimes referred to more narrowly as attitudinal or dispositional barriers) are individually held beliefs, values, attitudes, or perceptions that inhibit participation in organized learning activities. Adults who cite as barriers "lack of interest" or state that they "are too old to learn," "don't enjoy studying," "are tired of school," and so forth are expressing some of the wide variety of beliefs and attitudes that strongly influence participation behavior. While many of these factors might be considered psychological in nature, the term psychosocial is employed to emphasize the role of social forces generally, and of membership and reference groups specifically, in forming and maintaining attitudes toward participation in education.

While there is no question that situational and institutional factors can be major impediments to continuing learning, we shall focus on informational and psychosocial barriers to participation. The constraints of daily life and the deficiencies of institutions are not difficult to fathom as forces operating against participation. Informational and psychosocial barriers, on the other hand, are less obvious and in some ways more fundamental in accounting for participation or lack of participation, particularly among the disadvantaged sectors of the adult population.

Informational Barriers

In 1962, Johnstone and Rivera found that one-third of all adults had no knowledge whatever of educational resources for adults in their communities. They went on to observe:

> Studies of public knowledge on practically any social event, issue, or resource invariably uncover a sizeable number of poorly informed people. Since these frequently constitute from one-fifth to one-third of the whole adult population, the present result is by no means an unexpected one.[43]

More recent studies confirm Johnstone and Rivera's findings. Not only are many adults unaware of educational opportunities, but about one-fourth of the adult population does "not know where to go or whom to ask to get information about learning opportunities."[44]

Levels of awareness, as several studies have shown, vary greatly in relation to socioeconomic status and community size. Johnstone and Rivera found that 85 percent of high SES adults living in middle-sized cities "know of at least one place where adults could receive instruction, whereas the comparable figure for persons of low socioeconomic status in small towns or rural areas was 19 percent."[45] While these findings reflect the differences between urban and rural areas in the availability of educational resources, they show even more the influence of socioeconomic status on awareness of community resources and on information-seeking behavior in general. Obviously, if many adults are ignorant of available educational opportunities and do not even know how to obtain information concerning such opportunities, then many potential learners are not going to participate in organized education for this reason alone.

Lack of information is likely to remain a major barrier to participation in adult education, especially for disadvantaged adults. The basic reason for this is that communication is a two-way process. Merely providing more or better information, particularly through conventional channels of communication, is unlikely to have any effect on persons who do not attend to these channels of communication and who make no effort to seek the kind of information that is disseminated.[46] This is not to say that the communications barriers are insurmountable in the case of disadvantaged adults. There is considerable evidence that the disadvantaged can be reached effectively, in part through more personalized means of communication.[47] Doing so, however, is both difficult and expensive.

The need for more and better information on educational opportunities has resulted in the rapid development of community-based educational information centers. What these centers are actually called, what they do, who sponsors them, how they are financed, and so on varies greatly.[48] All of them, however, serve in one way or another as brokers—that is, they attempt to match the needs and interests of learners with appropriate educational resources in the community. Federal legislation enacted in the late 1970s provided modest sums to establish networks of educational information centers in all 50 states. Whether these networks take hold and prosper remains to be seen.

Psychosocial Barriers

Psychosocial barriers to participation, like informational barriers, seem to be in large measure a product of the values, attitudes, and experiences associated with differing levels of socioeconomic status. Johnstone and Rivera's conclusions in this regard are supported by numerous other studies:

> Learning and education are perceived and evaluated in radically different ways by persons on different rungs of the social ladder. Lower-class adults not only value high educational attainment less, but they assess the worth of education strictly in terms of the tangible advantages which can be gained from having it. They see little value in obtaining knowledge for its own sake. . . . Lower-class adults fully realize that education can lead to employment opportunities and job security but education in no sense is defined as pleasurable. Indeed for the typical lower-class adult, the concepts of "learning" and "spare-time enjoyment" convey quite opposite meanings.[49]

While social class by no means invariably determines individual attitudes toward education and learning, on a general level it is difficult to dispute Johnstone and Rivera's analysis. This does not mean, however, that exceptions to the rule are rare or that the poor and undereducated are concerned only with gaining "tangible advantages."

The beliefs, values, attitudes, and perceptions that we have labelled psychosocial barriers to participation are multiple and varied and often interrelated in complex configurations. Unfortunately, researchers have made few attempts to go beyond superficial tabulations of reasons for nonparticipation voiced by survey respondents such as "don't enjoy studying" and "afraid that I'm too old to begin."[50]

Of the many attitudinal or perceptual barriers that have been identified in the literature, most could be classified into one of two rough categories. Psychosocial obstacles tend to be related either to education or learning as entities or activities, or to the self as a learner or potential learner. The first category encompasses negative evaluations of the usefulness, appropriateness, and pleasurability of engaging in adult education. Particularly among lower- and working-class persons, adult education may be seen as having little intrinsic value and little usefulness as a means of achieving personal goals. In many cases, too, engaging in organized educational activities is viewed as inappropriate for mature adults, especially for men. Finally, the process of learning may be perceived as burdensome, unpleasant, or even frightening rather than as enjoyable or stimulating.

Negative or deprecatory evaluations of oneself as a potential learner are probably less closely tied to socioeconomic status, but they are nonetheless prevalent among disadvantaged and working-class adults. Lack of confidence in one's ability to learn is a commonly voiced reason for nonparticipation, but for most adults it does not reflect a realistic assessment of aptitude, self-discipline, or any other factor likely to affect performance. Closely related to negative perceptions of ability are feelings that any effort to learn will result in failure and humiliation. There is considerable evidence to suggest that such fears are widespread among disadvantaged adults and among adults (e.g., reentering women) who contemplate returning to education after a long hiatus.[51] The fact that the logic behind the "fear of failure syndrome" is distorted does not mitigate its power as an obstacle to continuing education. It also raises disturbing questions about the long-term effects of a preparatory educational system in which competition plays such a central role.

As noted, social institutions and forces influence to a large extent what seem on the surface to be solely individual or psychological barriers to participation in adult education. Social forces not only give rise to many of these barriers but also operate to maintain and reinforce them. The institutions, persons, and groups in one's social environment—in the home, the work place, and the community—exert strong pressures on the individual to conform to prevailing values and norms. For example, it can take a good deal of courage for a construction worker to enroll in a high-school completion program if his fellow workers ridicule him and his wife thinks he is wasting his time. Likewise, a physician may hesitate to continue her professional education through a short course or seminar if her reference group (other physicians) views continuing education only as a vehicle for the remediation of incompetency.

As the case of the physician illustrates, social influences on participation are not confined to class, ethnic background, or socioeconomic status. Membership and reference groups also exert powerful pressures on participation, as do social roles. The roles of mother and wife were alluded to earlier in connection with the fear-of-failure syndrome. Why do middle-class homemakers often exhibit this syndrome but not their spouses? It would seem that the reasons have little to do with social class or gender, but a great deal to do with social role. To oversimplify, the role of such a homemaker, unlike that of her spouse, has probably not served to reinforce a sense of personal efficacy outside the environment of the home. Thus, although she may know on one level that she is intelligent and able, on another level she may not believe it because she has not continually tested and confirmed it through experience. Similarly, the social role of retiree or senior citizen can erode an older adult's sense of personal efficacy. For older adults, however, negative attitudes toward learning seem less influenced by age or social role than by socioeconomic status.[52]

Powerful as they are, the structures and processes of society only partially account for attitudes and perceptions concerning education. Personal psychological characteristics, past experience with formal schooling, and many other factors clearly play a role. Furthermore, despite the values and norms in lower- and working-class society that militate against participation in adult education, a great many disadvantaged and working-class adults do value adult education and do participate. There is no question that psychosocial barriers to participation are formidable, but they are by no means always insurmountable. Negative attitudes and perceptions can be changed by better information, through counseling, and especially by adult educators who make an effort to work with and through the groups and institutions in the community and work place that exert such powerful influences on individual behavior.

THE DYNAMICS OF PARTICIPATION

In order to understand why adults engage in education we need to specify the nature of the factors that affect participation, how they are related to one another, and how they operate to affect actual behavior. In short, we need a theory of participation. Unfortunately, no such theory has been developed. Participation research in adult education, with a few notable exceptions,[53] has given scant attention to theory, and the social sciences have neglected theory building in the more general domain of social participation. To the extent that adult education represents a deliberate investment in human capital, participation can be at least partly explained using the conceptual tools of economics.[54] Economic models and concepts, such as "opportunity cost," clearly merit further development in adult education, but they would seem to have limited application outside the realm of work-related education.

There are many ways in which theory building doubtless will proceed as future researchers attempt to explain and predict participation phenomena. Some will emphasize psychological concepts and processes, while others will look to sociology, economics, decision theory, or a blend of disciplines for useful insights. Some theories will address participation behavior at a general and abstract level, while others will focus narrowly on participation in particular kinds of educational activities or on the participation behavior of specific groups. While a diversity of new concepts and perspectives is necessary if our understanding of participation is to grow, the interplay between individual and social-environmental forces must be central in any attempt to illuminate why adults continue their education.

A Psychosocial Interaction Model

A model might be thought of as a rough version of a theory. It rationalizes or imposes order on reality, but its concepts and propositions are crude and highly abstract, lacking a theory's specificity and therefore its explanatory power. Model building, nonetheless, is often useful in developing theory, and even a simple model is of some value in helping one grasp the dynamics of complex phenomena such as participation in adult education.

In the following pages, we shall pull together much of the earlier discussion in this chapter by proposing a model of participation and commenting on its major characteristics and assumptions. The model emphasizes social-environmental forces, particularly socioeconomic status, not because individual traits or attitudes are unimportant but because less is known about their influence on participation.

• **Pre-Adulthood Components of Model.** The left side of Figure 4.1 depicts in sketchy form the key factors in pre-adult life that influence adult behavior in general, including participation in adult education. There is nothing new here, but simply the conventional social science generalizations concerning the status attainment process. Initial individual and family characteristics (particularly I.Q. and SES) strongly influence subsequent experiences in school (all preparatory education through graduate school) and the values and aspirations that one acquires through the socialization process as it unfolds during the pre-adult years. The amount and quality of preparatory education, and the values and aspirations an individual acquires in the process of becoming an adult, are depicted in the diagram as major determinants of adult socioeconomic status (SES). Adult SES usually is defined in terms of educational attainment, occupational status, and income. Educational attainment, as noted earlier, is a particularly potent predictor of participation in adult education.

• **SES and Learning Press.** The right side of Figure 4.1 depicts the major variables that, during adulthood, are presumed to influence participation in adult education. Each variable represents in reality a continuum, but in the model, in order to clarify the complex interrelationships, all are shown as having three values—high, medium or moderate, and low. Adult SES is portrayed as the first and dominant influence in a sequence of variables affecting the probability that an individual will participate in adult education. Although SES is very important in relation to participation, we need to specify further how it exerts its effects by creating a new variable called "learning press." Learning press is defined as the extent to which one's total current environment requires or encourages further learning. High learning press is related to high SES (and low to low) in that learning press is determined by general social participation (e.g., participation in civic, cultural, religious, and recreational activities and organizations), occupational complexity (e.g., technical, professional, and managerial employment), and life-style (e.g., personal taste, leisure-time preference). All these components of learning press are heavily influenced by SES. To illustrate this point, we might observe that higher SES persons (such as teachers, managers, and doctors) are characterized by a high learning press environment because: (1) they tend to be involved in

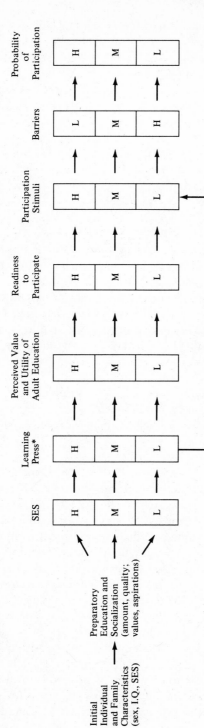

*Function of level of social participation, occupational complexity, and lifestyle.

Figure 4.1   Psychosocial Interaction Model of Participation in Organized Adult Education

many groups, organizations, and activities and this high degree of general social participation creates needs and occasions for further learning; (2) they are employed in complex, knowledge-based occupations that engender demands and opportunities for continued learning; and (3) they lead life-styles that encourage individual self-improvement and self-expression, which in part can be satisfied by participation in adult education. Persons toward the lower end of the SES continuum, in contrast, are less likely to exhibit a high degree of social participation, usually hold jobs that are relatively routine and require limited skills, and tend to lead life-styles that diverge from the middle-class values and norms associated with self-improvement and self-expression. In short, the learning press of their social-occupational environment is generally low.

• Perceived Value of Adult Education and Readiness to Participate. So far the model has dealt mainly with social or environmental rather than individual or psychological forces. While it is possible for an individual to ignore the learning press of his or her environment, it is highly unlikely. Instead, a particular learning press tends to foster certain attitudes and perceptions toward the value and utility of adult education. To the extent, therefore, that one's total current environment requires or encourages further learning, one will perceive adult education as having, at least potentially, high personal value or utility. When learning press is less pronounced, as it generally is for persons toward the lower end of the SES continuum, adult education is less likely to be perceived as potentially useful or valuable. An individual's perception of the value of adult education quite obviously will affect that individual's disposition or readiness to participate.

• Participation Stimuli and Barriers to Participation. General readiness to participate may be high, but readiness must be activated by one or more specific stimuli before participation can be expected to occur. A stimulus might be an external "trigger event" (or its anticipation) such as a job change or a divorce, or it might reflect instead the activation of internal needs or desires related, for example, to self-expression or self-improvement. A recent study by Aslanian and Brickell found that most adults are stimulated to continue their learning because of external "trigger events" and that nine of ten such events occur in the family life and work arenas.[55] A specific stimulus, or related set of stimuli, can be conceived as varying along a continuum of intensity or power. Similarly, participation stimuli vary in frequency from one person to another. The arrow connecting learning press and participation stimuli in the model indicates that there is a direct relationship between the intensity of one's learning press and the frequency and intensity of the participation stimuli one experiences. It follows that, in general, high SES and high learning press are related to higher levels of participation stimuli in terms both of frequency and intensity. It is important to note here that participation stimuli, while often having "objective" origins, are ultimately, like all perceptual phenomena, highly subjective. Thus, regardless of the objective situation (e.g., new baby or new job) some people will interpret the stimulus in terms of learning or education while others will not. If only on the grounds of simple conditioning, one would expect the former to be disproportionately represented among the high SES—high learning press group. Were selective perception of what we call participation stimuli not a reality, it would be less defensible to posit a direct connection between SES level and "level" of participation stimuli.

Even the presence of a specific, potent stimulus to participation does not ensure that a particular adult at a given time and place will engage in education. The path to action may be strewn with obstacles. These obstacles are the various barriers to participation—informational, institutional, situational, and psychosocial—discussed earlier. It is sufficient to note that the severity of these barriers is inversely related to SES.

To return to where we began, the probability of participation is lowest for adults at the lower end of the SES ladder and highest for those at the upper end. Although we can by no means totally explain this fact, the model in Figure 4.1 provides a coherent and useful picture of the dynamics of participation in organized adult education. The picture, to be sure, was painted with broad strokes, and to many it will appear gloomy. The function of a model or theory, however, is to depict reality as it is, not as one might like it to be. The model, in any event, depicts only general relationships of a variable or probabilistic nature. Its emphasis on social forces should not be construed as negating the importance of individual differences. As stressed earlier in this chapter, many less educated, disadvantaged adults, despite the odds against them, do in fact continue their education.

Implications

The model in Figure 4.1 suggests that adult education in countries such as the United States may, on balance, contribute to widening the general resource and life satisfaction gap between the least and most educated sectors of the population. If adult education, as we believe it does, yields significant benefits both for individuals and society, this is an important concern. Some of the public policy issues related to equal educational opportunity for adults are discussed in Chapter 7. Here we shall focus on the strategies adult educators can employ to serve more effectively the old, the poor, the undereducated, and other hard-to-reach groups.

To refer back to our participation model, it is clear that little can be done by educators to alter either SES or the learning press that is so closely connected to it. However, the perceived value or utility of adult education and the barriers to participation that confront disadvantaged adults can be influenced. These two factors are intimately intertwined. If one perceives adult education's value or utility to be low, then one is likely also to perceive formidable barriers to participation. The converse is also true: formidable barriers to participation tend to engender negative perceptions of adult education's value or utility.

Institutional barriers such as inconvenient scheduling or lack of counseling services, and individual situational barriers such as child-care needs or lack of transportation are not insurmountable. Adult educators can attack such barriers by scheduling classes at convenient times and locations; by providing guidance, child-care, or transportation services; and by doing whatever else is necessary and feasible to encourage participation. Adult learners themselves often can find ways around these kinds of tangible barriers.

But what is to be done when people have no idea of the educational options available to them, when adults lack confidence in their ability as learners, and when socially generated and maintained values and attitudes lead people to perceive adult education as having little value? In an earlier work, Darkenwald concluded that "ways must be found to convey information through personal rather than impersonal means; to utilize peer, membership, and reference groups to heighten rather than dampen educational aspirations; and above all to adjust programs and services to meet the real, present needs of people."[56]

To accomplish these goals will require adult educators to supplement the traditional marketing approach to recruitment, with its emphasis on the individual, with what might be called a "social linkages" strategy focusing on groups and organizations. The rationale for this viewpoint was first set forth by Harry Miller in a work that is still regarded as a major contribution to the literature on participation. It is worth quoting at some length:

> So long as the adult educator confronts a situation in which both personal need and social force move together toward the educational satisfaction of some need, it is relatively efficient to employ a marketplace technique for educational offerings. A strong and visible demand is met by providing an adequate supply, through some impersonal marketing device such as a catalog or newspaper announcement. Those who are sensitized by need respond individually to the announcement and appear at the appropriate supply source.
>
> But a marketplace analogy does not work very well in situations where the forces involved are weak or conflicting, as all adult educators interested in programming outside the vocational area have known for a long time. Even in that area, attempts to provide training in usable skills for the unemployed . . . have often failed miserably, most often because they have proceeded on the marketing asumption.

The [strong relationship] of social class membership to the associational life of the society suggests . . . that we can encourage higher rates of participation in some types of adult education only by abandoning a market psychology and developing instead strategies for working with people in organizations to which they already have ties. . . . The most serious difficulties are clearly with the lower-lower class level, the very poor, with the most unstable work life, and the most desperate sense of alienation, who have the fewest group memberships of any social group. Yet they are the most in need of the most fundamental kinds of education, those contributing to survival in an industrial society beginning to run short of unskilled jobs. Although religious associations are a feature of lower-lower life, their evangelical nature does not encourage an educational orientation; civil rights organizations attract mainly the middle class. The greatest potential, perhaps, lies in the neighborhood and community organizations which are often a feature of urban renewal situations or which are part of deliberate attempts to develop political consciousness within a community-based organization effort. . . . This is to say, perhaps, that it we are to gain access to this class level through organizations, we must first create the organization.[57]

Miller implies that reaching the hard-to-reach—especially the very poor—will require radical changes not merely in recruitment strategies but also in the ways adult educators conceive of their roles and organize and carry out educational programs. Indeed, what may be required in many cases is the development of loosely structured, nonformal programs aimed at integrating learning with the groups, activities, and concerns of everyday life in the home, community, and work place.[58] Adult educators concerned with literacy, agricultural, and family life education in developing countries have of necessity employed such nonformal educational strategies for many years.[59] So, too, in some respects, has the Cooperative Extension Service in the United States. Other examples can be found in the work of the Highlander Center in Tennessee, where learning and social action have always been closely linked, and in the Swedish study circle movement in which factory workers are assisted in planning their own continuing education activities in the workplace itself.[60]

Social linkage strategies for reaching the hard-to-reach adult are applicable to any population of potential learners, not only the socially or educationally disadvantaged. Many programs aimed at older adults have proved successful because they have been planned and operated in collaboration with organizations, such as senior citizen centers, that play a major role in the lives of many older people.[61] Other examples of social linkage approaches to program development abound, often in the form of "co-sponsorship" arrangements between an educational institution and another agency or group in the community. Most adults want to continue their education and many desperately need to do so. The challenge to adult educators is to devise alternative strategies for reaching the hard-to-reach when conventional recruitment techniques are inadequate to the task.

NOTES

1. John W. C. Johnstone and Ramon J. Rivera, *Volunteers for Learning: A Study of the Educational Pursuits of American Adults* (Chicago: Aldine, 1965).
2. Abraham Carp, Richard Peterson, and Pamela Roelfs, "Adult Learning Interests and Experiences," in *Planning Non-Traditional Programs*, ed. K. Patricia Cross and John R. Valley (San Francisco: Jossey-Bass, 1974), pp. 11–52.
3. National Center for Education Statistics, *Participation of Adults in Education: 1978 Preliminary Report* (Washington, D.C.: U.S. Department of Education, 1980).
4. Carp, Peterson, and Roelfs, "Adult Learning Interests."
5. Allen Tough, "Major Learning Efforts: Recent Research and Future Directions," *Adult Education* 28, no. 4 (1978): 250–263.
6. National Center for Education Statistics, *Digest of Education Statistics, 1977–78* (Washington, D.C.: Government Printing Office, 1978), pp. 76, 34.
7. National Center for Education Statistics, *Participation of Adults in Education: 1978*, p. 5.
8. Richard E. Anderson and Gordon G. Darkenwald, *Participation and Persistence in American Adult Education* (New York: College Board, 1979).
9. Ibid.
10. Ibid.
11. National Center for Education Statistics, *Participation in Adult Education: Final Report, 1975* (Washington, D.C.: Government Printing Office, 1978).
12. Michael O'Keefe, *The Adult, Education, and Public Policy* (Cambridge, Mass.: Aspen Institute for Humanistic Studies, 1977), p. 15.
13. Ibid., p. 18.
14. Johnstone and Rivera, *Volunteers for Learning*, p. 3.
15. National Center for Education Statistics, *Participation in Adult Education: 1975*, p. 9.
16. Johnstone and Rivera, *Volunteers for Learning*, p. 3.
17. National Center for Education Statistics, *Participation in Adult Education: 1975*, p. 75.
18. Carp, Peterson, and Roelfs, "Adult Learning Interests," p. 34.
19. Richard E. Anderson and Gordon G. Darkenwald, "The Adult Part-Time Learner in Colleges and Universities: A Clientele Analysis," *Research in Higher Education* 10, no. 4 (1979): 357–370.
20. Carp, Peterson, and Roelfs, "Adult Learning Interests," p. 33.
21. National Center for Education Statistics, *Participation in Adult Education: 1975*, p. 63.
22. Carp, Peterson, and Roelfs, "Adult Learning Interests," p. 30.
23. Johnstone and Rivera, *Volunteers for Learning*, p. 4.
24. Ibid.
25. Carp, Peterson, and Roelfs, "Adult Learning Interests," p. 42.
26. Ibid., pp. 43–44.
27. National Center for Education Statistics, *Participation in Adult Education: 1975*, p. 59.
28. Cyril O. Houle, *The Inquiring Mind* (Madison, Wisc.: University of Wisconsin Press, 1961), pp. 15–16.

29. Roger W. Boshier, "Factor Analysts at Large: A Critical Review of the Motivational Orientation Literature," *Adult Education* 27, no. 1 (1976): 24–47.

30. Barry R. Morstain and John C. Smart, "Reasons for Participation in Adult Education Courses: A Multivariate Analysis of Group Differences," *Adult Education* 24, no. 2 (1974): 83–98.

31. Roger W. Bosshier, "Motivational Orientations of Adult Education Participants: A Factor Analytic Exploration of Houle's Typology," *Adult Education* 21, no. 1 (1971): 3–26.

32. Roger W. Boshier, "Motivational Orientations Revisited: Life Space Motives and the Education Participation Scale," *Adult Education* 27, no. 2 (1977): 89–115.

33. Norman Nie et al., *Statistical Package for the Social Sciences*, 2d ed. (New York: McGraw-Hill, 1975), p. 469.

34. Morstain and Smart, "Reasons for Participation."

35. Ibid.

36. Ibid.

37. Boshier, "Motivational Orientations Revisited."

38. Johnstone and Rivera, *Volunteers for Learning*, p. 17; Carp, Peterson, and Roelfs, "Adult Learning Interests," p. 46.

39. Ibid.

40. K. Patricia Cross, "Adult Learners: Characteristics, Needs, and Interests," in *Lifelong Learning in America*, ed. Richard E. Peterson (San Francisco: Jossey-Bass, 1979), p. 108.

41. Ibid.

42. Ibid., p. 106.

43. Johnstone and Rivera, *Volunteers for Learning*, pp. 201–202.

44. Cross, "Adult Learners," p. 126.

45. Ibid., p. 103; Johnstone and Rivera, *Volunteers for Learning*, p. 203.

46. Gordon A. Larson, "Overcoming Barriers to Communication," in *Reaching Hard-to-Reach Adults*, ed. Gordon G. Darkenwald and Gordon A. Larson (San Francisco: Jossey-Bass, 1980), pp. 27–38.

47. Gladys H. Irish, "Reaching the Least Educated Adult," in *Reaching Hard-to-Reach Adults*, ed. Darkenwald and Larson, pp. 39–53.

48. Gordon G. Darkenwald, "Educational and Career Guidance for Adults: Delivery System Alternatives," *Vocational Guidance Quarterly* 28, no. 3 (1980): 200–207.

49. Johnstone and Rivera, *Volunteers for Learning*, pp. 21–22.

50. Carp, Peterson, and Roelfs, "Adult Learning Interests," p. 46.

51. Jack Mezirow, Gordon G. Darkenwald, and Alan B. Knox, *Last Gamble on Education* (Washington, D.C.: Adult Education Association of the U.S.A., 1975); Helen Astin, ed., *Some Action of Her Own* (Lexington, Mass.: Lexington Books, 1976).

52. Johnstone and Rivera, *Volunteers for Learning*, p. 17.

53. See, for example, Roger W. Boshier, "Educational Participation and Dropout: A Theoretical Model," *Adult Education* 23, no. 4 (1973): 255–282.

54. Lutaf Dhanidina and William S. Griffith, "Costs and Benefits of Delayed High School Completion," *Adult Education* 25, no. 4 (1975): 217–230.

55. Carol B. Aslanian and Henry M. Brickell, *Americans in Transition: Life*

Changes as Reasons for Adult Learning (New York: College Board, 1980).

56. Gordon G. Darkenwald, "Continuing Education and the Hard-to-Reach Adult," in *Reaching Hard-to-Reach Adults*, ed. Darkenwald and Larson, pp. 9–10.

57. Harry L. Miller, *Participation of Adults in Education: A Force-Field Analysis* (Brookline, Mass.: Center for the Study of Liberal Education for Adults, 1967), pp. 14–16.

58. Carmen Hunter and David Harmon, *Adult Illiteracy in the United States* (New York: McGraw-Hill, 1979).

59. Lyra Srinivasan, *Perspectives on Nonformal Adult Learning* (New York: World Education, 1977).

60. Frank Adams, *Unearthing Seeds of Fire: The Idea of Highlander* (Winston-Salem, N.C.: Blair, 1975); Kjell Rubenson, "Participation in Recurrent Education: Problems Relating to the Undereducated and Underprivileged" (Stockholm: Stockholm Institute of Education, 1977).

61. Barbara Spencer, "Overcoming the Age Bias of Continuing Education," in *Reaching Hard-to-Reach Adults*, ed. Darkenwald and Larson, pp. 71–86.

Chapter 5
Agencies and Programs

This chapter is concerned with the environments of adult learning and education, particularly the institutions that provide educational opportunities for adults, their roles, distinctive features, and interrelationships. Although not all adult education takes place under organizational auspices, a point emphasized throughout this volume, what might be called the *enterprise* of adult education is institutionally based. It is principally this enterprise that concerns us here—the multiplicity of organizations that plan and conduct learning activities for adults.

Familiarity with the organizational dimension of adult education is important for several reasons. Most significant is that adult education as an enterprise, a profession, and a movement cannot be fully understood apart from the organizations that have nurtured it and given it definition and direction. Moreover, adult education's organizational providers are exceedingly diverse—so much so that many people find the field bewildering or comprehend only a small part of the total endeavor. Finally, an understanding of the organizational dimension is important because the role of the adult educator is defined in part by the settings in which the work of adult education goes forward. As we shall see, there are many similarities in what adult educators do in various institutional settings, but there are also notable differences.

This chapter begins with a general overview of adult education settings, which is followed by a detailed discussion of the kinds of agencies that provide adult education and the similarities and differences among them. Following this review of specific agencies and programs, the discussion shifts to the larger context of adult education as a social enterprise. Emphasis is placed on the increasing involvement of government through an analysis of the impact of legislation on the field and the role of federal and state agencies in policymaking, planning, and coordination. Attempts at voluntary coordination at the national, state, and local levels are also reviewed. The chapter concludes with a discussion of the dilemmas and limitations of planning and coordination in a field as diverse as adult education.

ADULT EDUCATION SETTINGS

The settings or contexts of adult education comprise a continuum, one end of which can be labelled "highly informal" and the other "highly formal." We might consider as highly informal any purposeful, systematic, and sustained learning activity that is not sponsored, planned, or directed by an organization. Thus, highly informal adult education occurs in "natural" social settings. Not surprisingly, the activities and institutions toward the formal end of the continuum have received the most attention in the professional literature. Most adult educators, or at least those who identify themselves as such, are employed by organizations such as colleges and professional associations that sponsor classes, workshops, and other relatively formal educational activities. Informal adult education, on the other hand, is less visible and perhaps perceived by most adult educators as less urgent or serious. However, one manifestation of informal adult education, self-education, has received increasing attention from researchers and policymakers. The research in this area suggests that most adults in any given year engage in one or more highly deliberate efforts to learn—efforts that are usually self-initiated and self-directed.[1] By the most conservative estimates, a large part of what adults learn purposefully and systematically is acquired on an individual basis without benefit of organizational sponsorship.[2]

Informal adult education as conceived here goes beyond individual, self-directed learning. Private instruction, which is more widespread than most people realize, is provided by free-lance teachers, who give individual or group lessons in virtually every subject and skill. In some areas "learning exchanges" have been established to match up people who want to learn a particular subject or skill with others who want to teach it.[3]

Private instruction has been a significant vehicle of adult education since the early eighteenth century.[4]

While private instruction is usually provided for a fee, adults sometimes learn from each other at no cost through groups that are independent of any organization and that exist principally for the purpose of mutual education. The original Junto founded by Benjamin Franklin is a well-known example. Similar clubs and informal groups can be found today in most communities. Some devote themselves to the discussion of books, poetry, or other forms of literature; others are concerned with political or religious subjects and still others with avocational interests, such as astronomy, gardening, or local history. An interesting variation is the phenomenon of "networking," in which people with common interests or problems, such as women executives, get together for purposes of mutual learning and support. Members of the network use each other as resources for learning, advice, and psychological support, often in pairs or small groups that form and re-form as needs and circumstances change.[5]

Adult education, then, is not confined to the courses, workshops, lecture series, or other activities sponsored by organizations. Adults can and do learn on their own, through private instruction, and in loosely structured, informal groups. Unfortunately, scholars and researchers have devoted little attention to informal learning in natural social settings. A fuller understanding of informal adult learning activities might help professional adult educators to facilitate learning more effectively both in natural social settings and in more structured environments.

TYPES OF AGENCIES

Trying to discern or impose order on the multiplicity of agencies involved in adult education is a frustrating and probably futile task if the goal is a rigorous typology or classification scheme. As Knowles observed some time ago, "No simple symbol, such as the red brick schoolhouse or the stadium-dominated campus, stands for the institutional sponsorship of adult education. The institutional field in which adult education operates is so varied and complex as to defy neat classification. . . ."[6] Before considering the organizational makeup of the field, it may be useful to ponder some of the reasons why rigorous classification is so difficult.

Problems of Classification

Organizational theorists have developed several general typologies, but most do not seem useful for categorizing adult education agencies. Blau and Scott's cui bono scheme does, however, appear relevant to our purposes since it is based on "who benefits" from an organization's activities.[7] Applying an adapted version of this typology to adult education illustrates some of the problems of classifying organizations in such a complex field. A modified version of the cui bono typology yields the following categories, which in effect constitute distinctive clienteles for adult education programming:

1. The general public or some portion of it,
2. Employees (including volunteers),
3. Members, and
4. Clients, patients, or customers.

Although crude, these categories have some value because they correspond in a general way to major types of provider organizations (e.g., schools and colleges, business and industry, professional associations, hospitals). They are useful too because clientele characteristics strongly influence the goals and methods of adult education and therefore the professional functions of program development and instruction. The typology is deficient, however, because many adult education agencies would fall into more than one category. Consider, for example, the case of a large, university-affiliated hospital. Such an organization might have an educational unit that provides: (1) in-service training for professional and nonprofessional employees and volunteers; (2) patient education; (3) continuing professional education for health professionals not necessarily employed by the hospital (a segment of the general public); and (4) health education for the general public in the hospital's service area. The cui bono typology, despite its logic, is of little use in classifying such an agency, for it would have to be included in three of the four categories. This kind of problem extends to most other adult education agencies. While it might seem that the educational units of business and industry, because of their emphasis on employee training, would fall only in the second category, the fact is that many corporations are heavily engaged in customer education to help purchasers make effective use of products and services and some (such as public utilities) even provide educational programs for the general public. Likewise, museums and libraries provide training for their personnel and educational programs for the public, labor unions are heavily engaged in education for both members and employees, and so on.

There are, of course, other conceivable ways of constructing a typology of adult education agencies. A distinction is sometimes made between the schooling of adults and adult education, the implication being that "schooling" is teacher- rather than learner-centered, more formal (involving classrooms, grades, credits, etc.), and based on a professionally dictated curriculum rather than learner needs and interests. While the distinction has some validity, it is apparent that many agencies, including schools and colleges, business and industry, organized labor, and others, engage both in the schooling of adults and in what might be characterized as less formal or more learner-oriented adult education. Likewise, the distinction between training, or performance-oriented adult education, and service- or community-oriented adult education is useful for some purposes, but it clearly cannot be applied as the sole criterion to classify institutions since many employers, such as industry and government agencies, engage in both forms of adult education, as do schools, colleges, and other organizations.

While a rigorous typology of adult education agencies would seem to be an impossibility, scholars in the field such as Knowles[8] and Houle[9] have suggested a broad classification scheme that seems to have a modicum of utility. Essentially, in Knowles's words, this scheme is based on the "relationship of adult education to other purposes of the agencies in which it takes place."[10] Adult education can be the primary or sole function of an organization, a secondary function of an educational agency, a complementary function of a quasi-educational agency (such as a library or professional association), or a secondary and supportive function of a noneducational agency (such as a business corporation or prison). These four categories are used as an organizing framework in the overview of adult education agencies that follows.

INDEPENDENT ADULT EDUCATION ORGANIZATIONS

In the nineteenth century, institutions devoted primarily or exclusively to adult education, such as the lyceums or Chautauqua, probably played a larger role in the education of the adult public than such agencies do today.[11] Nonetheless, independent adult education organizations are more numerous than one might think and certainly diverse. Their number has been growing in recent years and probably will continue to do so in the 1980s and 1990s. In terms of numbers of adults served, the proprietary and correspondence schools have long played a major role and will be described in some detail. Also worthy of note are the nontraditional, external degree organizations that developed rapidly in the 1970s and show every sign of continued vitality. First, however, we shall consider the smaller, often overlooked agencies, which in general are oriented to the needs of local communities.

Community-Based Agencies

Agencies in this category include nonprofit locally or regionally oriented adult schools, residential adult education centers, learning exchanges (or networks), free universities, and other grass-roots adult education enterprises. Private, nonprofit community adult schools are sometimes found in communities where the public schools are unable or unwilling to support adult education. While few in number and often limited in scope to avocational, recreational, and personal development offerings, they are nonetheless an enduring part of the adult education scene. How many such schools there are in the United States and Canada is not known, but in New Jersey, for example, there are about six or seven.[12]

Nonprofit residential adult education centers, while prevalent in Scandinavia (there called folk schools), are rare in North America. These should not be confused with residential education centers operated by large organizations such as industries, labor unions, government agencies, and universities. One of the best-known independent residential schools is the Highlander Research and Education Center in Tennessee. Geared to education for social action, it played a major role in union organizing efforts in the South in the 1930s and 1940s, in the civil rights movement in the 1950s and 1960s, and more recently in community development and environment improvement efforts in Appalachia.[13]

Learning exchanges, as noted previously, serve as a vehicle for matching people who want to teach something with others who have something they want to learn. Perhaps the largest is The Learning Exchange in Evanston, Illinois, which serves approximately 20,000 adults who receive instruction in some 3,000 subjects.[14]

So-called free universities, which offer no credits or credentials, are often located near regular universities, although close to half the 200 or so that have been identified have no such ties.[15] Similar in some respects to independent adult schools, free universities usually provide a wide range of offerings in the arts and crafts and practical skills, along with courses in a more sophisticated vein on such topics as energy, the environment, women's issues, and political and social ideology. To some degree, the free universities constitute a national movement, with leadership provided by the Free University Network headquartered in Manhattan, Kansas.

Finally, it is important to note the private literacy education organizations that are organized nationally but operate at the local level through state or regional branches. The two best-known are Literacy Volunteers of America and the Laubach organization, both of which recruit and train volunteers to work one-on-one with illiterate adults. These organizations often cooperate with local libraries, prisons, churches, and public school adult education agencies.

Proprietary Schools

Privately owned profit-making schools have a long and controversial history. They include business schools, technical schools, correspondence schools, and others, like the Dale Carnegie Schools, that are difficult to classify. A few are owned by large corporations such as Bell and Howell, and others are organized like chain stores with units in various cities (e.g., the better-known secretarial schools), but most are small, single-unit organizations that are highly specialized. The most recent statistics indicate that there are some 9,000 such schools in the United States, about three times the number of colleges and universities.[16] Not all proprietary schools serve a primarily adult clientele. Many young people just out of high school enroll in these institutions on a full-time basis, particularly in the secretarial schools and those in the popular technical fields such as health and computer technology. In other fields, such as real estate and insurance, virtually all the students are adults. In the most recent year for which statistics are available, some 735,000 adults enrolled in private vocational, trade, or business schools, and another 457,000 enrolled in correspondence schools. Thus, in 1978 about 8 percent of all adults participating in organized educational activities were enrolled in proprietary and correspondence schools.[17]

External Degree Agencies

Some external degree agencies, such as Empire State College in New York State, are autonomous adult education organizations, while others are units of universities, school systems, or state governments. Despite the fact that many such agencies are attached to traditional educational institutions, their distinctiveness and strong orientation to adult needs argue for their treatment as independent, or at least quasi-independent, adult education organizations.

The term *external degree* refers to a wide variety of institutions and practices that sometimes seem to have little in common other than being nontraditional. There are, however, some general characteristics of these agencies that differentiate them from more traditional educational forms. Perhaps the most fundamental, as Cross and Valley point out, is their "explicit recognition that education should be measured by what the student knows rather than how or where he learns it."[18] In practice, as Houle has noted, this means separating out one or more of the five basic functions traditionally performed by colleges or universities (or, in modified form, by public schools). These functions, which are not normally separated, include "enforcement of admission (or matriculation) requirements, provision of instruction, evaluation of the individual's competence in the content taught, awarding of the certificate or degree, and licensure to practice a profession."[19] Thus an external degree agency, such as the New York State Regents External Degree Program (an arm of the New York State Education Department), or Thomas A. Edison College in New Jersey, may offer no instruction whatever, but may certify prior educational achievement (in college or even in industry or the military service); award credit for successful completion of examinations; and, when certain requirements related to the number of credits and their subject matter distribution are met, award a degree. Other external degree institutions, such as Empire State College, perform similar evaluative and certifying functions, but in addition offer instruction through nontraditional modes including individualized learning contracts, correspondence study, television courses, and so on. Highly motivated and able adults, particularly those with prior college attendance and significant work experience, can earn an external degree rapidly and inexpensively. In addition, adults who cannot attend regular college classes (or do not wish to) are able to study independently when, where, and at a pace they themselves determine.

A more recent, and equally significant, development has been the adoption of external degree practices at the adult secondary level. The nontraditional (or competency-based) adult high school movement, pioneered in the mid-1970s by the Regional Learning Service of Central New York, has spread rapidly to Texas, Michigan, Illinois, California, New Jersey, Maine, Oregon, and many other states. It offers adults who did not complete high school a flexible alternative to the GED (high school equivalency) test and the conventional, classroom-based, evening high school. In most cases, regular (not equivalency) diplomas are awarded not by state agencies (although this does occur), but by local school boards. Practices vary widely even within the same state, but the Adult High School of South Plainfield, New Jersey, is reasonably representative.[20] In this program, one hundred Carnegie units are required for graduation, including two courses in American history, the only mandatory subject. Students must also perform satisfactorily on a test of basic skills. Credit can be earned for a year or more of successful work experience, basic military training, and completion of an approved apprenticeship program (worth 30 credits). Students also may earn credits through assessment of performance, for example, in typing or auto repair; through passing tests in a range of high school subjects; and for prior coursework and training sponsored by schools and colleges, including approved proprietary schools, and by employers and the armed forces. Regular classes are also offered in a variety of high school subjects, and independent study is an option in American history. If appropriate courses are not available in South Plainfield, a student may take them for diploma credit at other institutions, such as county vocational-technical schools or community colleges. The nontraditional adult high school, like its collegiate counterpart, is revolutionary in its implications. The credential is not awarded for mere "seat time," but principally on the basis of what a student knows or can do, regardless of when, where, and how it was learned.

EDUCATIONAL INSTITUTIONS

In the United States and Canada, as well as in Great Britain and many other industrialized countries, the preparatory educational system of schools, colleges, and universities plays a major role in adult education. Table 5.1 shows just how significant this role is. It also illustrates the trend in recent years for public two-year colleges and technical institutes to serve an increasingly larger proportion of adult education participants.

From Table 5.1 it can be seen that nearly half of all participants in organized adult education in 1978 were enrolled in four-year colleges and universities, two-year colleges and technical institutes, and in programs sponsored by the public schools. The role of postsecondary institutions in providing education to adults is considerably larger than that of the public schools. There were more than ten million enrollments in two- or four-year colleges and universities compared with fewer than three million in programs sponsored by the public schools.

With some exceptions (notably among some community colleges), adult education is not a primary goal or function of traditional educational institutions. Schools and colleges are devoted not to lifelong learning for people of all ages, but rather to the preparatory education of children and young people in formal programs of instruction leading to diplomas and degrees. Since World War II, and particularly in the last decade, there has been some upgrading of adult education's status, particularly at the postsecondary level, but in general adult education is a secondary or ancillary activity in schools and colleges and typically receives little financial support from the parent institution.

To say that adult education is still a secondary activity in most school and college settings is not to denigrate its achievements or vitality in the kindergarten-through-university system. On the contrary, many of the most comprehensive, innovative, and effective programs of adult education are sponsored by the public schools and by colleges and universities. Clearly, they are the two principal sources of comprehensive educational programming geared to the needs and interests of the general public. We shall consider first adult education in the public schools.

Table 5.1   Trends in Adult Education Enrollments in Education Institutions as a Percentage of Total Enrollments

INSTITUTION	1969	1975	1978
Elementary or Secondary School	15.1	11.0	9.4
Four-Year College or University	21.7	19.1	19.6
Two-Year College or Vocational-Technical Institution	11.9	17.7	18.4

SOURCE: National Center for Education Statistics, *Participation of Adults in Education: Preliminary Report, 1978* (Washington, D.C.: U.S. Department of Education, 1980).

Public School Adult Education

America's public schools have been a major source of adult education since the middle of the nineteenth century. According to Grattan, the earliest evening classes in elementary school subjects were offered by the public schools of Boston and Louisville in 1834. Initially, most of the students in these classes were working youths, although adults also enrolled. Evening high school instruction was introduced in Cincinnati in 1856 and in New York City ten years later.[21] This emphasis on basic or remedial education continues to characterize much of public school adult education, especially in the cities. By the turn of the century, and particularly following World War I, instruction in the three Rs and high school subjects was supplemented by English-language and citizenship training for immigrants and by broad-based programs of vocational education. In the 1930s, and especially after World War II, the adult curricula were broadened considerably to include recreational, avocational, and personal development or "enrichment" courses of a liberal or humanistic vein.

In contrast to 1880 (or even 1930), it is impossible in the 1980s to characterize the "typical" public school adult education agency (hereafter called adult school). It can be said, however, that adult schools tend to reflect the needs of the local communities they serve. In the larger cities, as well as in economically depressed rural areas, programs emphasize vocational training (often supported by federal funds through the Comprehensive Employment and Training Act), adult basic education, English as a second language, citizenship education, and high school completion. Avocational and general enrichment programming in such settings is usually minimal, if it exists at all. Remedial and vocational programming is heavily supported by federal and state funding. In suburban and small-town settings, adult schools often provide a mix of remedial/vocational and general interest programming, the latter financed mainly or totally by student fees. In the more affluent small towns and suburban communities, adult schools usually provide little or no remedial or vocational instruction, concentrating instead on avocational, personal development, and general enrichment offerings more suited to middle-class interests.

The importance of public adult schools as providers of adult education varies from state to state. Among the factors affecting the role of the public schools in adult education are history and tradition, state financial support for public school adult education, the presence of competing delivery systems (mainly community college systems), and the extent of professional leadership on the part of public school adult educators and state education department officials. In some states, such as North Carolina, Iowa, Washington, and Wisconsin, community colleges and technical institutes have become the primary delivery system for community-based public sector adult education. In other states, such as Illinois, New York, Florida, Indiana, Massachusetts, New Jersey, and Michigan, the public schools play a vital role in the adult education enterprise. Despite declining enrollments of elementary and secondary school students, adult education in the public schools does not appear to be expanding to the extent one might expect. This may be related in part to the financial problems of many school districts and to increased competition from the postsecondary sector, particularly the community colleges. Nonetheless, well-established programs with a broad range of offerings, adequate facilities, reasonably secure funding, and a nucleus of full-time, professional staff are likely to continue to flourish.

Community Colleges

The public two-year college is an American innovation that has spread rapidly, not only within the United States and Canada, but in recent years to other countries as well. More than any other institution, the community college exemplifies the ideal of lifelong learning. There is virtually no person, no subject, no educational method that falls outside the range of the community college endeavor. Because the community college is so all-encompassing in its purposes and programs, it can be best defined with a statement of what it does not do: It does not provide formal preparatory education for youngsters and it does not provide collegiate or professional education leading to credentials higher than the two-year associate degree. Within these limitations, community colleges in general offer virtually everything to everyone. In the adult education arena alone, community colleges may offer adult basic education, high school equivalency, noncredit personal development courses, English as a second language, vocational training, and continuing professional education for a variety of occupational groups, including in some cases lawyers, dentists, engineers, and other practitioners with advanced university degrees. They often provide as well programs for such special groups as senior citizens, reentry women, prisoners, civic leaders, single parents, and recovering alcoholics, to mention but a few. Instructional formats and delivery systems include workshops, seminars, conferences, symposia, television courses, correspondence courses, telephone courses, newspaper courses, and computer-assisted courses, many of which are offered in factories, office buildings, hospitals, churches, libraries, prisons, and other off-campus settings.

The vitality of adult education in community colleges is due to several factors. First, service to the entire community has been a principal tenet of the community college movement since its beginning.

In most states, legislation establishing community colleges has specifically mandated, or at least legitimated, adult education (or community service) as a major institutional function. A second factor has been relatively generous funding, enabling community colleges to hire full-time adult education specialists to develop effective and needed programs. A third factor is the flexibility that community colleges enjoy, partly because of their broadly defined mission and partly because they are less encumbered by the academic traditionalism of universities and the web of political and legal constraints that can immobilize a public school system.

As might be expected, the community college's flexibility is reflected in a wide variety of organizational arrangements for the provision of adult education.[22] In the degree-credit arena, some institutions operate on the "single college" model, making no administrative distinction between day and evening classes or between full-time and part-time students. On many campuses, particularly in urban areas, the majority of degree-credit students are adults enrolled on a part-time basis. In contrast to degree-credit studies, noncredit offerings are almost always offered through special adult education units usually referred to as continuing education or community services divisions. Community colleges are a major source of noncredit, postsecondary education for adults. A national survey conducted in 1975–1976 reported four million registrations in noncredit activities in community colleges, compared with roughly two-and-a-half million in universities and two million in four-year colleges.[23]

As these statistics suggest, community colleges are reaching out to the general public in much the same way as the local adult schools. More than a decade ago, Harlacher identified several "major trends . . . apparent in community service programs" in community colleges. The experience of the 1970s has confirmed these trends and it is likely that they will continue to characterize community services programs in the 1980s. According to Harlacher, the community college will:

> develop aggressive multiservice outreach programs designed to extend its campus throughout the entire college district;
> place increased emphasis on community education for all age levels and groups;
> utilize a great diversification of media in meeting community needs and interests;
> increasingly utilize its catalytic capabilities to assist its community in the solution of basic educational, economic, and social problems;
> be increasingly concerned about the cultural growth of its community;
> place greater emphasis on interaction with its community;
> increasingly recognize the need for cooperation with other agencies.[24]

Four-Year Colleges and Universities

Community colleges are in many respects more alike than different, but four-year colleges and universities often are more different than alike. One source of difference is that many four-year institutions are not publicly controlled. But even more important is the highly differentiated nature of colleges and universities in terms of mission, structure, program, and clientele. Even universities that seem similar, such as Princeton and Columbia, are in actuality very different in a number of important respects—including their involvement in continuing education for adults. To impose some kind of order on this diversity, we shall consider separately the degree-credit and noncredit adult education activities of colleges and universities.

Noncredit adult education activities in colleges and universities date back to 1816, when a professor at Rutgers University offered lectures in science to the public. Similar lectures in popular science were offered at Yale, Columbia, and Harvard in the 1830s and 1840s, but it was not until the 1890s that adult education began to be institutionalized in the form of "university extension." By 1919, 32 universities (only 4 of them privately controlled) had established extension divisions.[25] By 1976, 1,233 four-year institutions offered noncredit adult educational activities, a sharp increase from 680 institutions a decade earlier.[26]

In many smaller colleges, noncredit adult education is organized on an informal, decentralized basis, often as a supplement to a department's regular offerings. Most often, however, noncredit adult education is provided through a special administrative unit, usually designated "continuing education," but sometimes referred to as a division or school of general studies, community services, evening studies, or extension.[27] In terms of the type of programming offered, as well as instructional methods and delivery systems, noncredit activities in colleges and universities are generally similar to such activities in community colleges. One important difference, however, is that four-year institutions are seldom involved in adult basic education and nonprofessional vocational education and are much more involved in continuing professional education in such fields as social work, medicine, dentistry, law, pharmacy, and business management. In fact, at most larger universities, continuing professional education is regarded as the "bread and butter" of noncredit programming.

Degree-credit programming for part-time adult students is most clearly demarcated from noncredit programming at those institutions that sponsor what are generally referred to as evening colleges (also known as schools of continuing education or general studies, university colleges, and weekend colleges). A few evening colleges are formally organized, with their own special curricula and full-time faculties (for example,

Columbia's School of General Studies), but most are loosely structured, consisting basically of standard undergraduate courses which are taught in the evenings or weekends by part-time instructors. Historically, evening colleges have been associated mainly with urban colleges and universities, largely because such institutions are able to draw from a large pool of adult learners in the immediate locale. Early pioneers in this field were the municipal colleges and universities, such as the College of the City of New York and the University of Cincinnati, and the private urban universities such as Syracuse, Tulane, and Northwestern. While many of the more established evening colleges have changed little over the years, the nontraditional education movement of the 1970s resulted in many innovative programs and the widespread adoption of such practices as granting credit on the basis of examinations and life or work experience. While true external degree institutions, as discussed earlier, are few in number, what might be called quasi-external degree programs have multiplied rapidly in colleges and universities. A survey conducted in the mid-seventies identified approximately 300 "nontraditional" degree-credit programs among four-year colleges and universities.[28] The trend is still toward greater flexibility in where and how adults can earn college and university degrees.

Cooperative Extension Service

According to Boone, "the Cooperative Extension Service . . . is the world's largest publicly supported informal adult education and development organization. . . . With over half a century of recognized achievement, it is America's first (and only) *national* system of adult education."[29] The term "cooperative" comes from the fact that the Cooperative Extension Service (CES) is based on a system of joint funding and program planning involving federal, state, and local units of government. The basis of the system is a statutory relationship (Smith-Lever Act of 1914) between the U.S. Department of Agriculture and the state land grant universities. The principal operational role is assumed by the state universities, which develop annual program plans in consultation with county governments, farmers' groups, and other local constituencies. The U.S. Department of Agriculture provides general guidelines and approves and monitors the state plans. Although the CES is administered by land grant universities, its unique purpose and structure as well as its great significance in the development of adult education justify treating it as a special case of continuing education in colleges and universities.

At the heart of the CES is a commitment to the development and dissemination of practical knowledge. Research is undertaken by agricultural experiment stations and other units in the universities. University-based extension specialists in agriculture, home economics, youth development, and community development utilize this research to prepare instructional and informational materials and to train county agents and other local personnel (such as volunteers and nutrition aides) on an ongoing basis. The county agents in turn provide direct service to the public, answering requests for information and providing instruction to groups and individuals on an informal, noncredit basis.

The CES is organized into four major program areas: agriculture and natural resources; home economics; 4-H youth development; and, more recently, community resource development. The first emphasizes crop and livestock production, business management and marketing, and pest management and environmental improvement. The home economics program is broadly concerned with improving family life. Educational activities focus on foods and nutrition, family economics, family life education, family health and safety, and textiles and clothing. The 4-H program is not of course aimed at adults, although the staff is responsible for organizing and training more than half a million volunteer leaders.[30] The community resource development program is targeted on rural areas and towns of less than 50,000 population. Its major concern is improving the quality of life in rural communities through assistance to local government and other groups and agencies concerned with employment, housing, health, education, citizen participation, and governmental effectiveness. While this program is small and not well developed in many states, it is the only national effort aimed at broad community development, a process in which adult education often plays a central role.

While most people associate the CES with farmers and rural America, in recent years, especially through its home economics programs, it has become increasingly active in urban areas. The home economics program, staffed by some 4,000 extension home economists, 7,000 aides, and 700,000 volunteer extension homemakers, reaches approximately ten million families each year.

While much extension work involves information giving and technical assistance rather than education in the stricter sense of the term, there is little doubt that several million Americans each year participate in CES activities that are genuinely educational. The following list of distinguishing features of the Cooperative Extension Service is worth reflecting upon, for if the CES is as successful as it appears to be, every educator can benefit in some way from its experience.

> Informal teaching that is designed to make knowledge relevant and help individuals, families, businesses, and communities to identify and solve their problems.
> The extensive use of lay advisory committees or councils to assist with planning, executing, and evaluating the educational program.
> The extension of its reach and effectiveness by working with (and through) new and existing organizations

The training of local [volunteer] leaders.

The support by different levels of government which has encouraged responsiveness to national, state, and local problems.

The reciprocal relationship between services and research, which provides channels for new knowledge to flow to the people and allows human needs and problems to be transmitted to the scientists.[31]

QUASI-EDUCATIONAL ORGANIZATIONS

In addition to the organizations that exist for educational purposes, there is a large and amorphous category of organizations termed "quasi-educational" in that education "is an allied function employed to fulfill only some of the needs which [these] agencies recognize as their responsibility."[32] Within this broad category are: (1) cultural organizations, concerned at least in part with the general diffusion of knowledge and including libraries, museums, and certain of the mass media; (2) community organizations, such as churches, Y's, senior citizen centers, and other private, nonprofit agencies that exist "to offer services, or to serve as a vehicle for association, to members or to the general public";[33] and (3) occupational associations, which are voluntary membership organizations whose principal purpose is to advance the interests of a particular profession or occupational group.

Cultural Organizations

As noted above, the major commonality among cultural organizations is their concern for disseminating information or knowledge (including insight, understanding, and appreciation) to the general public. All these organizations are *educative* in that people can and do learn from them, often unintentionally, incidentally, or very informally. They are *educational*, in the sense of offering organized learning opportunities, to a lesser extent. Our focus here is on the role of cultural organizations in providing or facilitating purposeful and organized learning for adults. Their broader educative activities, while equally or perhaps more important, are beyond the scope of this chapter.

The public library's role in adult education is many-faceted, but the basic emphases appear to be: (1) providing individual assistance to independent adult learners; (2) organizing and conducting group learning activities for the general public and specific clienteles (such as the elderly), usually with an emphasis on informal group discussion coupled with readings, films, or lectures; and (3) facilitating the adult education activities of other agencies such as churches, colleges, adult schools, and various community organizations through the provision of facilities, materials, or various professional library services. Monroe provides a brief overview of the history of adult library education that highlights the major trends:

> The library adult education movement from the 1920s through the 1930s focused on the advisor guiding the reader in individual reading programs. . . . During the 1940s and 1950s, library adult education—in the wake of World War II and growing internationalism—turned on group discussion of human values and social problems through such programs as Great Books Discussion. . . . Beginning in the 1950s and carrying through the 1960s, the adult education programs of public libraries refocused on . . . the particular needs of special groups in the community.[34]

Today, the adult education emphasis in public libraries, especially the larger ones, seems to have shifted away from informal group activities to more ambitious efforts to serve serious independent learners (many of whom are enrolled in independent study programs) and adults handicapped by functional illiteracy. Clearly, libraries have the potential to play an important role in adult education, and not only as a "resource" for highly motivated, independent learners. The best statistics available suggest, however, that only 2 percent of adult education participants, including those engaged in self-education projects, use libraries as locations for learning. Whether the deliberately educational, as opposed to broadly educative, role of the libraries will expand in the 1980s is unclear.

Like public libraries, museums are an enormous resource for serious adult learning but their potential has yet to be developed except at a few pacesetter institutions such as New York's Metropolitan Museum of Art, the Franklin Institute of Philadelphia, and the Chicago Museum of Science and Industry. Museums are increasingly using a wide variety of educational methods such as exhibits (including mobile units and other outreach techniques), guided tours, lectures, classes, and various kinds of participatory activities (e.g., simulated space travel, descents into reconstructed coal mines, and interactive experiences with various technological devices such as computers and video systems). The potential for creating rich educative environments that engage adults (and children) in active learning is enormous and appears to be a growing trend, especially in historical and science museums. In 1965, museums provided organized classes and lectures for some 4.5 million adults,[35] a figure that by 1980 may well have doubled.

The mass media—television, radio, and newspapers—are also more educative than educational in the sense that adults regularly acquire information from these sources but less often use them in deliberate and systematic efforts to learn. Unhappily, commercial television and radio, and to a lesser extent most newspapers, are only marginally educative and seldom produce anything that could reasonably be called educational.

With the possible exception of cable TV, this situation is unlikely to change.

Public television (and radio), however, presents a very different picture. Nearly 300 stations (compared with only 70 in the early 1960s) affiliated with the Public Broadcasting Service have the potential to reach two-thirds of the American population.[36] While much of the programming is geared to news, public affairs, and entertainment, there seems to be an increase in strictly educational programming, including tele-courses (usually sponsored cooperatively with colleges and universities) and such quasi-instructional series as "The Ascent of Man" and "The Voyage of the Beagle." Stations licensed to universities and state broadcasting agencies (about two-thirds of the total) place more emphasis on instructional television, including training for government employees, than those licensed to nonprofit corporations such as Boston's WGBH. While only one percent or so of adults currently utilize television for the purpose of deliberate and systematic learning,[37] this figure should increase, unless federal appropriations are heavily cut, as the Public Broadcasting System continues to develop its educational potential through technological advances (e.g., involving satellite transmission), closer collaboration with other educational agencies, and increased production and sharing of educational programming.

Community Organizations

A staggering diversity of locally based, private nonprofit membership and service organizations provide learning opportunities of many kinds for adults in local communities. Included in this category are membership organizations such as service and fraternal clubs (Rotary, Jaycees), chapters of political and other national special interest groups (American Civil Liberties Union, League of Women Voters), and performing arts organizations, community centers, and anti-poverty or community action agencies. For most of the examples just mentioned, adult education is a minor concern, generally narrow in focus and informal. Other organizations in this general category, however, such as churches and other religious organizations, Y's, and health associations (Red Cross, American Heart Association) often devote a considerable part of their energies to organized adult education. A national survey of organized adult education activities (excluding staff and volunteer training) in such private, nonprofit community organizations found the following:

1. Twenty-nine percent of America's churches and synagogues offered organized adult education activities (more than a fourth in nonreligious subjects) to 3,604,000 adults.
2. Other religious organizations (national church groups, Salvation Army, etc.) served another 474,000 persons.

3. Y's and Red Cross chapters provided adult education for 3,050,000 persons at some 3,360 sites.
4. Civic organizations, such as senior citizen groups, political groups, and neighborhood centers served a total of 1,175,000 adults in organized educational programs.
5. Social organizations, such as social and literary societies, theater and music groups, and other "miscellaneous" organizations provided adult education to 370,000 participants.[38]

It might be noted that the total of nearly 11 million participants is more than five times that found in a national survey of individuals (rather than of the community organizations) in the same year. Yet the larger estimate seems plausible.[39] Since many of the educational activities in question are of short duration (60 percent lasted between 3 and 19 hours) and informal, individuals may in many cases forget such participation or not consider it "educational." In any event, community organizations— especially churches—are a major source of informal, but nonetheless organized, adult education.

Occupational Associations

Virtually every occupational group in our society is organized into one or more membership organizations that exist to advance the interests of their members. These organizations can be considered quasi-educational in that most of them are devoted, among other things, to their members' professional or occupational development and therefore are concerned with continuing education. A large number of associations are organized nationally, usually with chapters or branches at the state and local levels. Others are local (usually county- or city-based) or state groups. Within the health professions alone there are thousands of such associations serving physicians, dentists, nurses, pharmacists, public health officers, respiratory therapists, physical therapists, dental hygienists, hospital administrators, and so on. But the established professions such as medicine, law, engineering, architecture, and education are merely the tip of the iceberg; all occupational groups are organized in some fashion and many encourage or even require their members to maintain or enhance their proficiencies through continuing education.

While numerous occupational associations rely to some degree on educational institutions to organize educational programs for their members, many operate their own educational programs and a few depend on the services of specialized educational organizations, such as the combined American Management Associations, the American Institutes of Banking, and the American College in Bryn Mawr, Pennsylvania, which is the sole source of continuing education for certain specialists in the insurance industry. The role of occupational associations in adult education will almost certainly expand if only because more occupations are encouraging or requiring continuing education for maintaining licensure, certification, or membership. Whether this trend toward mandatory continuing education is desirable or not is a hotly debated issue, which will be examined closely in Chapter 7.

NONEDUCATIONAL ORGANIZATIONS

Noneducational organizations utilize education to enhance the achievement of such goals as making money, curing the sick, rehabilitating prisoners, or advancing the economic interests of workers. In such settings, then, education is more a means than an end. It might be argued that this is true of some quasi-educational organizations, such as occupational associations, and that it is not true of at least some hospitals, prisons, and trade unions. Whether education in a particular setting is best viewed as a means or an end, a goal or a facilitating function, is a matter of opinion. However, most government agencies, prisons, unions, and hospitals are not primarily educational organizations nor, for the most part, do they fit our definition of quasi-educational organizations. Nevertheless, the boundaries are admittedly blurred.

Business and Industry

The educational activities of American industry have mushroomed in the decades since World War II. This growth has been so great that the business corporation has become one of the principal educative forces in contemporary society. This has occurred for a host of reasons, including rapid technical change, the increasing complexity of most jobs, a sharp increase in individual mobility both within and across occupational categories, the widespread recognition that "human resources" are a valuable asset that should be "developed" on a continuous basis, and a plethora of governmental regulations that require corporations to provide training in a multitude of areas related to occupational safety, quality assurance, and compliance with various legislative mandates related to environmental protection, consumer rights, affirmative action, and so on.

While these and other reasons account for the rapid growth of education in industry, the importance of the corporation as an educative institution stems from its impact on people. Some 32 million Americans work for mid- to large-sized corporations that employ 500 or more employees.[40] They spend about half their waking hours for 30 to 50 years in such an environment and depend on the corporation not only for a livelihood, but also for the satisfaction of other vitally important needs. Moreover, the hidden curriculum of the corporation—the habits, values, attitudes, and beliefs that it deliberately but informally teaches—is surely a powerful form of education. In the long run, it may be as potent in its educative effects as the curricula of schools and colleges.

The stereotype of education in industry as narrow, job-related training is far from accurate.[41] While a great deal of training is job-specific and skills-oriented, the "corporate curriculum" encompasses much more than vocational education. Virtually every subject that is taught in schools and colleges is also taught by some businesses and industries. Programs for managers and supervisors include a range of subjects, for example, human relations, written and oral communication, business ethics, career planning, health and physical fitness, as well as various business topics related to marketing, finance, management theory, personnel supervision, law, accounting, and hundreds of other specialized concerns. Programs for scientists, engineers, architects, and other professionals employed in industry are likewise wide-ranging and sophisticated, sometimes even more advanced than Ph.D. training in the same fields at the nation's leading universities. Educational programming for lower-level employees, such as production workers, clerks, and secretaries, is generally less extensive and more narrowly job-related. Even so, many companies offer adult basic education to upgrade workers' reading, writing, and computation skills, along with on-site high school completion classes, usually in collaboration with a local school system or community college. In addition, most larger corporations provide tuition-assistance plans that enable employees to continue their education in a school or college with some or all expenses paid by the company.

While in most corporations education is highly decentralized, and classrooms can be found in virtually every plant or office building, there has been a trend in recent years for larger companies to conduct at least a portion of their programming in residential education centers that in some ways are like small universities. Xerox's International Center for Training and Management Development, described by its director, is one example:

> The Center . . . has accommodations to handle 1,014 students in residence at one time. The actual square footage is 1,200,000. We have very complete audiovisual capabilities, and closed circuit TV in all the classrooms. . . . The center is pretty much self-contained. We have a barber and beauty shop, medical facilities, gift shop, newsstand, small resource center, library, cocktail lounge, snack bar, and dining room that will accommodate 750 people at one time.[42]

The Xerox Center, like most others, operates yearlong at full capacity and provides an extensive array of courses in managerial and technical subjects. At the heart of the center is its Education Services Group, which the center's director describes as "a small cadre of professional educators,

Ph.D.'s who have responsibility for making sure that everything we do . . . is educationally sound . . . in terms of design, content, and teaching methodology."[43] The actual instructors are described as the company's best performers in sales and service. They are given intensive training in teaching methods in preparation for a three-year tour of duty at the center. The instructors are characterized as highly motivated, for if they perform well at the center they are guaranteed a promotion to a first-line management position. Xerox and similar corporations take education very seriously.

Not only do many companies operate their own educational programs and facilities, but they collaborate with colleges, universities, and other educational institutions to provide certain kinds of educational experiences for their employees. Courses, and even entire degree programs, are offered by colleges and universities on-site for employees of hundreds of companies in the United States and Canada. Other institutions, such as school systems, provide basic education, high school completion, and vocational training programs for business and industry personnel. Corporations also utilize the services of private consulting and training companies and organizations such as the combined American Management Associations. In a study of education/industry cooperation in New Jersey, Beder and Darkenwald found that approximately half the companies surveyed had collaborated with at least one educational institution in some kind of joint program between 1977 and 1979.[44]

The educational role of the business corporation is not confined to employee education and development. Many companies, for example, are heavily engaged in customer or consumer education for "good will" or product promotion purposes or to assist customers to make more effective use of the products or services they have purchased. Purchasers of industrial, scientific, or office equipment usually must be trained to operate and maintain such products. Sales personnel often perform this training, but many companies maintain special customer education departments for this purpose and others operate residential training centers where courses range in duration from a few days to several weeks. Digital Equipment Corporation, for example, offers about 100 different courses each year at its residential education center. A recent customer education course catalog ran to 239 pages. Many retail establishments such as supermarket chains and companies that sell sewing machines, home computers, building supplies, and the like also offer short courses for customers or potential customers. Various businesses also provide educational activities for the general public. Utility companies offer short courses on energy conservation, banks and brokerage firms on how to invest money, insurance companies on health and physical fitness, and so on.

The number of adults who participate in educational activities sponsored by business and industry can be only roughly estimated. According to the National Center for Education Statistics, approximately 3.2 million adults participated in 1978 in educational activities sponsored by business and industry.[45] A 1975 survey of mid- to large-size companies estimated participation in company sponsored courses at 4.4 million, with an additional 1.3 million participating in tuition aid programs.[46] A particularly significant statistic is that one-fourth of all adult education participants on 1978 reported that the cost of their education was paid by their employers.[47] Finally, it should be noted that educational opportunities and participation rates vary greatly from company to company. Where one works can be more important than where one lives in regard to resources for adult learning. At many high-technology corporations, such as AT&T, Xerox, and IBM, a large portion of the work force is continually engaged in both formal and informal learning. At one such company, Oregon's Tektronix Corporation, approximately 85 percent of the firm's 15,000 employees have participated in educational programs. In 1978 alone 6,872 employees completed 13,702 courses, most of them at the company's facilities in suburban Portland.[48]

The modern corporation exerts an enormous influence on the education of the public, and the extent of this influence is generally not recognized even within the business community. It should be added, however, that industry's educational activities may not in every case serve the best interests of its employees or the public. In some instances what business may consider education or training others may view as propaganda or indoctrination.

Government Agencies

The second largest employer in the United States is the government. According to the Census Bureau, approximately 15 million people are employed in government service, not including the approximately two million men and women in the armed forces.[49] Of these 15 million, roughly two-fifths are employed at the state and federal levels and three-fifths at the local level. Education and training activities at all levels of government are extensive. In fact, the rate of participation in organized educational activities appears to be higher among government workers than employees in private business and industry. Until recently, information about the general scope of education and training at various levels of government was difficult to obtain, but Peterson has produced an excellent review of the scattered literature on this subject from which most of the following data were obtained.[50]

A Civil Service Commission study found that in 1976 roughly one-fifth of the nation's 2.8 million federal employees participated in one or more organized learning activities of at least 8 hours duration. While most of the training was sponsored by a particular department or agency for its own employees, about one-third was provided by other government units and by nongovernment organizations such as consulting firms, professional associations, and universities. The bulk of the training was geared to employees' specific job requirements (29 percent) and to various topics classified under the broad category of management and supervision (30 percent).[51]

Education for state-level employees tends to parallel that at the federal level. Federal agencies concerned with commerce, labor, housing, education, health, and so on have their counterparts in each of the 50 states and these state agencies generally maintain their own training departments. While data on state-level training activities are scarce, the numbers involved and the expenditures are enormous. One study reported that in California in 1975, "just over 191,000 state employees were . . . involved in in-house training, and the state contributed slightly over $1 million for outside (career-related) education."[52]

Training for employees of local government is often conducted in cooperation with educational institutions, particularly state universities and community colleges. "In-house" training, however, is widespread. A 1975 survey of cities of over 10,000 population found that two-thirds sponsored their own training programs for municipal employees.[53] Agencies of state government also are a major provider of training for local government employees, as are private consulting firms, the International City Management Association, the American Management Associations, and the National Training and Development Service.[54]

Armed Forces

Education in the military, which today employs about two million men and women, is an immense and exceedingly varied enterprise. In peacetime the major activity of most military personnel, aside from their work assignments, is learning. While much of this learning is job-related, it has wider significance in that some 90 percent of all military occupational specialties are transferable to civilian jobs.[55] According to Carr and Ripley, "each year the military graduates more than one million individuals from about 5,000 separate training courses produced within the Department of Defense. At the same time, about a half million service men and women are involved in educational programs conducted by more than 1,000 civilian institutions."[56] When one considers that the great majority of armed services personnel return sooner or later to civilian life, the enormous importance of military education programs—both to the millions of individuals involved and the larger society that benefits from their skills—is readily apparent.

Each branch of the military operates both its own voluntary education program and specialized training programs (which are not voluntary) for various military occupational specialties. The voluntary education programs—General Educational Development (Army), Navy Campus for Achievement, Education Services Program (Air Force), and the Marine Corps' Voluntary Education Program—are "the military version of an adult education program in which the individual participates during off-duty time and for which he pays a portion, usually 25 percent, of the tuition."[57] The Air Force also maintains a Community College of the Air Force, which consists of an administrative headquarters and seven Air Force technical training institutes, each of which is regionally accredited as a two-year college.

Two major programs that serve military personnel in all branches of the armed forces are DANTES (Defense Activity for Non-Traditional Education Support) and the Serviceman's Opportunity College. DANTES offers a high school completion program at overseas locations, administers a worldwide credit-by-examination program, and publishes a catalog of correspondence study courses offered by accredited civilian institutions. The Serviceman's Opportunity College, jointly funded by the Department of Defense and the Carnegie Corporation, is not a single institution but rather a "network of more than 360 civilian institutions [that] supports military education through adaptable residency requirements and a generous transfer policy."[58] This kind of flexibility is particularly important for geographically mobile military personnel who wish to earn a college degree.

In addition to the programs sketched above, the military provides counseling and testing services, adult literacy instruction, human relations training, and many other educational services to its uniformed personnel. It is also heavily engaged in educational research and development. All told, it is one of the world's largest producers and users of adult education and a major force in the education of the American public. This is particularly true for millions of less advantaged men and women, who, were it not for their military service, would have encountered great obstacles to continuing their education.

Unions

In Western European countries, such as Britain and Sweden, organized labor has long been a major force in adult education. For a number of reasons, this has not been true of the labor movement in North America. Nonetheless, many individual unions are active in providing educational opportunities to their employees and members.

There are basically three dimensions to union-related education: apprenticeship training, labor or worker's education, and labor studies. Apprenticeship training, which is required before one can practice certain crafts and trades, such as plumbing and carpentry, involves some 2,000 hours of classroom and on-the-job training. The formal instruction is often provided by community colleges or vocational-technical institutions rather than by the unions themselves. Approximately half a million workers participate in apprenticeship programs each year.[59]

Labor education refers to nonvocational training designed "to enable workers to function more effectively as unionists, to help them understand society and fulfill their obligations as citizens, and to promote individual development."[60] While churches, Y's, adult schools, and political action groups were once major providers of labor education, today, according to a recent report by MacKenzie, unions and land grant universities are the only significant providers, together accounting for some 95 percent of all labor education in the United States. Of the approximately 200 national and international unions, about 25 percent maintain education departments that are active in labor education programming, most of it geared to union leadership development (typical courses include union administration, labor law, collective bargaining, and steward training). Other unions rely heavily on labor education centers at land grant universities such as Penn State, Rutgers, and West Virginia for similar leadership development programming. The AFL-CIO maintains a large residential education center—The George Meany Center for Labor Studies—which provides one- to three-week training programs for union officials from all parts of the country.

The term labor studies refers to an emerging field of interdisciplinary study that has grown rapidly in the last decade. Labor studies degree programs have been established at approximately 40 institutions.[61] In a sense labor studies is the formal, degree-credit counterpart to noncredit labor education programs. Most labor studies students are union employees or members.

With its 21.5 million members, organized labor could play a vastly expanded role in adult education. A few prominent labor leaders have advocated federal labor education legislation modeled after the Cooperative Extension Service. Legislation of this kind could have a major impact on promoting access to continuing education for American workers, but it is unlikely to be adopted without the vigorous backing of the AFL-CIO leadership—which so far has been lacking.

Correctional Institutions

The prison population in the United States is something on the order of 425,000. More than half of these individuals are incarcerated in state institutions, 150,000 are in local jails, and about 25,000 are in federal facilities.[62] The majority of inmates are poor, undereducated, and lacking in the skills necessary to get a job. Education and job training programs are extensive in the federal facilities, somewhat less adequate in most state prisons, and generally inadequate or nonexistent in local jails. While there are many innovative and apparently successful educational and job training programs in prisons, the general picture, as McCollum paints it, is unsurprising:

> The current range and quality of educational and vocational programs offered and the rate of prisoner participation vary widely. . . . Some institutions provide adult basic education (ABE) as well as classes at all elementary and secondary levels, including the opportunity to complete high school-equivalency (GED) courses. In addition, most prisons offer some vocational training. . . . Postsecondary programs also are generally available. . . . "Study release" for college courses is a new concept that is just beginning to receive significant support in a few prison systems.[63]

Most larger prisons employ their own educational personnel, particularly for vocational, ABE, and high school completion programs. Turnover seems to be high, probably because prisons are frustrating environments for teaching and learning.

Other Agencies

Many other kinds of noneducational organizations are actively involved in adult education. Hospitals and other health care agencies, as noted earlier in this chapter, offer in-service training programs for their employees, patient education, community health education, and continuing professional education for health care professionals in their service areas. Learning and education are important aspects of the day-to-day functioning of most hospitals and health centers. In the economic sector, several hundred trade associations, such as the American Iron and Steel Institute, provide a variety of educational programs for employees of their member firms. So, too, do broad-based national business organizations such as the Chamber of Commerce of the United States and the National Association of Manufacturers.[64] Many other kinds of organizations provide adult education to their members, employees, clients, or the public; in fact, there seems to be no type of organization that does not.

FEDERAL AND STATE ROLES

It is obvious from the preceding overview of adult education agencies and programs that there is no national system of adult education in the United States. As Knowles recently put it:

> Adult education in this country is not "organized" in the dictionary sense of being formed into a coherent unity or functioning whole. It is a complex mosaic of unrelated activities and processes that permeate almost all the established organizations in our society.[65]

While in general adult education is indeed unorganized, parts of the field are more organized than they once were, principally because of the increasing involvement of state and federal government. While still modest, the role of government has expanded greatly since the early 1960s, primarily as a result of new federal legislation aimed at expanding educational opportunity for disadvantaged adults.

While hundreds of federal and state enactments provide financial support for adult education (usually through narrowly targeted programs), only a few have had a broad impact nationally. Most of these were initiated in the 1960s. Notable exceptions are the Smith-Lever Act of 1914, which established the Cooperative Extension Service, and the Smith-Hughes Act of 1917, a broad program of support for vocational education, including adult vocational education. The ensuing discussion emphasizes the legislative programs of the 1960s, particularly the Adult Education Act of 1966, which was probably the most significant piece of adult education legislation since the passage of Smith-Lever. Its importance comes not so much from the size of the program in dollar or enrollment terms as from the impetus it provided for growing federal and state involvement in policymaking, coordination, and professional leadership for an expanding segment of the field.

Adult Education Act of 1966

The Adult Education Act of 1966, part of the Elementary and Secondary Education Act of that year, originated two years earlier with the Economic Opportunity Act, part of President Johnson's War on Poverty. The Adult Education Act established a national program of adult basic education (ABE) for the purpose of educating adults "whose inability to speak, read, or write the English language constitutes a substantial impairment of their ability to get or retain employment commensurate with their real ability." ABE was interpreted to mean education designed to: (1) "help eliminate such inability"; (2) "raise the level of education of such individuals"; (3) "improve their ability to benefit from occupational training"; and (4) "make them better able to meet their adult responsibility."[66]

In addition to providing for costs of instruction and program administration, the act mandated that a portion of the total appropriation be utilized for staff training and special projects of a research and development nature. The Adult Education Act has been amended several times, mainly to increase the scope and flexibility of the ABE program and give the states more control over staff development and special projects.[67] While the emphasis on serving the least educated has been retained, a portion of the funds now can be used for high school completion programs. A significant recent change allows state education departments to channel operating funds to community agencies other than public educational institutions.

The federal appropriation for ABE in 1980–1981 was $100 million. About 1.8 million adults were enrolled. The amount of money involved is only a fraction of what the Cooperative Extension Service, the military, or even AT&T spends for adult education each year. However, because it has been integrated into the powerful federal and state educational bureaucracies and because of its links to the massive labor training programs of the Comprehensive Employment and Training Act, the ABE program has come to be a focal point for much of the policymaking, coordination, and professional development activity that does exist in adult education in the United States.

Government Role in Planning and Coordination

Coordination of adult education at all levels of government has two basic and interrelated dimensions. One involves coordination among different legislated programs with similar or complementary objectives, and the other involves coordination among different kinds of institutions or delivery systems that provide similar or complementary adult education services. A complete analysis of the issues in coordinating adult education is beyond our scope. Consequently, the discussion here focuses on two legislated programs—ABE and manpower training under the Comprehensive Employment and Training Act—and the problems of articulation between the school-based delivery system and the postsecondary system.

The Comprehensive Employment and Training Act (CETA) is a multi-billion-dollar program designed to combat unemployment and underemployment. While most of the funds, until recently, have been used to provide public service jobs for the unemployed, job training, as well as adult basic education for those deemed in need of it, have been major components of CETA. Despite its heavy educational emphasis, CETA is administered through the U.S. Department of Labor, not the Department of Education. It is highly decentralized, with many important decisions, such as who will be trained for what by whom, made by so-called prime sponsors, that is the CETA units of county or municipal governments. There are also state-level CETA organizations, again attached to departments of labor or their equivalents, which are responsible for various aspects of policymaking, planning, and coordination. A few CETA prime sponsors run their own vocational training and adult basic education programs, but the great majority contract for these services with community colleges, vocational-technical institutions, proprietary schools, and public school adult education agencies.

As might be expected, problems of planning and coordination involving CETA and related adult education programs begin in

Washington and spread downward through the state capitals to the local level where the actual programming takes place. The difficulties of coordinating these programs have long been recognized and repeated efforts made at the state and federal levels to remedy them through legislation and administrative directives mandating collaboration in planning and implementing CETA, ABE, and vocational education. These attempts to minimize waste and confusion in programs for undereducated and underemployed adults have met with mixed success.[68]

It is perhaps understandable that two federal departments, education and labor, and their state counterparts would encounter difficulty in coordinating educational programs for adults. Coordination of adult education is a problem, however, even within the U.S. Department of Education and most of the 50 state education agencies. This is partly caused by the fact that federal and state education agencies are oriented toward institutional "levels" and adult education, like vocational education, cuts across the elementary/secondary and postsecondary levels. Further compounding the situation is the semiautonomous status of vocational education, a result of heavy federal funding. Vocational education itself is fractured into levels.

A brief review of adult education's place in the U.S. Department of Education illustrates the problem. Adult education functions are assigned to two major offices in the department: the Office of the Assistant Secretary for Vocational and Adult Education and the Office of the Assistant Secretary for Postsecondary Education. The former office includes a division of adult education (under a deputy assistant secretary for adult learning and school-community relations), which administers the programs of the Adult Education Act, and another unit, under a different deputy assistant secretary, for adult occupational education. The second unit is responsible for adult programs funded under the Vocational Education Act. In the Office of the Assistant Secretary for Postsecondary Education there is a deputy assistant secretary for higher and continuing education who oversees some ten operating units, only one of which— community services and continuing education—has anything to do with continuing education. This unit's main function is to administer the community services and continuing education program authorized under Title I of the Higher Education Act; this is a small program that provides only short-term funding.

It should be clear from this brief description how fragmented adult education in the U.S. Department of Education is. Federal legislation has in effect established separate dominions for adult basic education, adult occupational education, and adult higher education. For the first and last of these there are even separate presidential advisory councils: the National Advisory Council on Adult Education and the National Advisory

Council on Extension and Continuing Education. The dominion of ABE enjoys a larger staff and higher official status in the department because the program it administers is much larger and more politically secure than the postsecondary community services program.

Fragmentation like that in the U.S. Department of Education is visible at the state and local levels as well. A number of states have even established separate departments or regulatory agencies for postsecondary education. This development seems to have exacerbated the problem of coordination in those states that use both the public schools and postsecondary institutions as delivery systems for ABE, adult vocational education, and related programs. In other states where community college or postsecondary vocational-technical education systems are the sole providers of both adult basic education and federally funded adult vocational education, there may be fewer problems of coordination. However, there is little evidence as to whether this is so.

An additional ramification of governmental control and coordination is the growing trend toward state regulation of public institutions that receive state support for adult education through enrollment-based reimbursement formulas. In some states limitations have been placed on the amount of money that can be generated by enrollment-based subsidies, thereby curtailing the expansion of certain adult education activities. State agencies can also exert considerable regulatory power through defining the kinds of courses or programs eligible for support and by restricting the scope or focus of adult education in different institutional sectors. Like education in general, publicly supported adult education has in the last decade been subjected to ever-closer scrutiny and control by economy-minded legislators and bureaucrats. This trend is not likely to reverse itself in the 1980s.

VOLUNTARY COORDINATION

The role of government in coordinating adult education centers mostly on federally funded state-grant programs such as ABE and the adult education activities of publicly financed educational institutions, particularly at the postsecondary level. These programs and delivery systems, including those beyond the purview of federal and state education agencies, such as CETA and the Cooperative Extension Service, comprise only a part (albeit an important one) of the total adult education enterprise in the United States. Government has little to do with coordinating adult education outside the sphere of publicly funded programs and institutions. Business and industry, unions, community health and social service agencies, museums, libraries, occupational associations, churches, and many other important providers of adult education remain beyond the

scope of direct governmental control. As a consequence, any cooperation and coordination involving the broader spectrum of providers of adult
education has been limited to voluntary efforts.

National and State Levels

Adult education lacks a powerful national organization to represent the
interests of the entire field and to facilitate cooperation and coordination
at the national level. The one organization that comes closest to playing
such a role is the Coalition of Adult Education Organizations (CAEO).
The CAEO counts among its members the Adult Education Association of
the U.S.A., the National University Continuing Education Association,
the National Home Study Council, the National Association of Educational Broadcasters, and many other national organizations concerned
with adult education. Among its major purposes are:

1. To identify and focus on major issues in adult and continuing
   education.
2. To facilitate the exchange of information about resources, actions,
   and plans of its member organizations.
3. To facilitate joint planning of projects to serve the field of adult
   and continuing education.
4. To promote the support of governments, foundations, and agencies to achieve equal educational opportunity for all persons.[69]

According to a recent assessment by Griffith, the accomplishments of
the CAEO since its founding in 1969 have been limited. Nonetheless, he
concludes that because the CAEO is the only national body that
represents the total field "it is on this foundation that leaders of the adult
education profession must design their structure for coordinated action in
the future."[70]

At the state level, as discussed in Chapter 1, sustained efforts at
voluntary coordination, where they exist, are carried out primarily by
professional associations of adult educators. In many states, however,
there are multiple associations representing different institutional interests, most notably the public schools and higher education. Sometimes, as
in Michigan, New Jersey, and, more recently Illinois, these interests have
managed to work together effectively in a single association. Even in
these states, however, the adult education associations consist mainly of
people employed by public schools and higher education institutions.
Adult educators who work in industry, libraries, and other nonschool
settings seldom are members. Griffith is probably correct in concluding
that at the state level "the forces that tend to fractionize the field of adult
education continue to be almost equal in strength to those favoring
coordination."[71]

Local Councils and Committees

Councils or committees consisting of representatives of local organizations that sponsor adult education abound. Usually, they are constituted on a municipal or county basis. The major function they perform is to serve as a vehicle for informal communication and coordination, although they may also conduct needs assessment studies, publish directories of local programs and services, and engage in political lobbying. Strangely, such councils in the larger cities, such as New York and Chicago, were quite active 20 or 30 years ago but have since declined or disbanded. Establishing a secure financial base has always been a problem for such organizations, but that does not explain their decline in the years when adult education has grown most rapidly. Perhaps it has been this growth itself, much of it supported by public funds channeled to schools and colleges, that has undermined the broad-based community support for the field that existed when adult education was less visibly associated with educational institutions. Despite the discouraging trend in some larger cities, local councils and committees continue to play an important role in coordinating the activities of a broad range of adult education agencies in communities across the nation.

LIMITS OF PLANNING AND COORDINATION

Few would deny that state and federal governments have the right and obligation to ensure that public funds for adult education are utilized as effectively as possible. Planning and coordination are necessary not only for reasons of economy, but also to improve the quality of services provided to adult learners. There is always of course the danger that government intervention will result in effects opposite from those intended. For example, too much regulation can stifle the responsiveness of institutions to public needs or diminish the benefits to adult learners of healthy competition among agencies. It is not always easy to discriminate between responsiveness and opportunism or between healthy competition and that which is wasteful. Whatever one's opinions, the trend toward a larger governmental role in controlling and coordinating publicly funded adult education is likely to continue. So far, the benefits have probably exceeded the costs.

Voluntary coordination entails fewer risks, although incentives and resources for positive and effective action are all too often lacking. A major problem is the absence of adequate funding to enable organizations such as the Coalition of Adult Education Organizations, state professional groups, and local adult education councils to undertake systematic and sustained efforts toward comprehensive planning and coordination. Without stable funding and paid professional leadership, these voluntary organizations cannot be expected to function in the future any more effectively than they do today.

Existing governmental and voluntary attempts at planning and coordination on the national level are, as we have seen, limited in scope and effectiveness. Nonetheless, a major issue today is whether the government should play an expanded role in the planning and management of adult education. This seems to be happening in some Western European countries, with their long traditions of centralized control of education. The impetus for these developments in European nations has come in part from the influential Organization for Economic Cooperation and Development (OECD), to which Canada and the United States also belong. In one of its many policy papers on the subject, the OECD outlined four options for the future development of adult education in member countries:

1. To let it evolve, as in the past, in a spontaneous and sporadic fashion without reference to any explicit public intervention;
2. To strengthen and coordinate the existing range of activities but not to perceive it as an active instrument of public policy in the social and economic arenas;
3. To strengthen and coordinate the existing range of activities while simultaneously pursuing a positive policy of support for specific activities judged to be national priorities . . . ; and
4. To create a comprehensive service of adult education as an integral element of broadly conceived educational systems and to relate its functions to the social, economic, and cultural objectives of the nation.[72]

The policies of adult education in the United States today could be said to correspond somewhat to the third option, if indeed such federal programs as ABE and vocational education and the work of the Cooperative Extension Service constitute national priorities. The option recommended by the OECD, however, is the fourth: that is, the establishment by the government of a comprehensive, nationwide adult education system. Such a course of action, while possibly viable in Sweden or Denmark, would be inappropriate for a nation like the United States. The multitude of diverse adult education agencies in the United States could not be reconstituted, redirected, or ignored in the interest of establishing a single national system. That private sector, nonschool agencies would cooperate in such a plan is particularly unlikely. Not only would the financial, legal, and political barriers to such a scheme be insurmountable but there is no reason to believe that a "comprehensive service" would be any improvement over the current, unplanned system of adult education.

CONCLUSION

Governmental policymakers and planners accustomed to thinking in terms of monolithic delivery systems that can be targeted on specific social or economic goals are bound to be frustrated by adult education's enormous diversity and complexity. Yet it may very well be that the profusion of purposes and agencies that characterizes the adult education enterprise in the United States is not a problem to be overcome but rather the basic source of adult education's vitality and effectiveness. No one institution or delivery system or "comprehensive service" could possibly address more than a fraction of the educational needs and interests of the adult public in the United States. Moreover, the needs of the public and the organizations to which adults belong or for which they work are continually changing. Even to monitor such changes would be a herculean task for any single agency or group of planners.

To some extent, adult education in the United States functions in a manner analogous to that of a free market economy. There is limited governmental planning and regulation, and educational services are provided by a variety of organizations largely in response to public demand. The great advantage of this state of affairs is that many needs are met and the quality of programs and services for adult learners is often enhanced through the competition of the educational marketplace. There are of course disadvantages to a free market system of adult education, some of which have previously been noted. Perhaps the most serious is that many adults cannot afford the cost of continuing their education. Federally funded programs, such as ABE, and state subsidies for adult education in publicly controlled educational institutions have mitigated but not resolved the problem. Most adult educators agree that it is not only unjust, but detrimental to the public good, that many poor and disadvantaged adults are denied the benefits of continuing education because they lack the necessary financial resources. The major challenge of the 1980s and 1990s would seem to be not the establishment of a national system of adult education, but rather the fostering by the government of a more equitable utilization of existing resources for lifelong learning so that no sector of society will be denied the opportunity for continued learning and development.

NOTES

1. Patrick Penland, "Self-Initiated Learning." *Adult Education* 29, no. 3 (1979): 170–179.
2. Abraham Carp, Richard Peterson, and Pamela Roelfs, "Adult Learning Interests and Experiences," in *Planning Non-Traditional Programs*, ed. K. Patricia Cross and John Valley (San Francisco: Jossey-Bass, 1974).

3. James M. Heffernan, Francis U. Macy, and Donn F. Vickers, *Educational Brokering: A New Service for Adult Learners* (Syracuse, N.Y.: National Center for Educational Brokering, 1976).
4. Lawrence A. Cremin, *American Education: The Colonial Experience 1607–1783* (New York: Harper & Row, 1970).
5. Judith Simon and Elaine Belz, "A Look at Network Learning Systems," *Lifelong Learning* 4 (December 1980): 22–24.
6. Malcolm Knowles, "The Field of Operations in Adult Education," in *Adult Education: Outlines of an Emerging Field of University Study*, ed. Gale Jensen, A. A. Liveright, and Wilbur Hallenbeck (Chicago: Adult Education Association of the U.S.A., 1964), p. 42.
7. Peter M. Blau and W. Richard Scott, *Formal Organizations* (San Francisco: Intext, 1962).
8. Knowles, "Field of Operations in Adult Education."
9. Cyril O. Houle, "Adult Education," in *Encyclopedia of Educational Research*, ed. R. Ebel (New York: Macmillan, 1969).
10. Knowles, "Field of Operations in Adult Education," p. 42.
11. C. Hartley Grattan, *In Quest of Knowledge* (New York: Association Press, 1955).
12. Sharan Merriam, "Independent Adult Schools," *Lifelong Learning* 1 (November 1977): 19–21, 25, 30.
13. Frank Adams, *Unearthing Seeds of Fire: The Idea of Highlander* (Winston-Salem, N.C.: Blair, 1975).
14. Ronald Gross, *The Lifelong Learner: A Guide to Self-Development* (New York: Simon & Schuster, 1977).
15. Ibid.
16. National Center for Education Statistics, *Programs and Enrollments in Non-Collegiate Postsecondary Schools: 1973–74* (Washington, D.C.: Government Printing Office, 1976).
17. National Center for Education Statistics, *Participation of Adults in Education: 1978 Preliminary Report* (Washington, D.C.: U.S. Department of Education, 1980).
18. K. Patricia Cross and John Valley, "Non-Traditional Study: An Overview," in *Planning Non-Traditional Programs*, ed. Cross and Valley, p. 1.
19. Cyril O. Houle, *The External Degree* (San Francisco: Jossey-Bass, 1973), p. 19.
20. James A. Lenox and Sharan Merriam, "The Weekend Adult School: An Experiment in High School Completion," *Lifelong Learning* 3 (December 1979): 24–25, 31.
21. Grattan, *In Quest of Knowledge*, p. 218.
22. Gunder A. Myran, *Community Services in the Community College* (Washington, D.C.: American Association of Junior Colleges, 1969).
23. National Center for Education Statistics, *Noncredit Activities in Institutions of Higher Education for the Year Ending June 30, 1976* (Washington, D.C.: Government Printing Office, 1978), p. 17.
24. Ervin L. Harlacher, "Community Colleges," in *Handbook of Adult Education*, ed. Robert M. Smith, George Aker, and J. R. Kidd (New York: Macmillan, 1970), p. 227.

25. Grattan, *In Quest of Knowledge*, pp. 185–190.
26. National Center for Education Statistics, *Noncredit Activities*, p. 3.
27. Ibid., p. 15.
28. Janet Ruyle and Lucy Ann Geiselman, "Non-Traditional Opportunities and Programs," in *Planning Non-Traditional Programs*, ed. Cross and Valley, p. 69.
29. Edgar J. Boone, "The Cooperative Extension Service," in *Handbook of Adult Education*, ed. Smith, Aker, and Kidd, p. 265.
30. Extension Service, U.S., Department of Agriculture, *Cooperative Extension Service Programs: A Unique Partnership Between Public and Private Interests* (Washington, D.C.: Government Printing Office, 1976).
31. H. C. Sanders, quoted by Boone, "Cooperative Extension Service," p. 266.
32. Wayne L. Schroeder, "Adult Education Defined and Described," in *Handbook of Adult Education*, ed. Smith, Aker, and Kidd, p. 37.
33. National Center for Education Statistics, *Adult Education in Community Organizations 1972* (Washington, D.C.: Government Printing Office, 1974), p. 2.
34. Margaret E. Monroe, "Public Libraries and Museums," in *Handbook of Adult Education*, ed. Smith, Aker, and Kidd, p. 246.
35. American Association of Museums, *A Statistical Survey of Museums in the United States and Canada* (Washington, D.C.: American Association of Museums, 1965).
36. Carnegie Task Force on Public Broadcasting, *Summary Report* (New York: Carnegie Corporation, 1977).
37. Carp, Peterson, and Roelfs, "Adult Learning Interests and Experiences," p. 30.
38. National Center for Education Statistics, *Adult Education in Community Organizations*, pp. 3–4.
39. Ibid., pp. 33–35.
40. Seymour Lusterman, *Education in Industry* (New York: Conference Board, 1977), p. 5.
41. Harold F. Clark and Harold S. Sloan, *Classrooms in the Factories* (New York: New York University Press, 1958).
42. Willard H. Duetting, "Welcoming Comments," in *Proceedings of the Invitational Conference on Continuing Education, Manpower Policy and Lifelong Learning* (Washington, D.C.: National Advisory Council on Extension and Continuing Education, 1977), p. 8.
43. Ibid.
44. Harold W. Beder and Gordon G. Darkenwald, *Cooperation Between Educational Institutions and Business and Industry in Adult Education and Training* (New Brunswick, N.J.: Center for Adult Development, Rutgers University, 1980).
45. National Center for Education Statistics, *Participation of Adults in Education: 1978*.
46. Lusterman, *Education in Industry*, p. 11.
47. National Center for Education Statistics, *Participation of Adults in Education: 1978*.

48. Huntly Collins, "Corporate Campus: Learning Your Way to a Better Job," *Change* 11 (July–August 1979): 68.

49. U.S., Bureau of the Census, *Statistical Abstract of the United States: 1979* (Washington, D.C.: Government Printing Office, 1979).

50. Peterson, *Lifelong Learning in America*, pp. 32–33.

51. U.S., Civil Service Commission, *Training Effort Government-Wide* (Washington, D.C.: Government Printing Office, 1977).

52. C. Seaton, *Report on Formal Instructional Programs by Business, Industry, Government, and Military in California* (Sacramento, Calif.: California Post-secondary Education Commission, 1977). Quoted in Peterson, *Lifelong Learning in America*, p. 33.

53. C. A. Brown, "Municipal Training Programs: 1975," in *Urban Data Service Reports #8* (Washington, D.C.: International City Management Association, 1976).

54. Peterson, *Lifelong Learning in America*, p. 33.

55. Ibid., p. 36.

56. Thomas W. Carr and Richard M. Ripley, "Armed Forces and Veterans' Education," in *Serving Personal and Community Needs Through Adult Education*, ed. Edgar J. Boone, Ronald W. Shearon, Estelle E. White (San Francisco: Jossey-Bass, 1980), p. 200.

57. Ibid., p. 201.

58. Ibid., p. 204.

59. Peterson, *Lifelong Learning in America*, p. 31.

60. Lawrence Rogin, "Labor Unions," in *Handbook of Adult Education*, ed. Smith, Aker, and Kidd, pp. 301–302.

61. John R. MacKenzie, "Labor Education," in *Serving Personal and Community Needs*, ed. Boone, Shearon, and White, p. 208.

62. Sylvia G. McCollum, "Adult Education in Corrections," in *Serving Personal and Community Needs*, ed. Boone, Shearon, and White, p. 177.

63. Ibid., pp. 168–169.

64. Malcolm Knowles, "Field of Operations in Adult Education," p. 58.

65. Malcolm Knowles, "The Growth and Development of Adult Education," in *Building an Effective Adult Education Enterprise*, ed. John M. Peters (San Francisco: Jossey-Bass, 1980), p. 12.

66. "Rules and Regulations for the Adult Education Act of 1966," cited in Jack Mezirow, Gordon G. Darkenwald, and Alan B. Knox, *Last Gamble on Education: Dynamics of Adult Basic Education* (Washington, D.C.: Adult Education Association, 1975), pp. 2–3.

67. Vincent De Sanctis, "The Adult Basic Education Legislation: 1964–1979," *Adult Literacy and Basic Education* 3 (Winter 1980): 245–253.

68. Harold W. Beder and Gordon G. Darkenwald, *Occupational Education for Adults: An Analysis of Institutional Roles and Relationships* (New Brunswick, N.J.: Center for Adult Development, Rutgers University, 1979).

69. William S. Griffith, "Coordination of Personnel, Programs, and Services," in *Building an Effective Adult Education Enterprise*, ed. Peters, pp. 97–98.

70. Ibid., p. 98.

71. Ibid., p. 103.

72. Organization for Economic Cooperation and Development, "Comprehensive Policies for Adult Education," cited by Griffith, "Coordination of Personnel, Programs, and Services," p. 90.

Chapter 6
International Adult
Education

The complexity and scope of adult education worldwide makes coverage of the topic within a single chapter a challenging undertaking. However, while there are substantial differences in adult education from one country to the next, some commonalities can be found among industrialized nations as well as among nations of the Third World. This chapter will begin with a brief overview of adult education in Western industrialized nations and then explore, in more detail, characteristics of adult education in Third World countries. The nature of adult education in Third World nations offers an interesting contrast to that of the United States.

ADULT EDUCATION IN INDUSTRIALIZED COUNTRIES

Extracting generalities about adult education from several countries depends to some extent upon a common definition of what is being investigated. As discussed in Chapter 1, adult education may be identified with lifelong learning, or with formal, informal, nonformal, or recurrent education. In addition, the form that adult education takes in various countries differs, and one can easily become frustrated attempting to draw comparisons among Danish folk schools, Britain's Open University, and American adult schools. If emphasis is placed on the learning of adults the task becomes easier. As Verner states:

> The need to learn continuously is common to all mankind, although the ways in which this need is met vary from one culture to another. Since every society develops some pattern of habitual response to this need to learn, it is readily apparent that adult education *per se* is universal in time and space, although the method of adult education is not.[1]

Studies of adult education from a world perspective have centered upon the learning in which adults are engaged. *Learning to Be* is, in fact, the title of the report of UNESCO's International Commission on the Development of Education. For the purpose of collecting data in countries throughout the world, UNESCO proposed acceptance of the definition used in the International Standard Classification of Education (ISCED): "organized programs of education provided for the benefit of and adapted to the needs of persons not in the regular school and university system and generally 15 or older."[2] Similar to UNESCO's definition is that used by the Organization for Economic Cooperation and Development (OECD), representing 25 industrial nations. OECD defines adult education as:

> any learning activity or program deliberately designed to satisfy any learning need or interest that may be experienced at any stage in his or her life by a person who is over the statutory school-leaving age and whose principal activity is no longer in education. Its ambit thus spans nonvocational, vocational, general, formal, or nonformal studies as well as education with a collective social purpose.[3]

The second point of the OECD definition alludes to the various functions of organized adult education found in industrialized countries. Historically, these functions have been:

1. providing remedial and basic education for those who had not gone to school or who had not profited from school or who had left school at an early age;
2. giving already educated adults an opportunity to further their intellectual and cultural development with or without reference to the conferment of academic credentials;
3. enabling a relatively small number of actual or potential working-class leaders to further their education so that they might increase their usefulness to their fellow-workers;
4. providing occupationally related courses for relatively restricted groups;

5. providing courses designed to promote good citizenship through the encouragement of popular educational movements;

6. providing courses for the socialization of immigrants.[4]

Third World countries, of course, share several of these goals, but, as will be discussed later, adult education in such countries becomes a means to the overriding end of nation building. Another difference lies in the fact that industrialized countries, characterized by greater economic wealth and more leisure time, can afford the luxury of allowing their adults to pursue "intellectual and cultural development."

While the functions of adult education are similar in industrialized nations, there are differences in its administration and financing and in the configuration of its agencies and programs. There are several reasons for this phenomenon. As Knowles points out, institutions of adult education typically exemplify a response to a specific need rather than a part of an overall national design.[5] Verner offers further insight into the reasons for the uniqueness of adult education in different cultures. His seven "propositions" help explain the growth (and sometimes demise) of a particular form of adult education, as well as why transferring adult education forms from one culture to another often causes problems:

1. Every society has a need for continuous learning, but the nature and content of the need varies from one to another so that a specific need existing in one society is not necessarily common to others.

2. Different societies develop unique methods* to meet their need for continuous learning; consequently, a system of adult education established in one is not necessarily appropriate for another.

3. The method developed to meet a specific need for learning in one culture is not necessarily suited to the same need in a different culture.

4. A method developed at one place and time in one culture can be applied to the same need at other places at the same time in that culture.

5. A method developed to meet a specific need in a culture at one moment in time is not always suited to the same need in the same culture at a different moment in time.

6. A method developed to meet a specific need in a culture at one moment in time may meet a different need in the same culture at a different moment in time.

7. A method developed to meet a specific need in a culture at one moment in time may meet a different culture's need at a different moment in time.[6]

*Verner uses the term "method" to mean the pattern of organization.

ADMINISTRATION

The sporadic growth of adult education in most industrialized countries has led to a plethora of public and private agencies assuming responsibility for its existence. Consistent with Verner's observations about cultural and time-bound aspects of adult education, no observer of international adult education would cite a single system as superior to others, or recommend the adoption of a particular administrative model. What can be agreed upon is that each country should insure, through legislative or other appropriate means, that the learning needs of adults are addressed. At the World Conference on Adult Education held in Tokyo in 1972, representatives from 83 countries endorsed the recommendation that "adult education be recognized as a specific and indispensable component of education, and that legislative or other measures be taken which support the development of broadly based adult education services."[7]

Issues related to the administration of adult education from a worldwide perspective center upon the extent of centralization and coordination and the amount of integration with the country's formal school system. The variety of ways in which adult education is organized reflects these concerns. In some countries adult education is administered through a special division within the ministry of education. This would seem to ensure a recognized status for adult education within the total educational system, as well as provide a ready mechanism for articulation with other levels of education. Sweden, Norway, and Yugoslavia, for example, consider adult education equal with other sectors of the educational system. An OECD report on international adult education notes, however, that in practice the interrelationship between the two levels is tenuous in most countries.[8] The advantages and disadvantages of separating "adult education from the general education service, either explicitly or *de facto*," are pointed out by Lowe:

> Separation emphasizes the distinctiveness of adult education, helps to ensure that adult education is not despised as the pariah of the educational system, and reduces the risk that a ministry of education will constrain it in a conventional straitjacket. The disadvantages of separation are that if adult education is everyone's business it is effectively no one's business; it leads to unnecessary expenditure and to further dispersion of scarce resources; it makes the recruitment of competent full-time staff even more difficult than it is at present because nearly all educators feel that their careers are insecure when they have to step outside the formal education system. Above all, it militates against the adoption of a lifelong educational model.[9]

Aside from its integration into the educational system, usually into a ministry of education, there are several other ways adult education is organized internationally. Israel, for example, has a separate national board for adult education, administered by the national government.

Germany also has a special national agency called the Deutscher Volks-hochschul. Public funds are used to provide programs for adults through-out the country. Scandinavian countries have several national agencies among which adult education functions are distributed.[10] Finally, many countries have national nongovernmental associations. England, Switzer-land, and Australia, among others, each have one national association, Canada has 2 (one for each cultural language group), and Sweden has 12 national associations.[11]

In reality, the administration of adult education in industrialized nations occurs through a variety of public and private agencies. Such a state of affairs reflects the voluntary nature of adult education and its capacity to respond to needs as they arise. Ironically, this situation places something of a burden on the adults who wish to "find a continuum of learning programs in which one endeavor leads naturally and smoothly to another," and who thus are "forced to integrate" a learning program on their own.[12] Even in a relatively small country like Denmark which has a ministry of education responsible for adult education, a number of other ministries are also involved to a great extent: the Ministry for Social Services, Ministry for Defense and the Ministry for Labor are also responsible for a number of activities. A recently published survey showed that no fewer than 38 central organs were involved with adult education either administratively or in some other decisive way—and that no fewer than 100 different types of educational establishments partici-pated in adult education activities.[13]

The situation is similar but even more complex in a large, highly diverse country such as the United States. Knowles points out that a multitude of coordinative organizations have arisen from the institutional, subject matter, and geographical bases of adult education. Within each dimension there are subgroupings, some more organized than others. Knowles concludes that "the relationship of these various parts to one another and to the whole field of adult education has not been sys-tematized and made clear."[14]

FINANCE

The sources and extent of financial support for adult education are an equally complex issue. Even gathering information for the purpose of comparison poses problems, as the OECD report indicates:

> Many adult education programs are run by public authorities with responsibility for the general education service or by agencies for which adult education is only a secondary or incidental concern.
> For central or even local government the expenditure on adult education may be so small a percentage of the gross expenditure

on education that it is administratively not worthwhile to keep a
separate account and to arrange for special audits.

When adult education programs are provided by the public authorities it is often difficult to disentangle the central government
from the local government contribution.

Adult education programs are often administered and organized by
personnel with other responsibilities.

There is the danger of double counting. Many public authorities give
substantial grants to nongovernmental adult education agencies.
Both the donor and the recipients usually show the grants as part
of their expenditures.

Some institutions indirectly support adult education by providing
special services (such as the public library).[15]

Case studies of adult education in nine industrialized countries—
Austria, Canada, Denmark, Germany, Italy, the Netherlands, Sweden,
the United Kingdom, and the United States—bear out the problem of
estimating expenditures. The authors of each study comment on the lack
of accurate financial information and warn that what is presented is, at
best, "suggestive," "crude," "scanty," or "speculative."[16]

While it is not possible to compare specific expenditures among
countries, some generalizations can be made with regard to the sources of
funding and the issues involved. Each country finances its adult education
through some combination of public funds, private expenditures, and
student fees. The amount of support differs from country to country and
program to program. In a UNESCO report on the financing of adult
education, "four out of seven industrially advanced countries declared
that the state made available 50 percent of the funds; one (the United
Kingdom) reported 45 percent, Poland roughly 11 percent, and Switzer-
land less than 2 percent."[17] In Canada, Japan, and the United States,
private expenditures (the bulk of which is attributable to employers)
exceed public outlay.[18]

The issues involved in financing adult education center around the
question of support for nonpublic agencies, the extent of government
responsibility, and the establishment of priorities for spending. Governmental funding of nonpublic agencies hinges, to some extent, upon
the philosophical issue of whether the service provided would ordinarily
be a public responsibility. Adult basic education in the United States, for
example, is heavily subsidized regardless of who offers the classes.
Austria, Canada, Denmark, Norway, Sweden, and the United Kingdom
also are among those countries that heavily subsidize nongovernmental
agencies.[19]

Adult educators in all countries agree that the field should receive more national public support. It is not so easy to determine what form that support should take. Suggestions range from financing recurrent education through awarding an allowance "sufficient to maintain a standard of living comparable with that attained during employment"[20] to the following list of finance-related items formulated by OECD members:

1. occupational training;
2. subsidies towards paid educational leave;
3. the building, equipment, and maintenance of centers specially designed for adult education;
4. the training of professional adult educators;
5. providing salaries of full-time administrative and teaching staff outside the employment sector and profit-making agencies;
6. preparatory and in-service training of full- and part-time staff;
7. supporting prescribed costs of activities of adult education organizations and the associations to which they may be affiliated if their own resources are insufficient for these purposes;
8. developmental programs in the areas, for example, of literacy and community development;
9. educational research with special reference to adult education.[21]

No country of course comes close to assuming responsibility for the whole range of activities listed above. Each country sets its priorities within the limits of its resources and according to its philosophical stance toward adult education and adult education's place within the total educational system. Lowe makes the point that financial questions should be considered within the larger context of establishing a comprehensive adult education program. Such a comprehensive plan could be facilitated by first taking account of both public and private providers, placing adult education within the general context of social economic policy, making a calculated attempt to link adult education with existing social institutions, and setting the priority of financial support with unmet needs.[22] Finance is an issue that cannot be separated from other aspects of adult education.

DELIVERY SYSTEMS IN INDUSTRIALIZED NATIONS

One of Verner's propositions for understanding international adult education was that different societies develop unique methods to meet their need for continuous learning.[23] Some delivery systems in industrialized countries provide primarily vocational adult education, others serve nonvocational needs, and others provide both vocational and nonvocational learning opportunities. Following is a sample of the variety of delivery systems found in industrialized nations.

Folk High Schools

Popular in Scandinavia, folk high schools are state-supported, self-governing, residential schools that offer a wide range of generally nonvocational courses. Discussion groups, study circles, and project work are the most common instructional formats. Courses vary in duration from one week to 4 to 6 months. Folk high schools differ in their specialization. Some emphasize cultural topics such as language, music, art, and literature; others emphasize gymnastics and athletics; and some offer preparatory courses for later professional study. Denmark is also experimenting with the family folk high school, where both parents and children may participate.[24]

External Degree Programs

Inspired by Britain's Open University and the University of London, several countries (Australia, Israel, Canada, Japan, the United States) now provide flexible opportunities for adults to study part-time for a college degree even though they may not meet formal university entrance requirements. Such programs are characterized by the awarding of credit either for passing examinations in a content area, or for having had relevant life experiences or training not sponsored by colleges and universities. Nontraditional instructional modes such as correspondence courses, tutorial arrangements, and televised instruction are common to external degree programs.[25]

Polyvalent Adult Education Centers

The multi-purpose polyvalent centers provide opportunities for working people "to update their knowledge or skills in respect to their various needs—technical, academic, cultural, and civic."[26] Ideally these centers respond to the needs of the local community. Versions of polyvalent centers include the workers' and people's universities in Germany, Yugoslavia, and the U.S.S.R.; certain technical colleges in the United Kingdom; and the Center for Social and Economic Co-operation in France.[27]

People's and workers' universities are unique adult education institutions, not to be confused with institutions of higher education. In Yugoslavia, the people's universities are established in rural areas and offer programs in agriculture, health, and household management. The workers' universities are primarily urban and appeal to workers. Programs offer general basic education, vocational-technical training, and ideological-political education. Funded by unions, local and district administrations, and factories, workers' universities constitute the largest focus of Yugoslavian adult education efforts.[28]

In the U.S.S.R., people's universities are sponsored locally by industrial establishments, collective farms, cultural and technical societies, and various government agencies. Different people's universities serve different interests. There are, for example, people's universities of technical progress, public health universities, and cultural people's universities. In 1974, approximately seven million adults were enrolled in 29,000 people's universities.[29]

Community Schools

The community school approach adopted in several industrialized and Third World countries attempts to make the school the focal point of community activities for children and adults of all ages. Lowe has called the community school "the most satisfactory type of adult education institution" for the following reasons:

1. it is economical since it guarantees maximum use of existing resources throughout the day and during weekends;
2. it destroys, or at least goes far towards destroying, the sense of alienation from the schools which affects many adults;
3. it facilitates the transition from school to youth activities and from youth to adult activities;
4. it provides a natural setting in which to bring together all age groups with minimum stress;
5. it allows for local community self-government and control of financial resources.[30]

Correspondence Education

Although it is difficult to estimate participation figures, most writers agree that correspondence education is a significant delivery system in adult education, particularly in Western countries, and particularly for vocational education. Estimates of the number of adults studying by correspondence in Great Britain, for example, range from 500,000 to 750,000 a year.[31] Sweden has three main correspondence organizations—one that is authorized to hold examinations for formal educational institutions, one that provides study materials that do not lead to any formal qualifications, and one that provides agricultural correspondence materials.[32] In the Netherlands, correspondence education is the most widely used form of adult education. Courses are offered largely by nonprofit schools and tuition is partially subsidized by the government.[33]

These represent only a sampling of the types of adult education found in industrialized countries. There are, of course, numerous other delivery systems such as community colleges, proprietary schools, agricultural extension services, government- and industry-sponsored programs, and so on, which reach large segments of a country's adult population. While some forms find acceptance in many countries (community schools, for example), other forms such as folk high schools or community colleges appear to be more culture-bound.

However, several general observations can be made about adult education in industrialized nations. First, most such countries lack a national policy of adult education and most countries are characterized by a variety of public and private administrative bodies and sources of financial support. Secondly, there is much rhetoric about the virtues of lifelong learning, but little substantial support. The United States, for example, passed enabling legislation for lifelong learning in 1976, but has yet to appropriate any funds. Thirdly, there is a rise in, or at least recognition of, the existence of nonformal, independent learning, and, concomitantly, innovative approaches to assisting adults in their own learning efforts. There are "education shops" in department stores in Great Britain, learning exchanges in the United States, and a television university in Germany. Finally, participation patterns in industrialized countries reveal that adult education has yet to reach those most in need. The following groups have been identified by OECD as educationally disadvantaged because of economic, social, or geographical factors: unemployed young adults, including school dropouts; certain rural populations; migrant workers; immigrants; the aged; urban poverty groups; unskilled and semi-skilled workers; unemployed and underemployed workers with little education; some categories of women (e.g., housebound mothers); and those experiencing language problems.[34] Providing opportunities and eliminating barriers to participation for these groups remains one of the greatest challenges facing industrialized countries.

ADULT EDUCATION IN THE THIRD WORLD

Adult education in the Third World offers an interesting contrast to that found in industrialized countries. Exploring adult education in Third World countries should contribute to a better understanding of international adult education.

The prominence of adult education in much of the Third World in terms of government support and public awareness is a situation to be envied by Western adult educators. Adult education plays a central rather than peripheral role in the nation-building efforts of these countries. Furthermore, adult education in Third World nations is relatively unhampered by traditional attitudes and past structures. It is, in many instances, more dynamic, innovative, and experimental. Some of the creative methods and delivery systems found in developing countries may well answer the needs of industrial nations. Finally, to the extent that all nations are interdependent, the problems and successes, failures and triumphs of Third World nations affect the industrialized world. Crop failures in East Africa, the acquisition of nuclear capabilities by Pakistan, or ethnic riots in Malaysia have repercussions throughout the world community. Education, and adult education in particular, is one medium whereby the urgency of world problems can be addressed, and the ideal of a world community brought closer to reality.

"Developing" or Third World Nations

What to call the nonindustrialized nations of the world has been a problem of pride and semantics. Thomas writes that "in the period where the word 'underdeveloped' was used to describe largely rural agricultural societies with large populations, low incomes, and per capita production, the discomfort [from its use] was to a large degree political."[35] The term *LDC's* (less-developed countries) carries the same negative connotation as *underdeveloped.* A more acceptable term has been *developing,* but this also has its problems. In the first place it reflects a Western bias which equates development with science, materialism, and technology. In an essay exploring the semantic implications of the term *Third World,* Merriam points out that the so-called poor developing countries are in some ways richer "psychologically and spiritually, enjoying a contentment and sense of tradition sorely lacking in the ulcer-ridden, hectic, depersonalized industrial societies. To many Buddhists, for example, inner peace is more valuable than a high gross national product."[36] A second objection to the term *developing* is that all countries are changing and "developing," the industrialized ones even faster than agriculturally based societies. While not without its limitations,[37] the term *Third World* is the more generally acceptable referent for the emerging, nonindustrialized nations of Africa, Asia, and Latin America.

The Third World includes about 70 percent of the earth's people; politically it ranges across the entire spectrum of systems and ideologies. Adult education in the Third World mirrors the common characteristics of these nations. Literacy programs, for example, reflect the fact that the majority of people in Third World nations are illiterate. There is a close association between illiteracy and poverty. "In the 25 least-developed countries where the *per capita* product is less than $100 a year, illiteracy rates are over 80 percent."[38] In addition to low per capita income, Third World nations have primarily agriculturally based economies, low gross national products (GNPs), poor nutrition and health, and a high birth rate which results in a very young population (half the population in developing countries is under 21). According to Lardner, the combination of demographics and economics results in:

1. A marked imbalance in the population structure with a growing predominance of persons under 15 years of age, whose contribution to the GNP is nil or certainly less than their consumption.
2. A reinforcement, whether agriculture stagnates or improves, of the movement of population to the towns.
3. A decline, as nationalism grows, in the opportunities formerly offered by international migration to accommodate populations in excess of the employment capacity of the national economies.
4. A growing problem in the allocation of resources between urban centers and rural areas, and between "productive" projects and "social-welfare" projects.[39]

Third World countries also are characterized by linguistic and cultural diversity. There are, for example, 14 major languages and about 500 dialects spoken in India, 3 separate and distinct cultures in Malaysia (Indian, Malay, Chinese), 250 tribal groups in Nigeria, and so on. Such diversity within even a single country poses problems for the government in terms of national educational goals and priorities.

Development and Its Relationship to Education

Adult education, as well as other levels of education, must be considered within the context of development in Third World countries. Traditionally, development has been defined synonymously with economic growth and measured in terms of an increase in either per capita income or the gross national product. In the past it has been assumed that Third World countries would follow in patterns of development set by the Western industrialized world. The "failure" of nations to develop according to Western expectations has led to a redefinition of the concept. Development is now much more broadly defined to include social and cultural as well as individual growth:

> Development is a process of self-realization, both individual and collective, and authentic liberation. As such, it cannot seek its tools or its models outside itself. It springs from, and can only spring from, within. If it does not correspond to an endogenous process of interrelated, integrated growth of societies, it is self-defeating. If it does not address itself to all components of development, to the collective promotion of society as a whole, it can only result in disruptive tensions, in disintegrating the social fabric.[40]

In a recent UNESCO publication, da Costa proposes 12 "musts" for development reflective of the broadened meaning of the term:

1. Development must be total . . . it must transcend purely economic dimensions in order to include social considerations . . . and the whole dimension of cultural and spiritual self-realization embracing creativity, quality of life, and the rights of man.
2. Development must be original, which is to say that imitation of models is undesirable.
3. Development must be self-determined. This applies to selecting a development style as well as assuring its application.
4. Development must be self-generated.
5. Development must be integrated. . . . Strong horizontal and vertical linkages must bind together the several productive units . . . and ensure complete communication and interdependence, and full integration with national supply and demand.
6. Development must respect the integrity of the environment, both natural and cultural, as well as the traditional structures.
7. Development must be planned and requires constant attention from and intervention by national authorities.
8. Development must be directed towards a just and equitable social order.
9. Development must be democratic, that is to say, it must respond to the choices made by the population as a whole.
10. Development must not insulate less developed countries or regions into "reservations" where they could barely survive and lead a marginal life free from the main flows of growth and dynamism.
11. Development must be innovative. It must neither depend on the importation of outmoded technologies from developed countries nor even advanced technology developed somewhere else.
12. Development planning must be based on a realistic definition of national needs and on consumption models that are consistent with the national characteristics of a country.[41]

The role of education in development has also undergone redefinition. When the Western industrialized model of development was transported to Third World nations, so, too, were European and North American educational systems. Educational programs, particularly compulsory primary and adult literacy, were thought to be the vehicles for attaining economic and occupational success. However, the relationship between amount of education and economic growth has proved tentative at best. Robert M. Hutchins, in *The Learning Society*, posits a convincing case for just the opposite view—that is, rather than education leading to economic growth, economically rich societies create advanced educational systems.[42] Hutchins points to Brazil as a country having a fast-growing economy but an educational level lower than it was before economic expansion began. Nineteenth-century pre-industrial Japan had a high literacy rate as well as widespread primary education.[43] Depending upon education to bring about economic growth is a fallacy, according to Hutchins, in that it attributes to education, "in competition with culture, powers it does not possess."[44]

Other critics have pointed out that the adoption of Western educational models has had anything but liberating and egalitarian effects. Curle claimed that formal education actually resulted in the continued "enslavement" of the masses by raising up an educated elite that ultimately became part of the colonial or national network exploiting the poor.[45] Furthermore, when education is extolled as the catalyst for economic growth it is not always coupled with a more realistic policy of labor development. Educated youth leave the village for a town where employment possibilities, if any, rarely coincide with academic preparation. The result has been a cadre of educated, unemployed or underemployed, dissatisfied youth.

Rather than positing some sort of causal relationship between development and education, most theorists today recognize the interactive effects of the one upon the other. The relationship is a spiral one in which "development is the action strand interwoven with education, both moving the whole system upward to higher levels of quality or forward to new bases. The consequences of such an integrated approach to change affect both developers and educators."[46] Stensland proposes the idea that education and development are related change processes and calls for national planning and programming based upon a social change rather than an economic productivity model. The interweaving of the two processes can be facilitated in several ways: (1) through recurrent education in which a person alternates periods of work with educational leave; (2) through the use of education as a way to prepare for development as well as participate in it, as Nyerere has attempted to do in Tanzania; and (3) through social action movements such as Freire's literacy and development work in Brazil and Chile.[47] UNESCO's worldwide study of education, summarized in *Learning to Be*, proposes lifelong education as the master integrative concept for both industrialized and Third World countries. Noting that "over a long term, education stimulates, accompanies, or sets a seal on social and political development, as well as technical and economic development," the study avoids linking the aim of education to economic development. Rather:

> The aim of education is to enable man to be himself, to "become himself." And the aim of education in relation to employment and economic progress should be not so much to prepare young people and adults for a specific, lifetime vocation, as to "optimize" mobility among the professions and afford a permanent stimulus to the desire to learn and to train oneself.[48]

Nyerere's keynote address to the International Conference on Adult Education and Development held in Dar es Salaam in 1976 also echoed this new notion of development and education. The purpose of development, according to Nyerere, "is the liberation of Man. . . . Development is for Man, by Man, and of Man. The same is true of education. Its purpose is the liberation of Man from the restraints and limitations of ignorance and dependency."[49]

An expanded concept of development necessitates a rethinking of the philosophies of traditional educational practice. This reevaluation leads to two major dilemmas for Third World nations. The first concerns the extent to which these countries should retain their colonial legacy. Lowe points out that this is no less a problem for adult educators than for those associated with any other social institution:

> The dilemma for the adult educator is whether to build on or to reject existing structures and customs. In some places institutions and practices ushered in by the old colonial regimes may be inflicting damage and yet be difficult to root out; in others, the borrowings may be beneficial but seem obnoxious simply because of their alien provenance.[50]

The second dilemma is determining where and how limited educational resources should be used and for what purpose. *Learning to Be* notes that the demand for education at all levels in all regions of the world "is of unprecedented dimensions and strength."[51] Countries are faced with the choice of allocating the bulk of their resources for one segment of the population or one program area or spreading resources thinly across many segments and programs. Lowe concludes that there is no stock answer to this dilemma. He favors a policy whereby priorities are determined and resources applied where they will have the most impact, with a concentration upon community development in rural areas.[52]

In many Third World nations the education of adults is a national priority. Countries simply cannot wait for their youth to acquire the skills and knowledge necessary to address the urgent task of national development:

> The education of the young is . . . a necessarily slow process. In this context adult education comes to play a very important part. Not because it is *per se* a quicker process—all developments that require a large degree of human change are slow processes—but mainly because it has time-saving and cost-reducing properties, such as a faster turnover rate. You do not need to grow up to use what you have learnt; the skills achieved can be used immediately.[53]

MAJOR PROGRAM AREAS

Adult education in the Third World seeks to eradicate illiteracy, raise political consciousness, improve living conditions, increase agricultural production, and develop skills for industrialization. In reality, all aspects of adult education are interrelated in the nation building efforts of Third World countries. As Nyerere states:

> Adult education is not something which can deal with just "agriculture," or "health," or "literacy," or "mechanical skill," etc. All these separate branches of education are related to the total life a man is living, and to the man he is and will become. . . . Adult education encompasses the whole of life, and must build upon what already exists.[54]

Without denying the interrelatedness of various aspects of adult education in Third World nations, one can find distinct program area emphases in nearly every country. The rest of this chapter will explore the five areas of literacy; civic and political education; health, welfare, and family life; agricultural education; and labor development. Major goals, adult education's role within the total development process, and unique and innovative delivery systems for each program area will be discussed.

Literacy

No other program area in the Third World has been the subject of so much rhetoric, writing, spending, and confusion as literacy education. Whether as a small-scale effort or as a mass campaign, whether local or international, the aims and objectives, successes and failures of literacy education continue to be debated and analyzed by educators throughout the world. Such attention reflects the complexity and importance of the topic.

Part of the complexity lies in defining what it means to be literate in any particular culture. In addressing that issue, Dauzat and Dauzat criticize those who "crusade for a national effort to make literacy a reality without establishing what that reality is." It is, they state, "a task significantly more difficult than finding a needle in a haystack, for at least one knows what a needle is and how it is different from the hay."[55] Defining literacy in terms of what it is not, or in terms of its properties, does little to clarify the concept. The authors conclude that, aside from having a language component, the definition may "forever be in developmental stages, . . . shaped by the changing types of literacy demanded by a changing world."[56]

Hunter and Harmon, in a Ford Foundation study of adult illiteracy, also conclude that definitions of literacy and illiteracy are relative. They prefer to differentiate between *conventional literacy*—the ability to read, write, and understand signs, labels, instructions, and so on necessary to get along in one's environment—and *functional literacy*—"the possession of skills *perceived as necessary by particular persons and groups* to fulfill their own self-determined objectives as family and community members, citizens, consumers, job-holders, and members of social, religious, or other associations of their choosing."[57]

Just as the concept of development and education's role in it has been subject to rethinking and reformulation, so has literacy and its place in the nation's development: hence, the movement from thinking of literacy as simply the ability to read and write to the notion of its functionality. The assumption that illiterates necessarily want or feel a need to become literate has also been abandoned. Harmon points out that literacy actually encompasses three stages, the first of which is motivational—at which point the illiterate conceptualizes literacy as a tool. The second stage, of attaining the skill to read and write, is then followed by "the practical application of these skills in activities meaningful to the learner."[58]

The confusion that has masked differences between simple and functional literacy has been compounded by unfounded assumptions regarding literacy and development. Hunter and Harmon list five such oversimplifications that have destined literacy campaigns to failure:

1. The assertion that economic development, increased gross national product, and modernization automatically follow or are contingent upon literacy.
2. The parallel claim that *anyone* who becomes literate is automatically better off economically, is better able to find employment, and becomes a better citizen.
3. The claim, even after narrow economic goals were decried as too utilitarian and limiting, that literacy might somehow bring about national development in the broadest sense of the term.
4. The equating of illiteracy with inferiority, backwardness, cultural poverty, and low intelligence.
5. The disregard for what individuals and groups themselves need and want within their own social settings and the imposition of programs believed to be "good" for them.[59]

Functional literacy, which has been adopted by Third World nations as one vehicle for development, has its own definitional problems. In its simplest terms, functional literacy is the attempt to tie the acquisition of reading and writing skills to vocational training, rural and agricultural development, family life, and so on. Reading and writing and the facilitation of a country's social, economic and political development thus become a simultaneous process.

Adiseshiah, in exploring the "functionalities" of literacy, underscores the complexity of the concept as well as its potential for "understanding, changing, and controlling the real world."[60] He describes four major functionalities of literacy: that which relates to the world of work either in a rural agricultural or industrial milieu; that which relates to sex and age groups (that is, literacy is functional for the large numbers of women and youth who have suffered discrimination); that which relates to individual and social values, and which leads to cultural development; and finally, that which

> relates to the right of the poor, illiterate, exploited, and disinherited man, who forms the 60 percent majority in the Third World countries, to organize himself and his fellow sufferers and fight against the existing power centers and decision-making processes, against the growing poverty he is living in and for an equitable and just social and political order.[61]

Adiseshiah's fourth functionality alludes to what some have called the cultural or political literacy espoused by Paulo Freire. For Freire, literacy is the tool for critically evaluating and comprehending one's social context. Such evaluation leads to combating society's oppressive forces and to taking an active part in shaping one's environment.[62] Freirian literacy compaigns have been conducted in Brazil, Chile, and Guinea-Bissau, and his methods and philosophy have had considerable influence in literacy campaigns in other Third World nations such as Tanzania.

Efforts to eradicate world illiteracy date back to eighteenth-century missionaries who taught people to read the Bible. Most literacy programs through the first half of the twentieth century were carried out by volunteer missions, churches, and other nongovernmental organizations.[63] The second half of the century has seen a proliferation of nationally and internationally sponsored literacy campaigns. A landmark in the development of worldwide literacy programs was the 1965 World Conference of Ministers of Education on the Eradication of Illiteracy. Participants recommended that traditional literacy programs be replaced with functional literacy campaigns in which "the very process of learning to read and write should be made an opportunity for acquiring information that can immediately be used to improve living standards . . . to train for work, increased productivity, a greater participation in civil life, and a better understanding of the surrounding world."[64] The conference led to the establishment of an Experimental World Literacy Program (EWLP) funded by UNESCO, the United Nations Development Program (UNDP), and the 13 participating countries (Algeria, Afghanistan, Ecuador, Ethiopia, Guinea, India, Iran, Madagascar, Mali, Sudan, Syria, Tanzania, and Venezuela). The objectives of the EWLP were to test and measure the impact of literacy upon social and economic development and to lay the groundwork for a world campaign to eradicate mass illiteracy.

Ten years and $32 million later, the Experimental World Literacy Program was judged a "failure" by some, a "learning experience" by others. What those involved with the experiment "learned" about literacy seems obvious from today's perspective. Briefly,

1. the needs and aspirations of illiterate individuals and groups should be taken into account in the identification of literacy objectives;

2. curricula should be functional in terms of a broad range of political, social, cultural, and economic knowledge and skills of use to new literates;

3. teaching methods should be varied and as active as possible, giving stress to "learning by doing";

4. international aid can complement—but should not attempt to replace—national initiative, both intellectual and material; and

5. the idea of follow-up must be replaced, where substantial numbers of new literates appear on the scene in largely illiterate countries, with the notion of building the infrastructure for a literate and continuously self-educating society.[65]

In contrast to EWLP, literacy campaigns in China and Cuba appear to be spectacular successes. The difference, according to several observers, rests in the realization and exploitation of literacy as a political force. Unless tied to some form of socioeconomic transformation, to the formation, in Freire's words, of a "critical consciousness," literacy campaigns can expect little success. In writing about the literacy campaign in Cuba, Kozol quotes Raul Ferrer, director of Cuba's Great Campaign:

"Why do [the literacy campaigns sponsored by UNESCO] fail?" he asked. "They have the money. They have the expertise. They have the international promotion. They have UNESCO. How is it possible, then, that they do not succeed?"

"It is because their starting point is anti-human. It is because they do not dare to use the words we use. They do not dare to speak of land reform, to speak about the sick and starving . . . nor about the ones who *make* those people sick and poor." . . .

"The literacy campaign," Ferrer announced, "was not a dry event. It must not be talked about as if it were. It was a passionate, turbulent, sometimes desperate—but, above all, it was a political event."

"The statistics of the end results are very good. Yet this was not at any time our chief concern. This fact was a by-product of a deeper goal. The great heart of the literacy struggle was the revolution."[66]

While not adopting the revolutionary goals of China's and Cuba's literacy campaigns, several other countries have experienced at least modest success in their efforts to eradicate illiteracy. In these cases literacy is closely linked to national development and popular participation in social, economic, and political life. Tanzania is a case in point. With the Arusha Declaration of 1967, Tanzania switched its adult education focus from meeting labor needs to meeting family and community needs at the local level. The declaration outlines a policy of self-reliance and national development with priority given to rural and agricultural development. Literacy work since 1967 has been an integral part of national and personal development. Tanzania's participatory approach to development and literacy is structured through the Ujamaa village concept. An Ujamaa village is a small, rural unit based upon the principle of cooperative living and working for the good of all, which stresses the traditions of "familyhood" (the literal meaning of *ujamaa*).[67] The Ujamaa village assumes responsibility for "planning and implementing literacy activities, greatly contributing to the success of the national literacy effort."[68] Other apparently successful approaches include those of Somalia, where a year's motivational phase preceded actual literacy training; Peru, where local community councils are used to launch literacy campaigns; and Guinea-Bissau, where local culture circles and the military are mobilized. These instances demonstrate the efficacy of combining functional literacy with a participatory delivery system.

Organizational structures such as Brazil's Mobral system, new institutions at national and regional levels, and new methods and materials have contributed to gains made in literacy despite seemingly insurmountable barriers. The absolute number of adult illiterates continues to increase, however, primarily due to the explosive population growth of the Third World countries. Efforts to eradicate illiteracy also are hampered by: (1) multilingual populations; (2) lack of trained teachers; (3) lack of coordination and articulation between national and local bodies, adult and school-based programs; and (4) lack of reading materials and follow-up campaigns aimed at preventing newly literate adults from slipping back into illiteracy.

In conclusion, the complexities, anxieties, and failures of literacy programs in the second half of the twentieth century are counterbalanced by some success, but more importantly by a more realistic and workable reconceptualization of the phenomenon as well. Literacy's relationship to all other aspects of life is summed up by a definition of literacy from *Learning to Be:* literacy is "not an end in itself [but] a means of personal liberation and development and of extending individuals' educational efforts, involving overall interdisciplinary responses to concrete problems. Literacy training is only a 'moment,' an element, in adult education."[69]

Civic and Political Education

In the broadest sense, all education is political. Whether education supports the status quo of stable societies or is used as a tool in nations undergoing dramatic change, it is "impossible to deny, except intentionally or by some angelic innocence, the political aspect of education."[70] In exploring the relationship between development and adult education,

Nyerere comments on the political nature of what he calls "generalist" adult educators. Generalists, he says,

> are the political activists and educators—whether or not they are members of, and organized by, a political party or whether they are community development workers or religious teachers. Such people are not politically neutral; by the nature of what they are doing they cannot be. For what they are doing will affect how men look at the society in which they live, and how they seek to use it or change it. Making the people of a village aware that their malaria can be avoided, for example, will cause them to make demands upon the larger community in which they live. . . . And if people who have been aroused cannot get the change they want, or a substitute for it which is acceptable to them, they will become discontented—if not hostile—towards whatever authority they regard as responsible for the failure. Adult education is thus a highly political activity.[71]

Generalists are followed by what Nyerere calls specialists—those who can respond after a demand has arisen or a problem has been identified. Such specialists can be health educators, agricultural experts, members of literacy teams, and so on.

The political nature of adult education is seen most dramatically in Third World countries that have undergone substantial transformations. In less than three decades, for example, China has moved from a semi-feudal, primarily illiterate country to one that is becoming modern, unified, and literate. Education is viewed as both a means and an end in China:

> The Chinese are convinced that the way in which you build a socialist society is through an educated proletariat of workers and peasants, but education is not measured simply by the level of schooling, the literacy rate, or the formal systems of conveying knowledge through books and classrooms. . . . The assumption is that all aspects of human nature are educable, thereby changeable, and that every situation where people come together has the potential for being an educational one.[72]

Regular political study, organized by workers' unions or communes, is an important aspect of adult education in China's efforts to bring about a proletarian world outlook. In other Third World countries, political education is part of other programs such as literacy campaigns. It might be recalled that Cuba's literacy campaign was characterized by its leader as a "political event," and Freire's literacy programs in Brazil, Chile, and Guinea-Bissau deliberately involved the development of a "critical consciousness" to bring about social and political change.

Less radical is the role of adult education in creating an awareness of national goals and development plans and of the individual's role in carrying them out. French-speaking African countries have adopted the term *les animateurs* to describe the individuals so critical to this process.

Les animateurs "are the creative people, the leaders in various spheres of life, who inspire and organize their friends and initiate development." They are the agents of change, in contrast to *les usagers*, "who make use of existing institutions and adapt themselves to their environment."[73] Adult education in these countries seeks out the *animateurs* and assists them in becoming more effective. Senegal, for example, has created a unique organization for just such a purpose. *Animation* refers to both the state organization and a network of local community leaders designed "to initiate and support a direct dialogue between organized communities and state and institutional authorities."[74] Pakistan has found that its village literacy centers have been instrumental in "promoting social cohesion and a new sense of civic responsibility."[75] Tanzania considers training leaders, providing basic education for adults who have not had an opportunity to attend school, and correcting the miseducation imposed during colonial times as important social functions of adult education.[76] The less radical forms of civic and social education strive for achieving some balance between newness and change and the appeal of traditional values and structures. As Coles observes:

> Both civic and social education are concerned with change; with the acquisition of new attitudes based on an understanding of why the world of today is different from that of yesterday but without too recklessly allowing all of the traditional forms and structures to disappear. But change everywhere is now the norm and whilst both general education and vocational training will also be helping people to adapt to the revised circumstances in which they are living, it is the especial aim of informal civic and social education to enable people to become willing and sensitive co-operators in the process.[77]

Role education (assisting people to perform more competently their roles in society), the community development process, cultural pursuits, and individual interests are all part of civic and social education.[78]

For some Third World nations the development of a sense of national unity and cultural identity is an urgent component of adult education. African nations in particular have had to face the problem of dealing with cultural and linguistic pluralism. According to Kashoki, cultural development encompassing "questions of preserving and promoting one's cultural heritage, evolving a national culture, forging a national identity, ensuring national unity, and promoting and/or selecting one language as a national language" preoccupies developing African nations as much as questions of economic development.[79] The trend in nations characterized by cultural diversity is, Kashoki notes, toward integration rather than assimilation, for the "existence of diverse groups is not necessarily disintegrative."[80] Such efforts are being supported by nationally sponsored cultural and civic education campaigns in several African countries.

This discussion of civic and political adult education illustrates the observation made earlier that it is difficult to delineate program areas of adult education in Third World nations. Nation building involves civic and political awareness, which is intertwined with literacy and aspects of community development, which all should lead to better living conditions for each citizen. Another part of the total picture is that aspect of adult education in Third World countries which addresses health, welfare, and family life.

Health and Family Life

Poor health, poor nutrition, a high birth rate, and high infant mortality are characteristic of Third World nations. Some countries in Africa, for example, "cannot provide even one doctor per 80,000 of the population. Infant mortality rises to as high as 700 per thousand in some of the new states. Many million hours of labor are lost annually through undernourishment, ill health, poor sanitary conditions, and inadequate medical care."[81] The importance of health education, particularly to a nation's development, is underscored by Harbison, who conceptualizes development in terms of the utilization of human resources. A nation's potential for development, Harbison writes, would be determined by, aside from measures of economic growth and educational attainment, "a measure of health, and this ideally would include data on life expectancy at various ages, infant mortality, incidence of critical diseases (such as parasites, malaria, and tuberculosis), and availability (that is, geographical distribution) of health services. Finally, some measure of nutrition of the total population . . . would be useful."[82] In contrast to modern countries where health and nutrition education has been left primarily to the schools, health education, Lowe points out, is "an essential component" of adult education in Third World countries.[83]

Whether in Asia, Latin America, or Africa, adult education programs aimed at improving health, nutrition, and sanitation conditions encounter many obstacles. Lack of trained medical personnel and health educators presents a major problem for most Third World countries. There is a resistance on the part of such personnel to leave urban centers for rural communities where the need is greatest, but the living and working conditions are particularly unattractive. Often, too, the urgency of rural health problems demands a short-term curative approach rather than a long-term preventive program. Limited resources are channeled into fighting communicable diseases such as malaria, tuberculosis, smallpox, and dysentery, leaving few, if any, for dealing with more subtle problems of mental health, chronic disease, and physical handicaps. Finally, combating tradition, superstition, and medical quackery may present the greatest challenge to health education programs in Third World countries.

Health and family life education in the Third World is often part of functional literacy or community or rural development programs. In the Philippines, for example, the functional literacy program teaches reading, writing, arithmetic, and citizenship skills and provides information about vocations and industries, and health and sanitation. Health and sanitation education includes "the development of essential skills, practices, and attitudes related to home sanitation, such as proper installation and use of toilets, proper disposal of garbage, proper construction of drainage . . . and closer cooperation in community health activities."[84] Kenya considers health education, which includes instruction in prevention of disease, hygiene, nutrition, child and family planning, and sanitation, as part of "fundamental" adult education.[85] For most Latin American countries, health education is one aspect of broad rural development programs. Rural development is a multidimensional concept aimed at transforming "stagnant, traditional societies into productive, dynamic rural economies." Programs encompass

> much more than an increase in agricultural and livestock output and productivity. Village and small town development, extension of health and education services, expansion of local trade and commerce, organization of cooperatives, the provision of credit, the creation of local industries for processing agricultural products, and the improvement of housing, water supplies, sanitation, roads, and communications are all within its scope.[86]

Women are often the focus of health education programs in Third World countries. Traditionally, their primary role in these societies has been childbearing and child rearing and thus they are the logical focus for upgrading health and nutrition practices and improving the quality of family life. The potential for women to contribute to their nation's development is, even in their traditional roles as mothers, teachers, household managers, and community members, as great as the male wage earner's, yet they lag behind men in formal schooling, literacy, and employment skills. The plight of rural women is especially acute:

> Rural women who are deprived of education and training do work but the kind of work they do is traditional, e.g., traditional agriculture, cottage industry, or petty trading, while their main activity is confined to domestic work, childbearing and child raising. In this way women neither contribute to nor benefit from the process of development in a way compatible with their capacity or their numbers in society. On the contrary, they constitute an obstacle to development because they are swelling the ranks of the traditional sector.[87]

In the areas of health and family life, at least, educational efforts are often aimed at the women and are more often than not facilitated by the

formation of women's groups or societies. Social barriers to women's participation in development are sometimes creatively circumvented by the
women themselves. In one section of India, for example, all efforts to
convene women for educational meetings were thwarted by religious and
social mandates that kept them restricted to their homes. They were
allowed, however, to receive instruction in using the *ambar charkha*, an
improved spinning wheel. Village classes, followed by home instruction,
became the means of learning a craft as well as imparting information
related to improving the health and living conditions of each woman's
family.[88]

In other parts of the Third World, health and family life education has
been conveyed through puppetry, impromptu local theater, and visual
aids. In Mexico, for example, the proper use of contraceptives is described
to illiterates in the *fotonovela*, a photo-illustrated story. Final decisions on
content, sequence, and symbols are made by the people for whom the
materials are intended.[89]

In some countries large-scale nationally organized efforts appear to
have had some impact. Pakistan has established a rural health program
consisting of a network of village health centers, each serving 40 to 50
thousand villagers. These centers offer family planning advice, organize
talks and demonstrations on nutrition and sanitation, and educate villagers
in preventive health measures as well as treat communicable diseases.[90]
Tanzania's Institute of Adult Education has launched several mass campaigns, one of which was on the subject of health education. Mbunda
defines a mass campaign as "a program designed to solve a problem," with
the following elements:

1. There is an urgently felt need.
2. The need involves many; it is felt to be common to all.
3. To satisfy the need, the cooperation of all concerned is paramount.
4. This cooperation ought to be a result of participatory planning and
   commitment to personal implementation.
5. There is a time factor.[91]

The object of Tanzania's "Man Is Health" campaign was to reach one
million rural adults through 75,000 organized "listening groups" with
information on measures to prevent five common communicable diseases.
Hall discusses the methods used to reach such a large audience:

> The campaign made use of weekly radio programs, printed materials, study
> guides, and a special booklet for the study group leaders which dealt with
> specific instructions for running each discussion. The emphasis in the cam-
> paign was on discussion of the relevant health problems in the area and then
> decisions about what could be done to alleviate the situation. Many practical
> suggestions such as increasing the size of windows, building a latrine, filling in
> the holes where mosquitoes breed, and killing the snails which carry bilharzia

were put forward for the group members to discuss. One of the most important objectives of the campaign was to make it possible for people to see that they had some control over matters of health and they were not simply at God's mercy or being punished by others when they suffered from disease.[92]

One source reports that the "Man Is Health" campaign reached twice the number of participants originally anticipated.[93]

Several generalizations that can be drawn from adult health education programs in Third World nations might be considered by educators in the industrialized world. Third World health programs, for the most part, look to treating the causes as well as the symptoms of the problem; focus on groups, such as rural women, who will have the most impact in bringing about change; and employ delivery methods that are not only feasible (e.g., radio in Tanzania) but compatible with cultural norms and values.

Agriculture

In the latter part of the twentieth century the emphasis of development efforts in many Third World countries shifted from industrialization to rural development. With between 70 and 80 percent of the population of Third World nations living in rural areas, the aim of development is to "tap and develop the latent capabilities of the rural people through incentives for productive and rewarding employment, and to involve them in the affairs of their community and nation."[94] Programs in rural areas include functional literacy, health care, nutrition, public works, population control, and agricultural education. This section will focus upon educational efforts with regard to agriculture, one of the major concerns in rural development.

One source has delineated two major components of agricultural development: a "technical" aspect, which may include "soil testing, the introduction of new varieties or new crops, [and] the use of fertilizer and irrigation"; and an attitudinal component, "namely, to persuade the farmer to try something new rather than continue to cultivate the land in the same way as their ancestors had done for generations."[95] Both components rely upon educational delivery systems to effect change.

Agricultural development does not mean merely introducing a new fertilizer or persuading a farmer to rotate crops. Changes are related to a nation's total development direction, its social structure, and its political ideology. In comparing the agricultural successes of China with the problems of other countries, Chonchol points out that each Third World country must evolve its own model of development compatible with social structures, national resources, and other "realities":

> First, agricultural development in underdeveloped countries cannot succeed without profound changes in their economic and social structures and the adaptation of these structures to the needs of the large majorities, not to the privileges of small minorities.

Second, agricultural development cannot be left to the free play of market forces, particularly in poor countries. It must be planned. . . .

Third, agricultural development and modernization cannot take place in underdeveloped countries if they do not simultaneously develop an industrial base of support which makes them less dependent on the international market for agricultural inputs. . . .

Fourth, the theory of international specialization must be seriously reexamined. It is more important for underdeveloped countries to assure the fulfillment of their basic food needs for their own people on their own territories than to produce goods for the world market, while remaining dependent on others for food.[96]

The concerns expressed by Chonchol have been echoed by other observers who point out the necessity of an integrated national development policy that provides the support necessary to carry through development programs. A parallel can be drawn with literacy education. Teaching people to read and write is not enough to sustain literacy. Inexpensive and readily accessible reading materials must be available to new literates or the impact of the initial instruction quickly fades. So, too, must agricultural improvements start with farmers committed to good farming practices, who are then supported by access to markets, availability of credit, structures for collective organization, and so on. Education in various forms plays a crucial role in the agricultural development of Third World countries. Speaking of the African context Busia writes:

Old techniques handed down to [the farmers] are no longer adequate. They are now required to produce more, to learn to use new tools, to improve the soil by new methods of drainage or fertilization, or water supply and soil conservation, or grow new crops, or join others in cooperative farming and mechanization. . . . These are tasks for adult education.[97]

The primary adult education delivery system for agricultural development in the Third World is modeled after the U.S. Cooperative Extension Service. Many Third World countries have adopted both its administrative structure and educational methods. In Latin America, extension agents working for ministries of agriculture have, with some success, set up agricultural experiment stations; formed farmers', homemakers', and youth clubs; sponsored short courses, pilot projects, and demonstrations; and produced technical publications.[98] Extension efforts in Third World nations are not, however, always effective. Chow gives several reasons why this is so: countries are reluctant or unable to support the system financially once it has been established by a consultant nation; peasant farmers who operate within a very narrow margin of failure hesitate to take risks; there is a lack of trained agriculturalists and a reluctance on the part of qualified personnel to work at the local level; and extension agents are not a part of nor fully aware of farmers' problems and aspirations.[99]

Several Third World nations have made interesting adaptations of the

Western extension model. Extension workers in Senegal are selected by local villages to represent the community. The agent is an influential village resident who is—and will remain—a farmer. These village representatives are given intensive training and follow-up support through rural extension centers.[100] Kenya has established a network of residential Farmers' Training Centers (FTCs). "The centers provide simple food and accommodations, range in capacity from 20 to 100 beds, and offer short courses in basic agricultural methods and techniques to peasant farmers who pay a highly subsidized fee."[101]

In some countries agricultural education is an important dimension of more comprehensive development structures. The Ujamaa village network in Tanzania, the Communal Villages system in Mozambique, and a nonformal education program for farmers and mothers in the Philippines called Rayalaseem Development Trust (RDT) are examples of such structures.

Aside from techniques used by the extension service, other creative approaches to agricultural education can be cited. In use in Ecuador, for example, is a simulation game designed to replicate the economic and social realities of the peasant situation. "Hacienda" sensitizes villagers to questions of land reform, modernization, power structures, and strategies for political reform.[102] Tanzania's Ministry of Agriculture publishes a rural newspaper called *Modern Farming*. The paper, which is printed in large type, gives practical advice on many aspects of farming. Inexpensive and widely distributed through extension agents, it is often accompanied by leaflets giving more detailed information on specific farming practices.[103] Tanzania also conducted a mass campaign, "Food Is Life," aimed at increasing food production. Reading materials used in conjunction with discussion groups and radio programs were used throughout the country. Perhaps the most unusual method of publicizing the "Food Is Life" campaign was the use of textiles. "In the farthest areas of the country, women were met wearing the 'Food Is Life' *khanga* [material worn as dresses, skirts, head coverings, or shirts], silently delivering the message as they walked to the communal farm or to the well."[104]

Radio is widely used for agricultural education as well as for other development projects. Lowe estimates that as of the mid-1970s there were, worldwide, over 400 radio programs addressed to farmers:

In Ghana a central broadcasting unit prepares programs for farmers and fishermen, as well as for their womenfolk with a view to improving their domestic skills. Listeners come together in groups averaging 25. The programs are in the form of "magazines" and include illustrative situation sketches and answers to listeners' queries. . . . In 1962 the African Institute for Social and Economic Development (INADES) was inaugurated in Abidjan (Ivory Coast), with the object of providing radio programs for illiterate farmers. Similar programs are now available in Burundi, Cameroon, Chad, the

Central African Republic, Ethiopia, and Zaire. The key principle is to treat village communities as totalities and to try to involve all the villagers in a given community. Courses are directed at three groups—small farmers, middle-level workers, women. . . . Great success is claimed for these programs.[105]

In summary, agricultural education in the Third World is an important aspect of the overall development process. To be most successful, it would seem, agricultural education must be integrated with other areas of community and national concern. The Third World countries, increasingly aware of the pitfalls of adopting techniques and structures from other settings, are experimenting with the delivery systems and instructional methodologies most compatible with their own cultural contexts. Finally, as DeVries points out, adult education's impact is affected by the larger context of the development process:

> Agricultural development depends on a large number of factors such as: good marketing systems, attractive prices, relevant new technology, favorable and stable government policies, and the availability of credit and agricultural extension. The success of extension efforts therefore . . . depends . . . also on the complex social, political, economic, and physical environment in which it operates.[106]

Vocational Training

Much of adult education in the Third World reflects the needs of rural, agriculturally based economies. However, in most instances, nation-building efforts also involve giving attention to a country's industrial sector. Broadly interpreted, labor development includes the distribution of resources between both the agricultural and industrial sectors. Because of changing consumption patterns and technological advancements, labor needs are in constant flux in developing nations. Vocational education more often than not has failed to produce the numbers of skilled and semi-skilled workers needed to meet the demand. Zymelman writes that the mismatch between need and supply is partially the result of the "unquestioned copying of foreign institutions . . . where the educational system proceeds independently and unrelated to the development of the labor markets."[107] Zymelman also points out that formal vocational education is considered less desirable than general education because of the selection mechanism of schools in most developing countries:

> Those lucky enough to have been selected proceed to universities and other institutes of higher learning to become leaders of industry, government, education, etc. Employers perpetuate the system by choosing those already selected by the educational system in preference to those that may have as much relevant training, but lack the formal credentials. The result is a vicious circle where vocational training becomes less and less prestigeful.[108]

While grappling with the problems of producing a skilled labor force through the formal school system, Third World nations recognize and cater to the potential within their adult population. "Vocational education for adults will doubtless flourish in the coming years," Lowe feels, "because it can be viewed as a profitable form of capital investment and a possible antidote to unemployment."[109] As in industrialized countries, formal vocational and professional training and retraining occurs through universities, technical schools, and vocational training centers. A considerable amount of work-related education is also conducted through private companies. In Zambia, for example, a survey of workers in the private sector revealed that three-fourths had received or were undergoing training through their employers.[110]

Much of adult vocational education in the Third World, however, is nonformal in nature—that is, outside the regular school system. Nonformal education, and in particular nonformal vocational education, serves many needs in developing societies. Harbison's discussion of six such functions can be summarized as follows: (1) nonformal education "provides a wide range of learning services which lie beyond the scope of formal education," such as training workers in factories; (2) nonformal training and education functions as "an alternative or substitute for formal education," as in the case of apprenticeship training; (3) "nonformal education is a means of extending skills and knowledge gained in formal education"—technicians who combine formal instruction with on-the-job experience are an example; (4) "nonformal education in many countries may be the only available learning opportunity for large proportions of the populations"; (5) nonformal education may help "counterbalance some of the distortion created by formal education"—that is, it allows people without credentials access to higher-level jobs; and (6) nonformal education "provides greater opportunity for innovation."[111]

Nonformal delivery systems for vocational training in Third World nations are many and varied. Perhaps the most comprehensive such nonformal educational system is found in Colombia. SENA (Servicio Nacional de Aprendizaje) is a semiautonomous organization within the Colombian Ministry of Labor that "develops and operates a vast array of training services for workers in commerce, industry, agriculture, animal husbandry, hotel management, and catering as well as medical services (nurses) and even vocational training in the military."[112] SENA services include providing classes in over 100 training centers, consulting to business, conducting labor needs assessments, training within business and industrial settings, and dispatching mobile training units to urban and rural centers. SENA concentrates on training persons already employed and so does not compete for the most part with the formal school system, which emphasizes preemployment training. Harbison notes that SENA-type programs endorsed by the International Labor Organization are in operation in most Latin American countries and under consideration in many Asian and African nations. Despite some shortcomings, Harbison writes, such programs are particularly suited to developing countries:

> The payroll tax is an effective means of raising large sums of money without putting strain on the budgets of ministries of education. The semiautonomous organizational structure allows for participation by employers and trade unions in programming free from the encrustations of traditional ministries. And the emphasis on on-the-job or close-to-the-job training results in more relevant skill generation.[113]

In contrast to national training schemes, several countries are experimenting with rural, locally sponsored vocational education delivery systems. Kenya, for example, has established village polytechnics which focus on developing skills particularly applicable to rural life, e.g., carpentry, leather work, and so on.[114] Botswana has a system of practical skill training called the Botswana Brigade Movement. Brigades are formed based on local demand. Training typically centers around building and trades, farming, dressmaking, motor mechanics, brick making, pottery, and crafts. The Botswana Brigade provides a member with up to 3 years training, with the learning of the skill taking place mainly on the job.

> In return the student contributes his or her work and production towards the wealth of the Brigade. This system has the advantage of not requiring large sums of money being injected into it since each Brigade is expected to generate its own resources through marketing its products, or selling the manual skills being learnt.[115]

A popular medium for vocational education in Third World nations is the mobile training unit. Brazil's UMIT program is a school on wheels that provides vocational skill training and continuing education opportunities for adults. Each mobile unit consists of a large truck and trailer and is staffed by a team of specialists. UMIT is presently operating in over 46 rural school districts. The staff uses a variety of instructional materials and holds sessions in community schools or residences. Instruction focuses upon basic technical training in business, industry, agriculture, and domestic arts, and also includes some enrichment and orientation courses.[116] Similar to Brazil's UMIT program is the Mobile Trade Training School (MTTS) program in Thailand. The aim of the program is to offer short, low-cost training in nonagricultural skills to out-of-school youth and adults. The schools use temporary buildings and offer a dozen or so trade courses for one to 3 years in one location before moving to another district.[117]

Nonformal delivery systems for adult vocational education in Third World nations suffer from some of the same problems that afflict vocational education in industrialized countries. Some persons receive training for which there are no jobs, while no training is provided for jobs where shortages exist. There is often a lack of trained teachers, the quality of instruction is uneven, and evaluation of program effectiveness is generally lacking. Chesterfield and Schutz point out too that such programs "lack much of the legitimacy associated with formal schools, do not perform a credentialing function, and fail to provide continuing possibilities of self-actualization over time."[118]

Workers' education is another dimension of labor development related to the industrial urban setting. Trade and industrial unionism is a growing force in Latin America and in some parts of Africa and Asia. Tanzania has established workers' councils to insure participation in planning and organization, and has required all factories, government offices, and East African Community Institutions to implement programs in workers' education.[119] The International Labor Organization (ILO) has a workers' education program to assist Third World nations to improve the effectiveness of vocational and technical training as well as to promote workers' participation in development through worker education. Activities include international and regional seminars dealing with labor participation in development, study fellowships, development of educational materials (e.g., guides, films, and visual aids), training organized by regional advisers for workers' institutes and union officers, and the efforts of advisory missions. Advisory missions have assisted in the building of permanent workers' education institutes in India, the Middle East, and the Caribbean; developed audiovisual aids in Malaysia; and assisted in research and workers' training in Singapore and Kenya.[120]

In summary, nation building in the Third World is determined by the interrelatedness of many dimensions of living. The work setting provides one avenue for engaging people in their country's development efforts. Creative delivery systems for developing and enhancing vocational/technical skills as well as the participation of workers in decision making and policy formation can have a major impact on national development.

CONCLUSION

The five program areas of adult education in the Third World—literacy, civic and political education, health and family life programs, and agricultural and vocational education—are all related to a nation's development. While a country may concentrate efforts on a particular program area for a period of time, the interrelatedness of forces affecting each individual citizen and the country as a whole makes dealing with only one aspect of development impossible. Thus, health, family life, civic education, and agricultural development are often subsumed under the rubric of community development. Functional literacy programs teach basic skills within the context of all these other program areas. Notably lacking in Third World adult education is support for liberal education, leisure time, or personal development courses. In commenting on this situation, Lowe notes that "an undue emphasis" upon other program areas "may well produce a higher economic output but in the meantime great damage may have been done to the quality of life in a society."[121] Likewise, individual self-development rarely is a goal of adult education except in terms of the way it adds to the collective efforts of a nation's citizenry to realize national development priorities. Finally, mass campaigns and in particular the use of radio characterize much of Third World adult education. One writer has called radio "the most potent method of mass education" presently in use in Third World nations.[122] When combined with listening groups and structured activities, radio is an effective educational medium that reaches even the most remote village.

Numerous problems beset all aspects of adult education in the Third World. One of the most serious is the lack of trained adult educators and other specialized personnel. Furthermore, those who are trained often resist relocating in rural areas where their skills are most needed. Secondly, women have not been afforded the same educational opportunities as men, and in nearly all Third World nations they lag behind men in literacy, skill development, and employment capability. Fortunately, this situation is changing as the potential women hold for effecting change in both family and community is recognized. Lack of coordination and follow-through is yet another problem. Wholesale adoption of the delivery systems and administrative structures of industrialized nations is frequently unsatisfactory. Developing a system of adult education that "fits" into a country's particular sociocultural context is desirable, yet it takes time and a good bit of experimentation. Finally, financing, or perhaps more accurately the allocation of available resources, is especially problematic for Third World nations, most of which are extremely poor.

The world community has in many ways responded to the educational and development needs of Third World nations. International cooperation and commitment to adult education have grown considerably in the last several decades. In addition to the Adult Education Division of UNESCO, other United Nations agencies such as the Food and Agriculture Organization and the International Labor Organization have added adult education components to their technical assistance programs. Among other international organizations that support adult education are the Council of Europe, the Organization for Economic Cooperation and Development, the World Confederation of Labor, and the World Bank. Regional associations in all parts of the world, individual countries, and private foundations also have recognized and supported educational efforts in many Third World countries. Several international education organizations such as the International Council on Correspondence Education, the International Congress of University Adult Education, and the Federation of Library Associations focus largely upon adult learners. Finally, the International Council for Adult Education, established in 1973, has as its primary objective the promotion of "all forms of adult education as a means of enhancing peace and security in the world, international understanding among peoples, and the advancement of less developed countries."[123] The council advises other agencies and member countries; organizes conferences, seminars, and training courses; publishes materials; and is in the process of setting up regional information centers.[124]

Learning To Be emphatically underscored the need for international cooperation in educational development:

> All countries at all development levels should . . . be brought into the common effort towards international solidarity, which at the same time should give special consideration to developing countries. There is more and more general agreement that the fight against ignorance is as important as the fight against hunger, the success of which requires linking efforts to develop agriculture in countries short of food with a generous redistribution of world food surpluses. Similarly, in education, efforts in developing countries must be combined with the world potential which could be made available to them.[125]

With regard to aid to Third World nations, the report points out that the "real, specific content of aid is as important as its volume. Effective aid creates the conditions in which it will no longer be necessary by developing the potential which the assisted country requires in order to do without assistance."[126]

The relationship between industrialized and Third World nations goes beyond that of donor and recipient. Adult educators in industrialized nations have much to gain from a knowledge of Third World development efforts. *Learning To Be* points out that "great as the industrialized nations' resources may be, their ambitious educational undertakings would be in danger of remaining at least partly sterile if they were to develop in a vacuum."[127] The very urgency of the problems of the Third World and their efforts to grapple with such problems is worthy of attention from adult educators worldwide. As Lowe concludes:

> In short, some of the most exciting work and the biggest challenges in the field of adult education are to be found in the developing countries. If they, in their wisdom, look for help to UNESCO and to specialists in other countries, adult educators in the developed countries would be well advised to take keen note of what they are doing and how, faced with unprecedented problems, they are turning to unprecedented solutions.[128]

NOTES

1. Coolie Verner, "Cultural Diffusion and Adult Education," in *Comparative Studies in Adult Education: An Anthology,* ed. Cliff Bennet, J. Roby Kidd and Jindra Kulich (Syracuse, N.Y.: Syracuse University Publications in Continuing Education, 1975), p. 146.

2. United Nations Educational, Scientific, and Cultural Organizations. (UNESCO), *Proposals for the Collection of Adult Education Statistics,* 1974, p. 5.
3. *Learning Opportunities for Adults,* vol. 1, *General Report* (Paris: Organization for Economic Co-operation and Development, 1977), p. 7.
4. Ibid., p. 9.
5. Malcolm Knowles, *A History of the Adult Education Movement in the United States* (New York: Krieger, 1977).
6. Verner, "Cultural Diffusion and Adult Education," p. 151.
7. Quoted in James Robbins Kidd, *A Tale of Three Cities: Elsinere-Montreal-Tokyo* (Syracuse, N.Y.: Syracuse University Publications in Continuing Education, 1974), p. 28.
8. *Learning Opportunities for Adults,* vol. 1, p. 41.
9. John Lowe, *The Education of Adults: A World Perspective* (Paris: UNESCO Press, Toronto: Ontario Institute for Studies in Education, 1975), p. 163.
10. *National Organizations for Co-operation in Adult Education* (Toronto: International Council for Adult Education, 1974), p. 5.
11. *Learning Opportunities for Adults,* vol. 1, p. 45.
12. Ibid., p. 44.
13. Quoted in *Learning Opportunities for Adults,* vol. 1, p. 44.
14. Knowles, *A History of the Adult Education Movement,* p. 189.
15. *Learning Opportunities for Adults,* vol. 1, pp. 58–59.
16. *Learning Opportunities for Adults,* vol. 4, *Participation in Adult Education.*
17. Lowe, *Education of Adults,* p. 175.
18. *Learning Opportunities for Adults,* vol. 1, p. 64.
19. Ibid., p. 63.
20. Berrit Hansen, *Recurrent Education: Denmark* (Paris: Organization for Economic Co-operation and Development, 1976), p. 33.
21. *Learning Opportunities for Adults,* vol. 1, p. 67.
22. John Lowe (Address delivered at the Annual Meeting of the Adult Education Association of the U.S.A., Portland, Oreg., 1978).
23. Verner, p. 151.
24. Per Himmelstrup, "Denmark," in *Learning Opportunities for Adults,* vol. 4.
25. Cyril O. Houle, *The External Degree* (San Francisco: Jossey-Bass, 1973).
26. Lowe, *Education of Adults,* p. 84.
27. Ibid., p. 85.
28. UNESCO, *Adult Education in Yugoslavia,* prepared by M. David, 1962, pp. 85–103.
29. Anatoli Darinsky, "People's Universities in the USSR," *Convergence* 7, no. 1 (1974): 51–54.
30. Lowe, *Education of Adults,* p. 81.
31. Maureen Woodhall, "United Kingdom: Adult Education and Training," in *Learning Opportunities for Adults,* vol. 4, p. 339.
32. OECD Secretariat, "Sweden," in *Learning Opportunities for Adults,* vol. 4, p. 276.
33. A. J. Curzon, "Correspondence Education in England and in the Netherlands," *Comparative Education* 13 (October 1977): 249–261.
34. *Learning Opportunities for Adults,* vol. 1, p. 32.
35. Alan M. Thomas, "Convergence," in *Adult Education and Nation Building,* ed. John Lowe (Chicago: Aldine, 1970), p. 228.

36. Allan H. Merriam, "The Semantic Implications of the Term 'Third World,' " *International Studies Notes* 6, no. 3 (Fall 1979): 13.
37. Ibid.
38. Leon Bataille, ed., *A Turning Point for Literacy* (New York: Pergamon Press, 1976), pp. 4–5.
39. Godfrey Lardner, "Adult Education and Economic Development," in *Development and Adult Education in Africa,* ed. Carl Gösta Widstrand (Uppsala, Sweden: Scandinavian Institute of African Studies, 1965), p. 17.
40. Majid Rahnema, quoted in Helen Callaway, "Learner-Centered Innovations in Literacy Work" in *A Turning Point for Literacy,* ed. Leon Bataille (New York: Pergamon Press, 1976), p. 185.
41. Joao Frank da Costa, "Twelve 'Musts' for Development," *UNESCO Courier* (November 1979): 10.
42. Robert M. Hutchins, *The Learning Society* (New York: Praeger, 1969).
43. Ibid., pp. 43–44.
44. Ibid., p. 39.
45. Adam Curle, *Education for Liberation* (New York: Wiley, 1973), pp. 115–116.
46. Per G. Stensland, "The Educational Core of Development," in *Adult Learning: A Design for Action,* ed. B. L. Hall and J. R. Kidd (New York: Pergamon Press, 1978), p. 7.
47. Ibid.
48. UNESCO, *Learning To Be,* prepared by Edgar Faure et al., 1972, pp. xxxi–xxxii.
49. Julius K. Nyerere, "Development Is for Man, by Man, and of Man: The Declaration of Dar es Salaam," in *Adult Learning: A Design for Action,* ed. Hall and Kidd, p. 27.
50. Lowe, *Adult Education and Nation Building,* p. 8.
51. UNESCO, *Learning To Be,* p. 34.
52. Lowe, *Adult Education and Nation Building,* p. 9.
53. Carl Gösta Widstrand, *Development and Adult Education in Africa* (Uppsala, Sweden: Scandinavian Institute of African Studies, 1965), p. 85.
54. Nyerere, "Development Is for Man," p. 29.
55. Sam V. Dauzat and JoAnn Dauzat, "Literacy: In Quest of a Definition," *Convergence* 10, no. 1 (1977): 37.
56. Ibid., p. 40.
57. Carman St. John Hunter and David Harmon, *Adult Illiteracy in the United States* (New York: McGraw-Hill, 1979), p. 7.
58. David Harmon, "Illiteracy: An Overview," *Harvard Educational Review* 20, no. 2 (1970): 228.
59. Hunter and Harmon, *Adult Illiteracy in the United States,* pp. 14–15.
60. Malcolm Adiseshiah, "Functionalities of Literacy," in *Turning Point for Literacy,* ed. Bataille, p. 65.
61. Ibid.
62. Paulo Freire, *Pedagogy of the Oppressed* (New York: Seabury Press, 1970).
63. Harmon, "Illiteracy," p. 231.
64. UNESCO, *World Conference of Ministers of Education on the Eradication of Illiteracy, Final Report,* 1965.

65. "Literacy in the World Since the 1965 Teheran Conference: Shortcomings, Achievements, Tendencies," in *Turning Point for Literacy*, ed. Bataille, p. 29.
66. Jonathan Kozol, *Children of the Revolution* (New York: Dell [Delacorte Press], 1978), pp. 82–83, 84.
67. Budd L. Hall, *Adult Education and the Development of Socialism in Tanzania* (Nairobi, Kenya: East African Literature Bureau, 1975), p. 24.
68. "Literacy in the World Since the 1965 Teheran Conference," p. 21.
69. UNESCO, *Learning to Be*, pp. 141, 207.
70. Paulo Freire, "Are Adult Literacy Programmes Neutral?" in *Turning Point for Literacy*, ed. Bataille, p. 198.
71. Nyerere, "Development Is for Man," p. 31.
72. Celeste Brody, "China: People Solving Problems," *Journal of Alternative Human Services* 4, no. 1 (1978), p. 27.
73. Paul Bertelson, "Problems of Priorities in Adult Education," in *Development and Adult Education in Africa*, ed. Widstrand, p. 26.
74. Ben Mady Cisse, "The People's Involvement in Development," in *Adult Learning*, ed. Hall and Kidd, p. 56.
75. Abdur Ruaf, *West Pakistan: Rural Education and Development* (Honolulu: East-West Center Press, 1970), p. 74.
76. Hall, *Adult Education and the Development of Socialism*, pp. 11–13.
77. Edwin K. Townsend Coles, *Adult Education in Developing Countries*, 2d ed. (New York: Pergamon Press, 1977), p. 41.
78. Ibid., pp. 41–43.
79. Mubanga E. Kashoki, "The Role of Languages in Development" in *Adult Learning*, ed. Hall and Kidd, p. 210.
80. Ibid., p. 214.
81. K. A. Busia, *Purposeful Education for Africa* (The Hague, The Netherlands: Mouton, 1968), p. 49.
82. Frederick H. Harbison, *Human Resources as the Wealth of Nations* (New York: Oxford University Press, 1973), p. 13.
83. Lowe, *Education of Adults*, p. 103.
84. Artemio C. Vizconde, "The Philippines," in *Adult Education and Nation Building*, ed. Lowe, p. 152.
85. R. C. Prosser, "Kenya," in *Adult Education and Nation Building*, ed. Lowe.
86. Harbison, *Human Resources as the Wealth of Nations*, p. 35.
87. Mohi El-Dlne Saber, *Development and Adult Education in the Arab States: An Analysis of Some Issues* (Toronto: International Council for Adult Education and the Arab Educational Cultural and Scientific Organization, 1977), p. 46.
88. Salig Ram Pathik, "Adult Education Through Ambar Charkha" in *Adult Education in India*, ed. Anil Bordia, J. R. Kidd, and J. A. Draper (Bombay: Nachiketa Publications, 1973).
89. Virgen Granados, Maria Elena Casanova, and Gordon W. Perkin, "A Candle Means Night," *World Education Reports* 20 (November 1979).
90. Rauf, *West Pakistan*.
91. Daniel Mbunda, "Educational Mass Campaigns for Development," in *Adult Learning*, ed. Hall and Kidd, pp. 195–196.

92. Hall, *Adult Education and the Development of Socialism*, p. 78.
93. Mbunda, "Educational Mass Campaigns for Development," p. 201.
94. Food and Agriculture Organization (FAO), *Toward a Strategy for Agricultural Development*, 1969, p. 40.
95. V. Patel and N. N. Shukla, *Lifelong Education and Community Learning: Three Case Studies in India* (Hamburg, West Germany: UNESCO Institute for Education, 1978), p. 9.
96. Jacques Chonchol, "Requirements of Agricultural Development" in *Hunger, Politics, and Markets,* ed. Sartaj Aziz (New York: New York University Press, 1975), p. 59.
97. Busia, *Purposeful Education for Africa*, p. 50.
98. J. W. Wenrich, "Spanish-Speaking South America" in *Adult Education and Nation Building*, ed. Lowe.
99. Marilyn Chow et al., *World Food Prospects and Agricultural Potential* (New York: Praeger, 1977), p. 226.
100. Ben Mady Cisse, "Senegal," in *Adult Education and Nation Building*, ed. Lowe.
101. Prosser, "Kenya," p. 82.
102. James Hoxegn, *Hacienda*, Technical Note no. 3 (Amherst, Mass.: University of Massachusetts, Amherst Center for International Education: ERIC Document Reproduction Service, ED 167, 480, 1972).
103. Hall, *Adult Education and the Development of Socialism*, p. 76.
104. Mbunda, "Educational Mass Campaigns for Development," p. 204.
105. Lowe, *Education of Adults*, p. 120.
106. James De Vries, "Agricultural Extension and Development" in *Adult Learning*, ed. Hall and Kidd, p. 149.
107. Manuel Zymelman, "Labour, Education, and Development" in *Education in National Development*, ed. Don Adams (New York: McKay, 1971), p. 113.
108. Ibid., p. 112.
109. Lowe, *Education of Adults*, p. 98.
110. Lalage Bown, "Zambia," in *Adult Education and Nation Building*, ed. Lowe.
111. Harbison, *Human Resources as the Wealth of Nations*, pp. 80–82.
112. Ibid., p. 85.
113. Ibid., p. 89.
114. Ibid., p. 90.
115. Coles, *Adult Education in Developing Countries*, p. 102.
116. Ray Chesterfield and Paulo Schutz, "Nonformal Continuing Education in Rural Brazil," *Lifelong Learning: The Adult Years* 2, no. 2 (1978).
117. Manzoor Ahmed, *The Economics of Nonformal Education* (New York: Praeger, 1975).
118. Chesterfield and Schutz, "Nonformal Continuing Education in Rural Brazil," p. 12.
119. Hall, *Adult Education and the Development of Socialism*, p. 85.
120. J. R. W. Whitehouse, "Workers' Participation for Development," in *Adult Learning*, ed. Hall and Kidd.
121. Lowe, *Adult Education and Nation Building*, p. 13.
122. Coles, *Adult Education in Developing Countries*, p. 105.

123. Lowe, *Education of Adults,* p. 208.
124. Ibid.
125. UNESCO, *Learning To Be,* p. 235.
126. Ibid.
127. Ibid.
128. Lowe, *Adult Education and Nation Building,* p. 16.

Chapter 7
Problems and Issues

In the first chapter, it was pointed out that many adult educators identify with the institutions that employ them rather than with the broader field. As a consequence, it has been difficult for the profession to organize to advance the interests of adult learners in general. Other chapters described fundamental disagreements concerning philosophy and values, opposing conceptions of adult learning and development, the barriers to full participation by the poor and elderly, the dilemmas of coordination and control, and the enormous challenge of illiteracy in Third World nations. This chapter extends the discussion of some of these matters and introduces new ones.

What is viewed as a problem or issue often is a matter of opinion and perspective. Adult educators with different values and backgrounds often disagree not only on what are the real problems and issues of the field, but also on why something is a problem or issue and what could or should be done about it. Administrators, for example, tend to see lack of adequate financial support as a crucial problem of adult education. Radical philosophers, on the other hand, view growing government support of adult education as a subtle means of manipulating the oppressed into continued acquiescence in an unjust social order. Virtually everyone concerned with the field has his or her own notions of its crucial issues and problems and a rationale for why they are important. The problems and issues addressed in the following pages, while not the only important ones, have been identified and debated in recent years by a range of individuals who are concerned about the field's future.

The first part of the chapter deals with some of the major concerns of adult education as a developing field of study and professional endeavor. Such a focus is particularly appropriate in a book intended mainly for graduate students preparing for professional leadership roles. A number of broader and more speculative issues are discussed in the second part of the chapter, in which the focus shifts to the future role of adult education as a social enterprise.

PROBLEMS OF A DEVELOPING FIELD

Adult education as a distinct field of study and professional application is still at best in its adolescence. Without an awareness of this fundamental reality one cannot really appreciate where the field is today, what its problems are, and where it might be headed. At first blush, this evaluation might seem untrue. What about the mechanics institutes, the Lyceum, Chautauqua, the Cooperative Extension Service, and other great institutions and events in adult education's history? There is no doubt that educators a century or more ago were busy with the work of what we now call adult education, creating programs and institutions to meet the learning needs of earlier generations of adults. Yet there were also people who ministered to the needs of orphans and the destitute, who built asylums, settlement houses, and other such institutions. They did not, however, call themselves social workers, as they do today. They had no collective identity. There was no body of common knowledge that formed the basis of their practice, nor any provision for formal training for the work they undertook. So, too, was the case with adult education. It was not until the 1920s that the field began to take form as a collective enterprise, the milestone event being the establishment of the American Association for Adult Education in 1926.

Even the date 1926 is misleading if we assume that any professional field or subfield must begin with at least a rudimentary body of knowledge and technique and a means for its transmission to practitioners. The knowledge base of adult education was beginning to develop in the 1920s and 1930s, but only very slowly. Edward L. Thorndike published the first major study of adult learning in 1928.[1] A number of courses in adult education were offered at Columbia University and a few other institutions and the first two doctorates were awarded in 1935.[2] But not until the 1960s did the field begin to grow rapidly. In the quarter century between

1936 and 1961, only 323 doctorates were awarded in adult education. The 1960s and 1970s saw better than a five-fold increase, with approximately 1,700 new doctorates granted in the 15 years between 1962 and 1977.[3]

Despite rapid growth in recent years, programs of graduate study and research in adult education are still a very small presence on most university campuses. Usually attached to schools of education, but seldom enjoying full departmental status, programs for the preparation of adult educators typically exist in an anomalous situation, striving for understanding and a niche in an environment heavily oriented to the education of young people. Research and graduate training in the education profession have been so overwhelmingly concerned with the schooling of children and young people that adult education seems to be in another world. As a result the field has for some years been faced with what might be called an identity crisis. In essence, the issue seems to be whether adult education ought to be a subfield within the education profession or a separate profession unto itself, like social work.

The Tensions of Growth

Like a rebellious adolescent, adult education has been torn by ambivalent feelings toward its parent field, or, rather, adoptive parent field, in that the movement of the 1920s was not nurtured primarily by professional educators. This ambivalence about the field's identity has largely been ignored in the professional literature, although we touched on the subject in Chapter 1, noting the role of leaders of the group dynamics movement in the forming of the Adult Education Association and in the naming of the AEA journal *Adult Leadership* (now *Lifelong Learning*).

It is neither possible nor pertinent to document all the conflicting viewpoints and tensions that have accompanied the field's development over the last three or four decades. It is, however, important to note that some leaders in the field, such as Malcolm Knowles, have emphasized adult education's distinctiveness from what is generally considered to be "education," while others, notably Cyril Houle, have stressed the continuities in the educational process and have identified adult education more closely with the educational establishment, particularly higher education. Another way to state the issue is that one segment of the field has been long concerned primarily with informal adult education in community settings, and with adult education for social action and community development, while another segment has emphasized the more formal side of adult education, particularly the role of colleges and universities in liberal education for adults, continuing professional education, and innovations such as the external degree.

The differences in perspective are not clear-cut, and in recent years have become even less sharply differentiated. To return to the issue of adult education's identity, the general momentum seems to have been toward separatism, toward dissociation from the broader field of education. In part this can be explained in terms of adult education's origins as a social movement and its rejection of the formalism and narrowness of schools and schooling. The separatist tendency also has been fueled, as suggested above, by the single-minded concern of the education profession with the schooling of children and youth.

Yet the future can and should be different. Adult education is, after all, *education*. The fact that its clientele is made up of mature people and that its purposes, methods, and settings are often distinctive does not negate this fundamental reality. Turning back from separatism does not mean denying adult education's distinct attributes, but rather developing them more fully within an education profession that has been reconceptualized to acknowledge the reality of lifelong learning. The redefining of education in more encompassing and accurate terms is already well under way. Adult educators should encourage it and take advantage of the opportunities for strengthening the field that it offers. One step in this direction would be for adult education researchers to abandon their intellectual isolation, symbolized so graphically by separate research meetings, and to work to develop the field through mainstream organizations such as the American Educational Research Association.

Adult Education's Knowledge Base

The effectiveness and stature of any applied professional field is directly related to its knowledge base. The knowledge base of adult education rests on two foundations. The first is other disciplines, most notably the social sciences. Research and theory in adult learning and development, organizational behavior, group process, communication, aging, adult socialization, and many other fields underpin both scholarship and practice in adult education. For the most part adult educators do not do basic research in such areas, but rather draw upon these fields for concepts that can be fruitfully applied to research in adult education and the improvement of professional technique. There have been significant advances in the social science arena over the last 30 years, and adult education, like other human service fields, has benefited enormously from them.

The second foundation of adult education's knowledge base is research focused directly on adult education itself. Some of this inquiry, for example, Clark's *Adult Education in Transition*[4] and Johnstone and Rivera's *Volunteers for Learning*,[5] has been conducted not by adult education researchers but by social scientists whose professional commitments lie elsewhere. In contrast, Boshier's studies of the motivational orientations of adult learners,[6] Tough's work on self-initiated learning projects,[7] and Mezirow, Darkenwald, and Knox's massive analysis of adult basic education[8] are examples of inquiries that center directly on adult education and have little to do with general problems in social science. It might be added that the studies just mentioned could be considered basic rather than applied research in the sense that they contribute to the general store of knowledge and understanding in the field rather than to the solution of narrow problems of limited general significance. This is not to suggest that applied research is not important. Furthermore, it is not always easy to distinguish between the two types of inquiry. Basic research is often, but not necessarily, bereft of immediate implications for specific professional concerns. For example, experiments to test the hypothesis that learning is enhanced when adults have the opportunity to participate in planning their educational experiences have obvious practical implications for program planning and contribute as well to the general pool of tested knowledge in adult education.[9] An example of a purely applied research project might be a needs assessment study carried out by a university extension unit to determine the courses in which the adults in a particular community would have the most interest. The results could be very valuable to program developers in making decisions on what courses to offer in the future. The study would not, however, add to the knowledge base of adult education, and its practical import for program developers at other universities would probably be slight.

Unfortunately, the store of tested knowledge about adult education itself is sorely deficient, although progress has certainly been made. The reasons for this state of affairs include the following: (1) the number of active researchers is very small; (2) funds for research in adult education have been and still are very scarce; (3) the research in the field is fragmented, with little cumulative development of knowledge on problems of central importance; (4) basic research that can add to the store of tested knowledge and contribute to the development of theory is neglected; (5) much of the research is poorly conceived and executed. These problems are by no means confined to research in adult education. They characterize to a greater or lesser extent virtually every area of professional study in education and applied human development. The number of researchers in adult education is, however, smaller than in most other fields. Basically, this reflects the size and number of graduate degree programs.

Coming up with the solutions to these deficiencies in research, other than the obvious ones of finding more and better-trained researchers and more money, is not at all easy. What may be most important at this stage of the field's development is that the problem be recognized and grappled with, particularly by professors and graduate students. Improving the quality of research training and thus of doctoral research could make a great difference in the rate of accumulation of significant knowledge.

Those involved in adult education are, and will always be, heavily engaged in the pressing demands of the real world. Even professors find it difficult to find time for basic scholarship. Nonetheless, fundamental research must be done, for not to expand the field's knowledge base is to preclude any hope for improving the quality of professional performance. And if it must be done, then of course it must be done well. This does not mean that all research in adult education should employ multivariate statistical methods. Methods of any kind are tools, not ends in themselves. What is required is that important questions, not trivial ones, be asked; that major lines of inquiry be developed systematically and cumulatively; that knowledge and understanding be pursued not simply for utilitarian ends; and that the methods employed in research be appropriate to the problem and skillfully applied.

Professionalism

No discussion of issues in adult education can avoid mention of the field's development as a professionalized occupation. The general topic has been ably reviewed by Griffith.[10] Rather than cover the same ground, we shall approach the key issues from a slightly different perspective while drawing selectively from his analysis.

Adult education, it is generally agreed, is not now a profession but rather an occupation in the process of becoming more professionalized. This is true of other fields in education such as reading, guidance counseling, and school administration. Nonetheless, it is fair to say that adult education has not come as far along the road of professionalization as many comparable vocations. Some of the reasons why have been discussed in this chapter and in earlier ones, especially the first. They include the tendency for adult educators to identify primarily with the particular institutional sector in which they work, rather than with the broad field; the limited visibility of the field and the lack of clear-cut career lines; the fact that professional preparation is not usually required for employment as an adult educator; and the limited, albeit expanding, base of knowledge and technique upon which professional development must ultimately depend. Despite these handicaps, it is probably true that adult educators could take certain concrete steps toward becoming more highly professionalized. The issue, however, is not only what steps could or should be taken, but whether it is desirable to take any steps whatever. The basic arguments have been summarized by Griffith:

> Professionalization of the field of adult education could have serious consequences if increased status and influence of professional adult educators were

coupled with a decreased commitment to serve the learning needs of individual adults and of the society. If the desire for professionalism is motivated by a commitment to improving the quality and quantity of adult learning opportunities, then the resulting changes will be in the best interest of all. Conversely, to the extent that the motivation is a veiled concern for self-aggrandizement, the tactics of exclusion and self-protection will not be in the interests of all. [11]

Many adult educators, including some professors and other leaders of the field, believe that enhanced professionalism would probably not be in the "best interest of all." To understand why, it is necessary to recall our earlier discussion of the origins of adult education as a social reform movement imbued with the liberal ideals of progressive social philosophy. From such a vantage point, the exclusionary practices and standards-setting associated with professionalism are seen as conservative, undemocratic, and incompatible with the voluntary and informal nature of true adult education. Professionalism, in this view, is synonymous with elitism, rigidity, credentialism, formality, and all the other vices of the educational establishment that adult educators have historically rejected.

Clearly, adult educators are not going to gain the kind of control over their work that doctors and lawyers exercise. It has not even been suggested that this is desirable. What, then, does professionalism actually mean in terms of possible next steps? Most of the discussion and debate at professional gatherings during the 1970s, particularly at the meetings of the Commission of Professors of Adult Education, centered on the establishment of a professional society that would limit membership to those deemed qualified on the basis of their professional training or its equivalent in professional accomplishment; the certification or licensure of adult education teachers and administrators, a matter of concern mainly to the public school sector of the field; and the accreditation of university training programs for adult educators. Of these concerns, the establishment of a national professional society would probably have the greatest impact on the long-term development of the field as a whole. Constituting such a society has typically been the first step taken by other professionalizing occupations, and in general it is a prerequisite for any further action that might be taken to regulate professional practice. Griffith, who advocates the establishment of such a society, describes its purposes as follows:

> Ideally, its concern would be with maintaining the quality and the provision of learning opportunities for adults by ensuring that professional adult educators would satisfy certain requirements in terms of academic preparation and demonstrated competence. It would promote collaboration among providing agencies and encourage the in-service training of volunteers and

paraprofessionals in the field. Expanding and improving the quality of learning opportunities for adults would remain its paramount concern, and no more time would be spent on exclusionary self-aggrandizing concerns than is endemic to all established professions.[12]

The formation of a professional society along these general lines may well be inevitable. Despite the reluctance of many to compromise what they see as their egalitarian principles, the fact is that no self-respecting occupation can evade responsibility for setting at least minimal standards for those who practice it.

There already exist several national associations that function to a certain extent as professional societies. They do not, however, require professional preparation or other such qualifications for membership. With the exception of the Adult Education Association, which has only a few thousand members, none is dedicated to advancing the interests of the total field. They represent instead narrow institutional interests. Nevertheless, these associations must be reckoned with if any attempt is made to form a true professional society. Leadership for a new society must come from the ranks of the associations that now exist (and that have no intention of disbanding).

In the absence of a ground swell of dissatisfaction with the present organizational arrangements in the field, there is not much likelihood of change. Dissatisfaction may be growing, particularly among professors of adult education, but as yet there has been no major expression of discontent. Moreover, many leaders in the field are understandably reluctant to establish a new professional society that would weaken the existing organizations. Consequently, the prospects for forming a society along the lines advanced by Griffith and others are not yet auspicious. Existing associations would almost certainly oppose such a move and no one of them would be likely to take on this role itself. Yet it might be argued that the need for such a society, or at least for the functions it would perform, is growing. One possible step might be for concerned leaders in the field to form a small society that initially would restrict its role to handling the professional upgrading functions not now performed by other organizations. Should it prove its value in this arena, the society might then find expanded responsibility feasible.

It should no longer be acceptable that anyone at all may lay claim to being an adult educator and obtain employment in this field. Learning by trial and error was a necessary and sometimes adequate form of professional preparation in the past, but it is not today. Low standards of performance may have had to be tolerated in the past, but they should not be in the future. Yet, in the 1980s individuals continue to enter adult education with no preparation for their work and little guidance or encouragement to gain the knowledge and skills they need. Professional regulation is certainly no panacea, but the present total lack of standards is difficult to justify.

ADULT EDUCATION AS A SOCIAL ENTERPRISE

Underlying the issue of identity discussed earlier is the fact that adult education's societal functions, or social ends, are in many ways distinct from those of preparatory education in schools and colleges. One distinctive function is to help people adapt to change in their own lives and in society at large. Another is to provide adults with a second chance to complete basic or higher education. A third function is to promote civic competence and responsibility by assisting citizens to understand more fully their common problems and to take effective action in resolving them. Still another end is to help individuals lead fuller lives through providing them with opportunities to learn whatever is personally meaningful. These are not the only functions that adult education serves, but they are suggestive of its broad significance in contemporary society. Adult educators who are true professionals are concerned about the social ends toward which their work is directed and acknowledge their personal and collective responsibility for the actions they take or fail to take on behalf of the public good.

In the following pages we can address only a few of the pressing issues related to adult education's larger significance in American society: equality of educational opportunity for adults; the trend toward what some have called "permanent schooling"; and the failure of adult education to address the crucial concerns of the times such as world peace, social justice, and environmental protection. There are obviously other urgent issues, but these seem not only to be of fundamental importance but also to offer the possibility of some degree of resolution.

Equal Opportunity

No adult who wishes to continue his or her education should be prevented from doing so on account of race, sex, age, ability to pay, or any other condition or handicap. This statement expresses unequivocally the ideal of equal educational opportunity for all adults, but this ideal is an impossibility now and in the foreseeable future. The goal is too sweeping and the cost would be staggering. College students, it is pertinent to note, must pay a large part of their educational costs. The public subsidies that are provided are justified in terms of achieving social equity and on the grounds that society as a whole will benefit from the skills and knowledge that individuals acquire in college. As far as adult education is concerned, in addition to part-time college study, such justifications are applicable mainly to basic education (ABE and high school completion) and vocational training for the unemployed. These of course are precisely the areas in which such arguments have been somewhat successful. Nonetheless, even for adult basic education the level of funding is inadequate. If political reality is acknowledged, the goal must be restated as equality of educational opportunity for adults whose inability to continue their education constitutes a social inequity and a liability for the society as a whole.

In Chapter 4 we discussed in detail the sectors of the adult population that are not being reached in proportion to their numbers, especially the poor, the ill-educated, and the elderly; the barriers that discourage their participation in adult education; and some of the practical steps that adult educators can take to aid the hard-to-reach adult. These concerns are also the subject of *Reaching Hard-to-Reach Adults,* edited by Darkenwald and Larson.[13] Rather than recapitulate this material here, we shall focus instead on some basic public policy questions concerning equal educational opportunity for adults.

• Is Adult Education Widening the Gap? A major issue concerns the contention that adult education, rather than contributing to social equality, works against it by providing a disproportionate share of educational resources to the more advantaged sectors of the adult population. As Cross puts it, "If the well educated seek out new learning opportunities while the poorly educated avoid them, then the learning gap will surely grow—right along with today's profusion of opportunities." The gap theory, she points out, "explains the reluctance of some to put more government funding into adult education."[14]

The notion that adult education contributes to widening the gap poses a serious threat to increased public support for continuing education and thus, ironically, to any hope of actually enhancing equal educational opportunity. As noted in Chapter 4, adults who continue their education are reasonably representative of the general adult population. It is true, however, that if one contrasts the participation rate at the extremes of the educational attainment continuum, the well-educated are getting "more than their share." This is certainly a matter for concern, but to conclude from such statistics that adult education is "elitist" and thus not deserving of public financial support is unwarranted. Consider, for example, the consequences of a drastic reduction in the various government subsidies for adult education in colleges and universities. As tuition costs increased, it would not be the privileged sectors of the adult population who would suffer. They could pay whatever they had to; but many working-class and middle-class adults would be unable to continue their education. The result would be a widening gap between those at the middle of the socioeconomic status continuum and those toward the upper end. Of course, the education gap between the lower and middle sectors would narrow, but this could hardly be a cause of satisfaction. The obvious point, which seems to elude the "widening gap" theorists, is that no one's interests are served by reducing public support for adult education. A wise public policy is not one that reduces educational opportunity for the majority, but one that increases opportunity for all, particularly the least advantaged. This is a principle that adult educators must be prepared to argue more forcefully if government support for education continues to decline.

• **A Right to a Basic Education?** A right is something that a person has a just claim to because it is good or proper or by virtue of law, nature, or tradition. Children have a legal right to a free public education through the high school years. Adults do not have such a legal right. Yet if a basic education is held to be good and proper, even necessary, for young people, and the right to it has the force of law, it would seem logical that the same arguments and legal entitlement should apply to adults. The main counterarguments appear to be these. First, those who are now adults did have a legal right to a free public education when they were younger. If they did not exercise that right fully, the problem is theirs, not society's. Second, it is not financially feasible for society to provide the necessary means to enable adults to exercise a legal right to a basic education. Finally, while not enjoying a legal right to a basic education, most undereducated adults have the opportunity to complete such an education through tuition-free programs supported by public funds.

These counterarguments do not seem persuasive. The first is narrowly legalistic and mean-spirited. The second is devoid of a rationale, simply asserting that the costs to society would not be proportionate to the benefits. The last, that since adults now have ample opportunities to complete a basic education they have a de facto if not legal right, is grossly misleading. Even if every community provided access to adult basic education, undereducated adults would still be greatly handicapped in exercising their "de facto" right. For one thing, tuition accounts for only a small part of total costs. Transportation, child care, and time spent learning rather than earning represent insuperable financial barriers for many undereducated adults. Second, because financial and personnel resources for adult basic education are so limited, the quality of instruction is often poor. Finally, full-time study is rarely possible for adults. This poses an enormous handicap for the functionally illiterate whose deficiencies may take many years to remediate when learning is limited to a few hours a week.

Adults lacking a basic education must have full rights and ample opportunities to secure one if equality of educational opportunity is to mean anything at all. It is difficult to see how this goal can be achieved in the absence of an individual educational entitlement for all adults who lack a high school diploma. Ideally, such an entitlement would provide adults sufficient funds to enable them to continue their basic education on a full-time basis. There are (as Barton has pointed out) many ways of structuring a national educational entitlement program.[15] This goal could be achieved in the 1980s if adult educators from all sectors of the field were to work hard for it.

At the root of all the arguments surrounding the issue of equal educational opportunity for adults is the simple question of who should pay; however, the answer is far from simple. Nonetheless, we propose that there be agreement on one basic principle: persons should not be discriminated against on the basis of age. If public support for a basic education or a college education is right for young people, then it is equally right for adults.

Lifelong Learning or Permanent Schooling?

Will support for lifelong learning eventually lead to an oppressive system of permanent schooling from cradle to grave? Will the historic emphasis of adult education on voluntary learning be replaced by an obsession with credits, credentials, and formal instruction? For more than a decade these questions have been raised by a small group of concerned adult educators. Ohliger dramatizes the issue with sardonic humor in the following vignette:

> A child is born in the United States in the year 1984. He can never look forward to getting out of school. From the "infant school" he starts attending at the age of six months to the "geriatric learning center" he dies in, he finds himself going to school all his life "for the good of society." . . . When he does die, a minister eulogizes him over his grave. . . . He points out that this man was very lucky, for he was born in 1984, the first year that the national "Permanent School Law" was in effect. . . . "And so we bid goodbye to this lucky man," the minister chants, "firm in the conviction that he will go to heaven where he will attend a "school for angels" into infinity."[16]

The picture sketched by Ohliger may be exaggerated, but the issue is a serious one. Lifelong compulsory schooling is hardly imminent, but at least two developments in recent years provide some cause for concern. The first is the expanding role in adult education of traditional educational institutions, and the second is the growing tendency to "prescribe" continuing education as a remedy for such problems as professional obsolescence.

• **The Schooling of Adult Education.** The "greying" of the American population has brought in its wake the emptying of classrooms and growing indications of what might be called "the schooling of adult education."

The phenomenon is most noticeable in the college and university sector. This is not to say that in the 1980s the schools will not also move to capture a larger share of what is termed the adult market. Most states in this decade will experience an accelerating decline in secondary school enrollments. It is conceivable that adult education could take up some of the slack, but whether this will actually occur on a widespread basis is uncertain. Nonetheless a trend has already developed in some states to convert surplus school buildings into comprehensive adult education centers.

We will not repeat the statistics cited in earlier chapters on the phenomenal growth of adult education in colleges and universities. It is enough to note that the number of colleges and universities offering noncredit adult education activities nearly doubled in the ten years between 1966 and 1976.[17] The number of degree-credit programs for adults probably increased at an even faster rate. During the same period hundreds of new community colleges were founded and adult education enrollments in these institutions increased by roughly a third.

What is pertinent here is not so much the growth of adult education in the postsecondary sector, but the more difficult and speculative question of where increased dependence on adult students might lead. Some fear that colleges and universities, desperate for new students, will increasingly dominate adult education, and that they will be neither willing nor able to make adjustments in their traditional ways of doing things to serve an expanded adult clientele effectively and appropriately. The most dismal scenario depicts colleges as shortchanging adult learners, making few changes in their curricula and instructional methods, offering meaningless credentials, and in general dampening the spirit of voluntary and self-directed adult learning. On a more general level, it is conceivable that the institutional ecology of adult education will shift radically and in doing so threaten some noncollegiate "species" and alter the character of the entire system.

These are legitimate concerns, but it is premature to conclude that the pluralistic and voluntary nature of adult education is in jeopardy. An expanded role for postsecondary institutions need not lead to a lesser role for other kinds of agencies such as churches, Y's, museums, and libraries. No type of institution is likely soon to enjoy anything approaching a monopoly in adult education. Nor is it inevitable that colleges and universities, as they expand their services to adults, will erode the voluntary, learner-centered qualities of adult education. Community colleges, by and large, do not seem to have done so, yet these institutions are increasingly serving a predominantly adult clientele. Whatever the consequences, the schooling of adult education will almost certainly continue as increasing numbers of youth-centered institutions become dependent on an adult clientele.

• **Mandatory Continuing Education.** The idea that adult education is a kind of treatment to be prescribed for the prevention or cure of performance deficiencies underlies the trend toward compulsory continuing education. The list of groups often considered to be in need of such treatment is a long one:

> traffic offenders and judges; parents of delinquents and public school teachers; illiterates on welfare; nurses; pharmacists; physicians; optometrists; nursing home administrators; firemen; policemen; psychiatrists; dieticians; podiatrists; preachers; veterinarians; many municipal, state, provincial, and federal civil servants; employees of all types pressured into taking courses, classes, or joining sensitivity training or organizational development groups; and, of course, the military. . . .[18]

While all these groups, and more, are in some places pressured or compelled to engage in adult education, it is mainly in the health professions that permanent schooling is close to becoming a reality. This is not surprising since the medical model of treatment (symptoms → diagnosis → prescription → cure) seems on the surface to be as applicable to knowledge or performance deficiencies as to other ailments. There are, however, problems with this reasoning.

The basic argument for compelling people to learn is that it is good for them and for society. If individuals lack the knowledge and skills to be good parents, safe drivers, or competent professionals then it is necessary for the proper authorities to see that these deficiencies are remedied. However, the symptoms are often incorrectly diagnosed, educational treatment does not guarantee learning, and the acquisition of knowledge or skills does not insure that they will be applied to improved performance. The assumptions that "proper authorities" know what is good for individuals subject to their control and that they are justified in compelling people to do what is deemed good for them or for society are also dubious.

The least-questioned assumption of the medical treatment model of mandatory continuing education is that the symptoms speak for themselves and that the appropriate treatment is invariably some form of education or training. Common sense shows that in many cases this is simply untrue. One has to be naive indeed to believe that lack of learning in the schools, reckless driving, chronic welfare dependency, or child delinquency are conditions that arise primarily from ignorance or individual incompetence. The behavior of reckless drivers may be stupid, but that hardly means that it derives from ignorance. In the case of school teachers, welfare mothers, or the parents of delinquents, to ascribe the cause of their problems solely to ignorance is to blame the victims for conditions that are partly or wholly beyond their control. Even in the health care professions, what may seem like a deficiency of knowledge or skill can be due to inadequate equipment, lack of supervision, conflicting expectations or regulations governing professional performance, and many other factors that have little to do with individual deficiencies in knowledge or skills. The idea that education is a panacea for every social problem is not only misguided, but dangerous. Dealing with such problems effectively is impossible when their real causes are not recognized.

That participation in organized educational activities is no guarantee of learning is evident to most educators. Less obvious is the error of confusing a need to learn with a need to participate in organized activities such as courses and workshops. Professionals surely need to continue learning all their lives, but as Houle has pointed out in his analysis of continuing learning in the professions, participation in organized activities is only one mode of continuing learning and not necessarily the most effective or appropriate under all circumstances.[19] Mandatory attendance at formal courses may even have the effect of discouraging the self-initiated and self-directed learning that for many professionals is more relevant to their needs than the formal opportunities that may be available to them.

In almost every instance where adult education is mandated for some group it is assumed not only that learning will occur, but also that it will be applied to improving proficiency at some task or role. Even under ideal circumstances, there is no guarantee that this will happen. When adults are forced to learn, there is even less assurance that knowledge will be put to use. It is particularly disturbing that these obvious truths have been ignored by proponents of mandatory continuing education for licensed professionals. The public has a right to be protected from incompetent practitioners, but mandatory continuing education is neither necessary nor sufficient to ensure that result. What is needed is to mandate competent performance through periodic evaluations and to deny relicensure to those who fail to demonstrate continued proficiency. Under this kind of quality assurance system, professionals would be highly motivated to maintain their competence through voluntary learning appropriate to their individual needs and circumstances. Unfortunately, the prospect of periodic performance evaluations is threatening to many professionals, whereas the idea of mandatory continuing education is not. It has been argued that mandatory education is a step in the right direction, but it is a small step indeed if the goal is to protect the public from incompetent practitioners.

Some would argue that any kind of compulsory participation in adult education is educationally and ethically unjustifiable. The issue seems to hinge on the meaning of the word *compulsory*. Employees of all kinds are expected or compelled to participate in certain training or educational programs. Is it ethically or educationally unjustifiable for employers to expect such participation? In general, the answer would seem to be no. The obligation to learn whatever is required to perform one's job is implicit when one accepts employment. Also implicit is the employer's obligation to provide opportunities for work-related education. In most cases, education or training benefits both the employee and the employer and is therefore not inherently exploitive or oppressive. It is, however, educationally unsound and in some sense oppressive for employees to have little or no control in planning or carrying out their own learning activities. Paradoxically, the most notorious examples of compulsory miseducation can be found in the in-service education programs of many school systems. Typically, school administrators decide what teachers need to learn, hire an outside expert to give a speech or workshop, and then expect teachers to apply what they learn, if anything, to their work in the classroom. Teachers and others subjected to such experiences have a right to resent and resist them, for their employers have failed in their responsibility to provide appropriate and effective educational opportunities for occupational development.

Can Adult Education Change the World?

In the 1920s and 1930s the leaders of the emerging adult education movement believed fervently that adult education could change the world. The greatest threat to democracy, they felt, was an uninformed and apathetic citizenry unable or unwilling to exercise wisely and fully its civic responsibilities. Over the years, the belief that adult education could contribute in a major way to improving the social and political order began to be eroded, in part perhaps because too much was expected too soon with too few resources. Rhetoric exhorting adult educators to combat poverty, injustice, civic apathy, and other social evils is seldom heard today although many of the old problems remain and new ones have appeared. Still, most adult educators would agree with Myles Horton's recent observations after 50 years of work in the cause of social change:

> I got into adult education because I got tired of hearing each generation say that our only hope is with the children—the next generation will clean up our mess, make our society better. I realized the world would only change if the people who are now running things, who are already adults, changed. So I decided that if we want a more decent society, we would have to work with today's adults on today's problems.[20]

Since 1932 Highlander, the residential adult education center Horton founded, has worked with the people of Appalachia and other parts of the South to organize labor unions, work for racial justice, and in general to improve living conditions and communities through a process of problem solving linked to collective action.[21] Yet despite its success and the importance of its work, Highlander is still a unique institution. Adult education for social action continues to be unorganized and sporadic, developing in one place or another in response to an immediate need or threat and then disappearing without a trace. Perhaps education for social change, because it is inescapably political and a threat to established interests, will never gain any measure of institutional stability. On the other hand, the cause may not be hopeless, for if Highlander can survive, then similar efforts could be developed in other parts of the country.

Less controversial than adult education for direct social action is what might be termed adult education for civic competence. Helping citizens to gain a better understanding of their common problems and take action to deal with them has long been a major concern of the adult education movement. World peace, social justice, environmental protection, energy policy, and urban decay are just a few of the pressing concerns that confront the United States and most other industrialized countries in the 1980s. The adult citizens of a democracy cannot escape personal and collective responsibility for the decisions that must be made in each of these crucial areas, because each of these problems is, in the broad sense of the word, political. There are to be sure hard facts and theories involved, and experts who can provide technical advice, but the problems would not exist if their solutions were clear-cut or merely technical. There are always competing values (e.g., military readiness versus arms control), contradictory "facts," and short- and long-term tradeoffs that must be evaluated intelligently by concerned and responsible citizens. The role that adult education could play in social problem solving would be to help citizens acquire the information and understanding they need to make informed judgments. This in fact is the principal educative function of the mass media, particularly television and the press. Unfortunately, the educative potential of the media appears to be inversely related to the difficulty of the problem at hand. Consider the economic and technical complexity of the issues surrounding the energy shortage and energy policy. Could most citizens be expected to make informed judgments on these matters on the basis of what they read in the newspapers or view on television? Surely the answer is no. And this is only one of many such issues. What, if anything, can be done?

Provided that adult educators and public policymakers recognize the urgency of the problem and the available options, much can be done. For example, the technological capacity is now available to mount nationwide and even international educational campaigns through various video delivery systems, including satellite transmission. Educational programs exploring all sides of complex public issues such as arms control or environmental protection could be developed or sponsored by a variety of national or international agencies. With careful planning and adequate publicity, televised instructional units could be supplemented with print materials and coordinated with local discussion groups held in schools, churches, libraries, and other community settings. Whatever the organizational patterns, the potential benefits of mass civic education could be great; but they will not be realized until the belief that adult education can help to change the world is once again firm.

It seems appropriate to conclude our discussion of adult education as a social enterprise with these words penned more than 50 years ago by the great adult education philosopher Eduard Lindeman:

> We do not pursue the path of learning solely for the purpose of putting more knowledge into our own behavior. Knowing-behavior, which is intelligence, is social in two directions: it takes others into account and it calls forth more intelligent responses from others. If then learning adults wish to live in a social environment in which their intellectual alertness will count for something (will get itself realized, i.e., in power, creative expression, freedom, et cetera), they will be as eager to improve their collective enterprises . . . as they are to improve themselves. Orthodox education may be a preparation for life but adult education is an agitating instrumentality for changing life. . . . Adult education will become an agency of progress if its short-time goal of self-improvement can be made compatible with a long-time, experimental but resolute policy of changing the social order. Changing individuals in continuous adjustment to changing social functions—this is the bilateral though unified purpose of adult learning.[22]

CONCLUSION

As a field of study, developing profession, and social enterprise, adult education is today entering a new and crucial era. What it will become, its integrity and direction, is being shaped by a swirl of events that cannot be totally predicted or controlled. Adult educators, individually and collectively, can nonetheless profoundly influence the field's development in this crucial decade. Yet for this to happen, the issues discussed here, and those identified as relevant by other scholars and practitioners, must be further explored and clarified through study and debate, and adult educators must resolve to work together for a common agenda.[23] In this chapter we sought to raise questions, outline the issues, and assert our views in the expectation that our readers will extend and clarify the analysis, continue the debate, and reach their own conclusions.

NOTES

1. Edward L. Thorndike, *Adult Learning* (New York: Macmillan, 1928).
2. Cyril O. Houle and Delores Ford, "Doctorates in Adult Education, 1976 and 1977," *Adult Education* 26, no. 1 (1978): 65–70.
3. Cyril O. Houle, "The Emergence of Graduate Study in Adult Education," in *Adult Education: Outlines of an Emerging Field of University Study*, ed. Gale

Jensen, A. A. Liveright, and Wilbur Hallenbeck (Chicago: Adult Education Association of the U.S.A., 1964).

4. Burton R. Clark, *Adult Education in Transition* (Berkeley, Calif.: University of California Press, 1968).

5. John W. C. Johnstone and Ramon J. Rivera, *Volunteers for Learning: A Study of the Educational Pursuits of American Adults* (Chicago: Aldine, 1965).

6. Roger W. Boshier, "Factor Analysts at Large: A Critical Review of the Motivational Orientation Literature," *Adult Education* 24, no. 1 (1976): 24–47.

7. Allen Tough, *The Adult's Learning Projects* (Toronto: Ontario Institute for the Study of Education, 1971).

8. Jack Mezirow, Gordon G. Darkenwald, and Alan B. Knox, *Last Gamble on Education: Dynamics of Adult Basic Education* (Washington, D.C.: Adult Education Association of the U.S.A., 1975).

9. J. William Cole and J. Conrad Glass, Jr., "The Effects of Adult Student Participation in Program Planning on Achievement, Retention, and Attitude," *Adult Education* 27, no. 2 (1977): 75–88.

10. William S. Griffith, "Personnel Preparation: Is There a Continuing Education Profession?" in *Power and Conflict in Continuing Education*, ed. Harold J. Alford (Belmont, Calif.: Wadsworth, 1980).

11. Ibid., p. 218.

12. Ibid.

13. Gordon G. Darkenwald and Gordon A. Larson, eds., *Reaching Hard-to-Reach Adults* (San Francisco: Jossey-Bass, 1980).

14. K. Patricia Cross, "Adult Learners: Characteristics, Needs, and Interests," in *Lifelong Learning in America*, ed. Richard E. Peterson (San Francisco: Jossey-Bass, 1979), pp. 81, 133.

15. Paul E. Barton, "Lifelong Learning: Getting Started," *School Review* 86 (May 1978): 311–326.

16. John Ohliger, "Adult Education: 1984," *Adult Leadership* 20 (January 1971): 223.

17. National Center for Education Statistics, *Noncredit Activities in Institutions of Higher Education, 1975–76* (Washington, D.C.: Government Printing Office, 1978).

18. John Ohliger, "Is Lifelong Adult Education a Guarantee of Permanent Inadequacy?" (Paper presented at the University of Saskatchewan, Saskatoon, Canada, March 1974), p. 2.

19. Cyril O. Houle, *Continuing Learning in the Professions* (San Francisco: Jossey-Bass, 1980).

20. "This School Helps Grass Roots Grow," *New York Times*, 7 September 1980, section 12, p. 4.

21. Frank Adams, *Unearthing Seeds of Fire: The Idea of Highlander* (Winston-Salem, N.C.: Blair, 1975).

22. Eduard Lindeman, *The Meaning of Adult Education* (Montreal: Harvest House, 1961), pp. 104–105.

23. Burton W. Kreitlow (ed.), *Examining Controversies in Adult Education* (San Francisco: Jossey-Bass, 1981).

Index of Names

Index of Subjects